The Islamic Conception of Justice

Other Works in English by Majid Khadduri

The Law of War and Peace in Islam (1941)
Independent Iraq (1951)
War and Peace in the Law of Islam (1955)*
Law in the Middle East (edited, with H. J. Liebesny, 1955)
Islamic Jurisprudence (1960)*
Modern Libya (1963)*
The Islamic Law of Nations (1965)*
Major Middle Eastern Problems in International Law (1968)
Republican Iraq (1969)
Political Trends in the Arab World (1970)*
Arab Contemporaries (1973)*
Socialist Iraq (1978)
Arab Personalities in Politics (1982)

*Published by The Johns Hopkins University Press

The Islamic Conception of Justice

Majid Khadduri

The Johns Hopkins University Press
BALTIMORE AND LONDON

The Johns Hopkins University Press, Baltimore, Maryland 21218
The Johns Hopkins Press Ltd., London

Library of Congress Cataloging in Publication Data

Khadduri, Majid, date–
The Islamic conception of justice.

Bibliography: p. 243
Includes index.
1. Islam and justice. I. Title.
BP173.43.K44 1984 297'.1978 84-5723
ISBN 0-8018-3245-4

The paper in this book is acid-free and meets the guidelines for permanence and durability of the Committee on Production Guidelines for Book Longevity of the Council on Library Resources.

This book was set in Garamond 49 type by BG Composition, Inc., based on a design by Susan P. Fillion. It was printed on S. D. Warren's 50-lb. Sebago Eggshell cream paper and bound in Holliston Roxite A by the Maple Press Company.

Contents

Foreword

This work on *The Islamic Conception of Justice* is intellectually organic. Unlike so many volumes on Islam in recent years, it is not occasioned by the resurgence of "Islamic fundamentalism" or the eruption of the Iranian Revolution. In a sense this volume has been in the making over the past thirty years, since 1955, when Professor Majid Khadduri published his standard volume on *War and Peace in the Law of Islam*. Throughout these decades, the international community of scholars has witnessed the prolific display of his multifaceted talents—above all, his numerous contributions to the study of politics and law in the Middle East, both in substance and theory.

In this volume, Professor Khadduri has for the first time brought to bear this twin commitment to the study of law and politics on one of the most difficult questions of our time. Seldom in the historical past have individuals and collectivities everywhere been so profoundly concerned with the quest for justice, a concept that is, indeed, elusive, but not by any means illusive. The primary objective of this volume is to inquire systematically into the writings of the leading Muslim scholars, both classical and modern, in search of an Islamic theory of justice, but the inquiry is consistently related to political dynamics and institutions in the history of Islam.

The author traces forth the development of the conception of justice from the rise of Islam to the present within the broader context of the Islamic public order. Guided by conceptual as well as empirical concerns, he examines the development of the concept of justice in Islam in terms of political, theological, philosophical, ethical, legal, and social categories rather than in a strictly chronological order. The bulk of the volume treats in depth the classical Islamic conception of justice in terms of these principal categories. This emphasis on the classical development deepens our understanding of the modern conception of justice, which is treated briefly with a keen eye to the processes of continuity and change in the evolution of the Islamic conception of justice.

Who may find this study useful? Nowhere else can Western students of Islam, regardless of their disciplinary emphasis, find such a comprehensive examination of the Islamic conception of justice within the covers of a single volume. In these pages, for example, they will find how the concept of justice has eluded such towering Islamic thinkers as al-Kindi, al-Farabi, Ibn Sina, and Ibn Rushd philosophically, al-Ghazzali, al-Razi, al-Mawardi and Nasir al-Din Tusi ethically, Abu Hanifa and Shafi'i legally, and Ibn Khaldun socially, not to mention such thinkers as Afghani, 'Abduh, 'Abd al-Raziq, and Khumayni in modern times.

Western students of comparative and international law may find this volume no less useful. The comparativists will be able to compare the examples of the divinely-based concepts of justice in the Judeo-Christian tradition in Western civilization with the classical examples in Islamic civilization. They will also be able to contrast the examples of the common-law and civil-law based concepts of justice with those of Islam in modern times. International lawyers, on the other hand, may find this volume useful variously. The so-called idealists, or optimists, will see in the Western-inspired efforts of Muslim states for secularization of law and the administration of justice an important indication of "progressive development of international law," including the gradual emergence of common standards of justice, despite cultural differences. The so-called realists, or pessimists, on the other hand, will find more ammunition in the resurgence of "Islamic fundamentalism" in contemporary times for the argument that the search for common universal standards of law and justice is doomed because, despite the processes of modernization, primordial loyalties, values, attitudes, and ethnic and linguistic particularities continue to undermine the new elements of commonality.

Finally, this study should interest general theorists. Professor Khadduri's search for an Islamic theory of justice avoids the concern of some previous authors with the foreign origins of the norms and maxims of Islamic justice in terms of the influence of the Greek, Persian, Indian, and other cultures. As such, his categories of "revelational," "rational," and "social" justice based on the Islamic experience, for example, should interest legal theorists who deal with the broad categories of "natural law" and "positive law." They should also interest political theorists who concern themselves with tension between "idealism" and "realism," or between theory and practice in the study of politics and foreign policy.

The author's own approach does not quite fit the idealist-realist dichotomy: his long-standing position is best described as of "empirical idealism." While Professor Khadduri believes that "justice is essentially a relative concept"—depending largely on the underlying social and cultural substrata—it should be inspired by higher values as well. In his own words: "The historical experiences of Islam—indeed the historical experiences of all mankind—demonstrate that any system of law on the national as well as the international plane would lose its meaning were it divorced from moral principles."

R. K. Ramazani
University of Virginia

Preface

Few subjects have aroused greater concern among men of various ranks and classes than the question of what is man's due as a member of society. True, perhaps men who belong to that section of society which feels deprived of its rightful due have spoken loudest about their concern for justice. But it is also true that men in other sections of society have sympathized with the underprivileged and voiced their concern about justice.

But what is justice? The answer varies from one school of thought to another and from scholar to scholar within the same school, as the dialogue on justice in Plato's *Republic* makes clear. Even men in high offices, whose function is presumably to dispense justice, seem to be dubious about their task. It is said that Judge Learned Hand, having once given Justice Holmes a lift to the Supreme Court, admonished him to do justice. "This is not my job," replied Holmes, "my job is to play the game according to the rules." In his work *Why Justice Fails*, W. N. Seymour tells us that the courts neither dispense justice nor do they apply the rules fairly. Nevertheless, all men concerned with justice are agreed on the need for it, but they have disagreed on both its elements and the method of realizing it on Earth.

It is the purpose of this work to study the experiences of Islam with justice and how its leaders and thinkers grappled with the problem of how the standard of justice is to be defined and determined in accordance with an order of ideals and values that would set the conscience of the public at rest. Islam's experiences with justice, not unlike the experiences of other nations, demonstrated that no people can claim possession of a scale of justice superior to others. Indeed, diversity of scales of justice enriches mankind's experiences with the means of how to resolve problems equitably on both the national and international planes, notwithstanding that it may also breed dissension and conflicts. No nation can afford today to ignore the experiences of other nations concerning how to establish scales of justice and resolve the problems arising from their application in comparable situations. At the height of its power, Islam had drawn on the experiences of other nations—Greeks, Persians, and others—and set the example that no nation can live in isolation from others. It is not the purpose of our study, however, to trace the origins of foreign elements and maxims of justice which Muslims have adopted from foreign sources—a process of transmission which is still continuing and which all nations have experienced in varying degree—but to discuss how those foreign elements have been harmonized with and ultimately assimilated into the Islamic public order. Above all, our concern is to discuss the rationale and the theoretical speculation of Muslim thinkers in order to meet immediate needs and expectations.

This book is not only intended for students in the Islamic field; it is hoped that it would be of interest to all who are concerned with justice as a means for the promotion of peace through the diffusion and exchange of ideas. Readers who are interested either in the theory of justice in general or the Islamic conception of justice in particular obviously need no advice on how to proceed throughout this book. But for the general reader, may I suggest that the purely theoretical portions, especially chapters 3 and 4 (and perhaps the first part of chapter 5) can either be skimmed or skipped without serious interruption in the process of development of the concept of justice from the rise of Islam to the present.

It is a pleasure to acknowledge the kindnesses of all who have given me assistance or counsel during the preparation of this work. I should like to acknowledge in particular the grant extended to me by His Royal Highness Shaykh Khalifa Bin Hamad Al Thani, Ruler of the State of Qatar, which made it possible for me to visit several Arab capitals and obtain material for the book and consult a number of scholars in the Arab World and Western countries. I should like also to thank Linda Vlasak who with meticulous care prepared the book and the compilation of the index for the press. My friend Professor R. K. Ramazani made several valuable suggestions during the final stage of the preparation of the text for the publisher. I should like finally to thank J. G. Goellner, Director of the Johns Hopkins University Press, who took a special interest in this book even before I began to write it and helped to ensure that it would be published in its present attractive format. None of them, however, is responsible for the opinions expressed in this work or for any error of content in it.

System of Transliteration and Abbreviations

In reproducing works by non-Western authors written in Western languages, in the Latin alphabet, no question of transliteration arises, as the established practice is to reproduce them as they stand. The problem of transliteration arises in reproducing names and words from non-Western languages, written in scripts other than the Latin alphabet, as Western writers have pursued different systems in the absence of a common standard acceptable to all.

In this book, as I have done in my earlier works, I have followed the system adopted by the editors of the *Encyclopaedia of Islam* and the Library of Congress with slight variations, particularly in omitting letters at the end of words that are not pronounced in the original language, such as Makka and Madīna (instead of Makkah and Madīnah). Moreover, names beginning with the article "al" have been used uniformly without distinction between the so-called shamsī and qamarī categories, such as al-Ṭaḥāwī and al-Dimashqī instead of aṭ-Ṭaḥāwī and ad-Dimashqī. Needless to say, place names that have been anglicized, such as Syria (for Surīya) and Cairo (for Qāhira), have not been transliterated.

The abbreviations most frequently used are the following:

Q. Qur'ān

1/632. The date cited in accordance with the Hijra and the Gregorian calendar.

B. This letter, if inserted between two parts of a person's full name, stands for Bin or Ibn, which means "the son of."

d. Died

n.d. ''No Date''—the date of publication of a certain source is not cited.

Law Whenever this term is used with a capital letter, it refers to the Sharī'a (Islamic law); the term Sharī'a will also be used wherever it is necessary.

1

Introduction

And fill up the measure when you measure, and with the just balance; that is better and fairer in the issue.

—Q. XVII, 37

And when you speak, be just, even if it should be to a kinsman.

—Q. VI, 153

Justice is essentially a relative concept. Whenever a man asserts that which he considers his just claim, were it to be valid, it must be relevant to an established public order under which a certain scale of justice is acknowledged. Scales of justice vary considerably from land to land, and each scale is defined and ultimately determined by society in accordance with the public order of that society. Yet no matter how scales differ one from another, they all seem to have certain elements in common and, broadly speaking, may be divided into two major categories.

One category is to be found in societies which assume that men are capable of determining their individual or collective interests and know that which they may need or to which they may aspire; they therefore can, individually or collectively, establish a public order under which a certain scale or scales of justice are likely to evolve by tacit agreement or by formal action. This kind of justice, a product of the interaction between expectations and existing conditions, may be called positive justice. It is admittedly imperfect and men always endeavor to refine and improve it by a continuing process of social change. The ideal or perfect justice is a mirage, and the real one develops by improvisation from generation to generation.[1]

1. Although a variety of notions of justice are known to exist in such a society, most of them seem to revolve around the two major schools—the utilitarian and the social contract. The most important recent critique of the theories of justice, in which the social contract theory is re-examined and refined, is John Rawls's *Theory of Justice* (Cambridge, Mass., 1971).

In a society which presupposes that man is essentially weak and therefore incapable of rising above personal failings, the idea that fallible human beings can determine what their collective interests are and lay down an impartial standard of justice is scarcely acceptable. In such a society a superhuman or divine authority is invoked to provide either the sources or the basic principles of the public order under which a certain standard of justice is established. Whether the superhuman authority is exercised by a gifted sage or an inspired prophet, the kind of justice that flows from such a source commands respect and can have a lasting impact on the administration of justice. Some of the ancient societies—the Hebrew, the Christian and the Islamic are but three examples—were committed to this viewpoint: God disclosed Himself through Revelations, communicated to men through prophets, in which His justice is embodied. The justice which flows from such a high divine source is considered applicable to all men and forms another category of justice. In contrast with positive justice, it may be called Divine or Revelational justice. It is the product of intuition, or divine inspiration, and is closely interwoven with religion and ethics. It coincides with Reason and may well fall in the category of natural justice. Aristotle used the term "natural justice" in the sense that it is the product not of social but of natural forces.[2] Following Aristotle, scholars often equated Divine or God's justice with natural justice, but, unlike the natural-law scholars who were concerned with the relation of justice to society, Christian and Muslim scholars focused their primary concern on the concept of justice in relation to God's Will and related it to the destiny of man.[3] Both held that Divine Justice is the ultimate objective of the Revelation, expressed in its early form in the sacred laws of Christianity and Islam. In the *Summa Theologica*, St. Thomas Aquinas termed the sacred law of Christianity the Eternal Law, and Muslim scholars called their Eternal Law simply the "pathway" (Sharī'a).[4] The concept of justice embodied in the Religion and Law of Islam, not to speak of Christian justice, evoked an endless debate among scholars concerning both its scope and character and how its standard is to be realized on Earth.

2. Aristotle, *Nichomachean Ethics*, 1134ᵃ18.

3. While some Muslim philosophers were prepared to equate Divine Justice with natural justice, the early theologians rejected this characterization, but later conceded a certain rational element in it (see chaps. 3–4).

4. See St. Thomas Aquinas, *Summa Theologica*, question 93: Of the Eternal Law; for the Sharī'a, see chap. 6.

The Sources of Justice

In Islam, Divine Justice is enshrined in the Revelation and Divine Wisdom which the Prophet Muḥammad communicated to his people. The Revelation, transmitted in God's words, is to be found in the Qur'ān; and the Divine Wisdom, inspired to the Prophet, was uttered in the Prophet's own words and promulgated as the Sunna, which subsequently came to be known as the Ḥadīth, or the Prophet's Traditions.[5] These two authoritative or "textual sources," the embodiment of God's Will and Justice, provided the raw material on the basis of which the scholars, through the use of a third "derivative source" of human reasoning called ijtihād, laid down the Law and the Creed.[6] The fundamental principles of the Law and the Creed, and the creative works of succeeding generations, formed the foundation of the renowned Islamic public order. From a scrutiny of all these sources and scholarly works, we shall seek evidence for the reconstruction and interpretation of the various notions and theories that have been spun by Muslim men of learning about justice. Since the scale of justice in any given society must be related to its public order, a few words about the nature of Islam's public order may be useful at this stage.

In Islamic theory, God is the Sovereign of the community of believers; He is its ultimate Ruler and Legislator. The Revelation and Divine Wisdom are the primary sources of the developing public order, presuming to meet the community's growing needs and expectations. The principles and maxims of justice derived from the Revelation and Divine Wisdom were considered infallible and inviolable, designed for all time and potentially capable of application to all men. In principle, the Law laid down by the Divine Legislator is an ideal and perfect system. But the public order, composed of the Law as well as state acts and the rulings (furū') and opinions of the scholars on all matters arrived at through human reasoning (ijtihād), are by necessity subject to adaptation and refinement to meet changing conditions and the growing needs of the community.

5. For the view that Divine Wisdom is embodied in the Sunna of the Prophet, see Shāfi'ī, *al-Risāla*, ed. Shākir (Cairo, 1940), p. 32; Trans. M. Khadduri, *Islamic Jurisprudence* (Baltimore, 1961), p. 75.

6. Human reasoning took the form either of analogy (qiyās), exercised by the individual scholar, or of consensus (ijmā'), exercised collectively by the scholars, presumably on behalf of the community (see Shāfi'ī, *op. cit.*, trans. M. Khadduri, *op. cit.*, chaps. 11–13).

Since the Divine Legislator did not rule directly over the believers, the enthronement of a Ruler to represent God on Earth, to whom God's authority was delegated, had become necessary to put the Law into practice and to rule with Justice.[7] A new form of government had thus been established based on Divine Law and Justice. This form of government, often called theocracy, is obviously not based on the principle that authority is exercised directly by God (whether as a Pharaoh or a Caesar) but by a representative who derives his authority not directly from God but from God's Law. It is therefore the Law, embodying the principles of Divine authority, which indeed rules and therefore the state becomes not, strictly speaking, a theocracy, but a form of nomocracy. The Islamic State, whose constitution and source of authority is a Divine Law, might be called a Divine nomocracy.[8]

The textual sources, consisting of the Revelation and Divine Wisdom, are the Qur'ān and the Sunna. To these constitutional instruments, the proximate source of authority, all the political leaders and contending parties appealed to assert their conflicting claims to power. Likewise, on the strength of these sources, the scholars sought to legitimize one claim against another by diverse arguments—theological, legal, and others—on the grounds of justice. Although the scholars agreed on the Divine nature of justice, they disagreed on how it should be realized on Earth and formulated various doctrines of justice reflecting the conflicting interests, local traditions, and aspirations of rival leaders and groups in their struggle for power. Legitimacy and justice were often used interchangeably by political leaders, and the scholars, in an attempt to rationalize the legitimacy of rival groups, provided one scale of justice or another drawn from the emerging public order. For an understanding of the standard of justice of each particular group or school of thought, it is proposed to analyze justice from all the aspects that came under discussion—political, theological, legal, and others—since a study of each one epitomizes not only the conflicting views about justice but also the methods of debate pursued by each group to formulate a doctrine of justice that would set the conscience of the community at rest and provide stability and continuity.

7. God to David: "We have appointed thee a Caliph on Earth so as to judge among men with justice" (Q. XXXVIII, 25).

8. For a discussion of this form of government, see M. Khadduri, *War and Peace in the Law of Islam* (Baltimore, 1955), pp. 14–18.

At the outset the debate on justice began on the political level. In a community founded on religion, it was indeed in the nature of things that public concern should focus first on the question of legitimacy and the qualification of the Ruler whose primary task was to put God's Law and Justice into practice. Since the Prophet, the first Ruler, died without providing a rule for succession, the question of legitimacy became crucial. Should any pretender to the throne seize power without a valid claim, his act would naturally be considered a travesty to Divine Justice. The debate thus was bound to center on the procedural question of the choice of the person who would have a legitimate claim to succeed the Prophet in accordance with the standard of political justice embodied in the textual sources.

Once the debate on political justice started, it never really ended. Like Pandora's box, it became exceedingly difficult to bring political differences under control. It led to schism in the body politic and the rise of rival credal groups and sects, each seeking to rationalize its standard of political justice on one credal ground or another. From the political level the debate gradually shifted to other levels—theological, legal, and others—although ulterior political motivation continued to reassert itself in one form or another. As the Islamic public order advanced, the debate moved to higher levels of sophistication, and scholars in fields other than theology and law—philosophers and other men of learning—were very soon drawn into it. For no great thinker, whether in Islam or in any other community, could possibly remain indifferent to a debate on a subject as engaging and central as justice. But before we proceed further, perhaps a clarification of the literary meaning of justice and other related terms would be in order.

The Literary Meaning of Justice

The meaning of the common usage of words expressing the notions of justice or injustice is not only important in the abstract sense, but also illuminating for an understanding of the manifold aspects of justice; since the literal meaning of words is ultimately the outgrowth of their social or every-day meaning, the writers and thinkers are likely to be influenced by it in the articulation and rationalization of man's needs and expectations in the struggle to achieve justice and other human ideals. Classical Arabic is renowned for its richness in vocabulary and literary expressions. Indeed, it is no exaggeration to say that for every concept or action describing or identifying a particular human activity, perhaps a dozen words in the major lexicons are likely to be found, notwithstanding that each word is not necessarily a synonym, as it may often imply a slightly different shade of meaning from the other. For instance, for the name of God (although this is not a typical example), it may be interesting to note, there are ninety-nine words called the asmā' al-ḥusna (the beautiful names), each denoting or expressing the meaning of one of His manifold attributes.[9]

For every aspect of justice there are several words and the most common in usage is the word "'adl." Moreover, there are several synonyms, perhaps the most important of which are the following: qisṭ, qaṣd, istiqāma, wasaṭ, naṣīb, hiṣṣa, mizān and others. The antonym of 'adl is not a modified spelling of the word 'adl denoting its negative meaning—as is the counter word "injustice" to "justice" in English—but an entirely different word called "jawr." There are also several synonyms of jawr; some express a slightly different shade of meaning such as zulm (wrongdoing), ṭughyān (tyranny), mayl (inclination), inḥirāf (deviation) and others.

Literally, the word 'adl is an abstract noun, derived from the verb 'adala, which means: First, to straighten or to sit straight, to amend or modify; second, to run away, depart or deflect from one (wrong) path to the other (right) one; third, to be equal or equivalent, to be equal or match, or to equalize; fourth, to balance or counter-balance, to weigh, or to be in a state of equilibrium.[10] Finally, 'adl (or 'idl) may also mean example or alike (Q. V, 96), a literal expression which is indirectly related to justice.[11]

In the conceptual sense, Ibn Manẓūr, the lexicographer, states that "the thing that is established in the mind as being straightforward" is the meaning of justice.[12] Anything which is not upright or in order is regarded as jawr or unfair. The two literal meanings of "straight" and

9. See 'Abd al-Qāhir al-Baghdādī, *Kitāb Uṣūl al-Dīn* [A Treatise on the Fundamentals of Religion] (Istānbūl, 1928), I, 119. A list of God's "most beautiful names" may be found in Daud Rahbar, *God of Justice* (Leiden, 1960), pp. 9–10.

10. See the following dictionaries: Ibn Manẓūr, *Lisān al-'Arab*, XIII, 457–58; al-Fayrūzābādī, *al-Qāmūs al-Muḥīṭ*, I, 431; II, 415–16; IV (pt. 2), 6; al-Zabīdī, *Tāj al-'Arūs*, VIII, 9–10; al-Maqqarī, *Kitāb al-Miṣbāḥ al-Munīr*, II, 541–42, 689–90.

11. See 'Abd al-Ra'ūf al-Miṣrī, *Mu'jam al-Qur'ān* (Cairo, 1948), I, 137–38; II, 34.

12. Ibn Manẓūr, *op. cit.*, XIII, 457; al-Jurjānī, *Kitāb al-Ta'rīfāt*, ed. G. L. Flügel (Leipzig, 1845), p. 153.

"departure" are implied in the conceptual sense of straightforwardness and uprightness. Needless to say, the notions of "right" and "wrong" are implied in the terms "'adl" and "jawr," as these terms are often used in the broadest sense to include moral and religious values. The notion of 'adl as "right" is equivalent to the notions of fairness and equitableness, which are perhaps more precisely expressed in the term istiqāma or straightforwardness.[13]

The notion of 'adl as equality or equalizing is used in the sense of equating one thing to another. This meaning may be expressed either in qualitative or quantitative terms. The first refers to the abstract principle of equality which means equality before the law or of having equal rights as implied in the Quranic dictum that "the believers are indeed brothers" (Q. XLIX, 10). The second, stressing the principle of distributive justice, is perhaps best expressed in such terms as naṣīb and qisṭ (share), qisṭāṣ and mizān (scale), and taqwīm (straightening).

Finally, the notions of balance, temperance and moderation may be said to be implied in the words ta'dīl, qaṣd and wasaṭ. The first, which literally means to amend or to adjust, expresses the notion of balance; the second and the third, which literally mean the "middle" or a place equidistant (or midway) between two extremes, may be taken to imply moderation and temperance. These notions of justice are perhaps more finely expressed in the principle of the golden mean. The believers are not only individually urged to act in accordance with this principle, but also collectively called upon to be "a nation in the middle" (Q. II, 137; XIII, 11).[14]

The foregoing notions of justice, which may be said to be implied in the common usage of 'adl, have been summarized in a letter reputed to have been addressed to the Caliph 'Abd al-Malik (d. 86/705), in reply to an inquiry about the meaning of the term 'adl, by Sa'īd Ibn Jubayr, who said:

> 'Adl (justice) may take four forms: [First], justice in making decisions in accordance with God's saying: "when you judge among men you should judge with justice" (Q. IV, 61); [secondly], justice in speech in

13. The notions of right and wrong were embodied in the ancient classical conception of justice which Islam subsequently adopted as part of its moral and religious traditions (Ibn Manzūr, *op. cit.*, XV, 266–72).

14. See Baghdādī, *op. cit.*, pp. 131–33; Shāṭibī, *al-Muwāfaqāt* (Cairo, n.d.), II, 163–67. For commentaries on "wasaṭ" (middle) to mean justice in the sense of moderation, see Ṭabarī, *Tafsīr*, ed. Shākir (Cairo, 1955), III, 142.

accordance with His saying: "when you speak, you should be equitable" (Q. VI, 153); [thirdly], justice in [the pursuit of] salvation in accordance with His saying: "protect yourselves against a day on which no person will give any satisfaction instead of another, nor will an equivalent be accepted from him, nor will intercession avail him" (Q. II, 117); [fourthly], justice in the sense of attributing an equal to God in accordance with His saying: "yet the unbelievers attribute an equal to Him" (Q. VI, 1).

As to [God's] saying: "you will not be able to be equitable between your wives, be you ever so eager" (Q. IV, 128); 'Ubayda al-Salmānī and al-Ḍaḥḥāk said that [man's inability to be equitable] meant with respect to love and intercourse. And [the saying that] so-and-so has done justice to so-and-so means that the one is equal to the other. [If] it is said that "no-one is equal to you in our view," it means that "no-one stands with us in thy stead." Justice in [the sense of] weight and measurement means [that a certain thing is] equal [to another] in weight or size. [If] you did justice between two things, you did justice between so-and-so and so-and-so, it means that you have made the two things, or between one and another, to be equal or the like of one another. The doing of justice for a [certain] thing means to make it straight. It is said that justice means the rating of a thing as equal to a thing of another kind so as to make it like the latter.[15]

The literal meaning of 'adl in classical Arabic is thus a combination of moral and social values denoting fairness, balance, temperance and straightforwardness. Logically, Divine Justice would be a synthesis of all these values and virtues; indeed such a conceptual meaning is the theme of the debate among theologians, jurists and philosophers and will be the subject of our inquiry in the pages to follow.

The Notion of Justice in the Qur'ān and Traditions

The Prophet Muḥammad, who seems to have been endowed with a deep sense of justice, found widespread inequity and oppression in the society in which he had grown up, and he sought to establish order and harmony within which a distinct standard of justice would be acknowledged. As a Prophet, he naturally stressed religious values, but he was also a social reformer, and his decisions provided precedents on the strength of which the issues that were to arise in succeed-

15. See Ibn Manzūr, *op. cit.*, XIII, 458; for translation of all relevant passages, see E. W. Lane, *Arabic-English Lexicon*, bk. I (pt. 5), 1972–75.

ing generations were resolved. The idea of justice was of particular interest to him, and he dealt with the problems of his day with uprightness, balance, and fairness. Nor was he indifferent to discrimination and inhuman acts, as exemplified in the legislation for the improvement of the status of women, emancipation of slaves (though slavery as a system was not abolished), and prohibition of infanticide and other unjust acts and practices. Moreover, he himself valued certain virtues honored by his followers and he incorporated them in his teachings. As he said in one of his often quoted utterances, his call was not to abolish but to "further the good morals" (li utammim makārim al-akhlāq) that had been in existence in society, and he felt compelled to confirm them.

In the tribal society of Arabia, where survival was perhaps the tribesman's primary concern, such virtues as honor, courage, and liberality were more highly prized than other virtues. These were epitomized in the word "muruwwa," consisting of everything that was taken to be praiseworthy and which may be called the Arab *summum bonum*.[16] The muruwwa continued to be viewed so high in Arab eyes in subsequent centuries that al-Maqqarī (d. 770/1369) in his definition of justice, stated that no one could claim to be just were he to compromise the virtue of muruwwa.[17] But in the exhibition of honor and courage the tribesmen were often brutal and oppressive, especially in the pursuit of *vendetta*, with the consequent subordination of the virtues of fairness and moderation to arbitrary rules of order. The poet 'Amr B. Kulthūm, composer of one of the well-known Seven Odes (al-Mu'allaqāt al-Sab'a) was not the only one who sang the praise of brutality and oppression attributed to his tribe.[18] The absence of a coherent social order and political unity in the tribal society of Arabia necessarily subordinated the scale of justice to the requirements of survival, and consequently the appeal to justice took the negative form of retribution, such as retaliation and the payment

16. For references to virtues in pre-Islamic literature, see the letters and proverbs attributed to Aktham B. Ṣayfī in al-Maydānī, *Majma' al-Amthāl*, II, 87–145; for the idealization of these virtues, see Shanfara's ode, "Lāmiyyat al-'Arab" in M. Badī' Sharīf, ed., *Lāmiyat al-'Arab* (Beirut, 1964). For the meaning of muruwwa, see Bishr Fāris, *Mabāḥith 'Arabīya* (Cairo, 1939), pp. 57–74.

17. Maqqarī, *op. cit.*, II, 542.

18. The Seven Odes were renowned not only for their literary excellence but also for their vivid description of Arab character and Arab way of life before Islam. See A. J. Arberry, *The Seven Odes* (London, 1957), chap. 6.

of blood-money, rather than the positive forms of fairness, balance, and temperance.

The Prophet, while conceding the value of courage and other virtues, felt keenly the need to assert religious and moral values to temper cruelty and harshness. For this reason, the Qur'ān and Traditions often warned believers against bigotry and oppression, and admonished them that in the fulfillment of their religious obligations they must above all be just. In the Qur'ān there are over two hundred admonitions against injustice expressed in such words as zulm, ithm, ḍalāl, and others, and no less than almost a hundred expressions embodying the notion of justice, either directly in such words as 'adl, qisṭ, mizān, and others as noted before, or in a variety of indirect expressions.[19]

Second only to the existence of the One God, no other religious or moral principles are more emphasized in the Qur'ān and Traditions than the principles of uprightness, equity, and temperance, partly because of their intrinsic value but mainly because of the reaction against the pre-Islamic social order which paid little or no attention to justice. The most important Quranic references to justice are as follows:

> God commands justice and good-doing . . . and He forbids indecency, dishonor and insolence. (Q. XV, 92)
>
> God commands you to deliver trusts back to their owners, and when you judge among men, you should judge with justice. (Q. IV, 61)
>
> Of those We created are a people who guide by the truth, and by it act with justice. (Q. VIII, 180)[20]

In the Traditions, the Prophet sought to explain the meaning of the abstract maxims of justice enunciated in the Qur'ān by specific examples, expressed in legal and ethical terms, to distinguish between just and unjust acts as well as to set underlying rules indicating what the scale of justice ought to be. Since the Prophet dealt essentially with practical questions, the theologians and other scholars found in the Traditions precedents on the strength of which they formulated their theories of justice. However, neither in the Qur'ān nor in the

19. The words 'adl and qisṭ alone recur in the Qur'ān in various forms over fifty times. See G. L. Flügel, *Concordaniste Corani Arabicae* (Leipzig, 1842).

20. For further references enjoining justice and prohibiting injustice, see Q. III, 100, 106, 110; IX, 72, 113; XXII, 42; XXXI, 16; and others.

Traditions are there specific measures to indicate what are the constituent elements of justice or how justice can be realized on Earth. Thus the task of working out what the standard of justice ought to be fell upon the scholars who sought to draw its elements from the diverse authoritative sources and the rulings and acts embodied in the works of commentators.

The religious character of the public order, however, imposed by its very nature certain restraints, and the community of believers, distrustful of the capacity of fallible men to legislate for society, discouraged radical departure from the literal meaning of textual sources. Small wonder that many scholars, under popular pressures, were often forced to renounce doctrines seemingly inconsistent with the literal meaning of the authoritative sources, despite the growing needs of society for innovations. However, most scholars felt that they were duty-bound to accept the interpretation of the standard of justice laid down by their predecessors more strictly than by those who sought radical changes.

Scope and Method of This Study

It is perhaps necessary to define at this stage the scope and method of our study, although the subject matter has been outlined in broader terms earlier. Its aim is to inquire into the nature and scope of Divine Justice and to reconstruct from the diverse writings of Muslim men of learning the Islamic theory of justice in all its aspects. It is true that the most permeating aspects of justice were the religio-political and legal, but all other aspects were interrelated and had bearing in varying degree on the life of believers over the centuries. For this reason, some of the seemingly abstract aspects, the philosophical and ethical in particular, were deemed necessary to deal with not only for their intrinsic value, but also because in presenting ideal formulations an implied criticism of existing conditions was revealed which was not always possible to express in official doctrines.

It is proposed in this study to combine the advantages of the idealist and realist methods. An attempt to relate idealism with realism, which may be called "empirical idealism," is a method which I have pursued in earlier studies. It is thus not our purpose to elucidate only the norms and values in abstract terms, but to relate them to the various political and intellectual groups and movements which strive to realize them in the form of standards of justice on Earth. More specifically, the concept of justice will be closely scrutinized as defined and determined by text-writers in the context of the public order. The realities of life were indeed not always ignored by theorists; for the scholars, who were considered the conscience of the political community, often echoed the needs and aspirations of believers in their doctrinal postulations of justice. The impact of those who tried to relate doctrines to realities is made nowhere more apparent than in our discussion on the discrepancy between the theory and reality in the scale of legal and social justice (chaps. 6–7 and 9). It is the aim of our method to present a systematic study of the Islamic conception of justice within the context of the Islamic superstructure as it evolved from the formative period.

2

Political Justice

O David, We have appointed thee a caliph on earth so as to judge among men with justice, and follow not caprice, lest it lead thee astray from the path of God.

—Q. XXXVIII, 25

Political justice, often regarded as the principal end of the state, is justice in accordance with the will of the sovereign. Aristotle, in making a distinction between a variety of narrow and wide forms of justice, considered political justice to be the widest in scope; its scale belongs to the state, which determines what is just and unjust.[1] The sovereign will may or may not be just, depending on whether state acts contain some elements of justice—legal, ethical or social—or whether they merely assert a particular interest, personal or otherwise. Since political justice is weighed in state acts, the sovereign will determines how much of the elements of justice state acts should contain. In the pursuit of the perpetuation of itself, the state may make concessions to vested interests which often compromise legal or social justice; it may even punish innocent opponents advocating radical ideals on the grounds of vitiating its acts. Political justice is thus a function of political aims; in the final analysis, however, it is the product of complex forces, varying from lofty ideals and social claims (some dictated by public pressure and others by group interests) to personal ambition, and often legal justice—not to speak of ethical or social justice—is subordinated to political convenience.[2]

If the state acts were contrary to the standard of justice embodied in

1. See Aristotle, *Politics*, 1253^{a}37; and the *Nichomachean Ethics*, 1134^{a}32.

2. For a study of the relationship between legal justice and political objectives, see Otto Kirchheimer, *Political Justice* (Princeton, 1961); cf. William Godwin, *Political Justice*, ed. H. S. Salt (London, 1890; 2nd ed., 1918), for the view that political justice is an expression of social ideals.

the public order, how long could they be enforced? It is true that they may temporarily be enforced, but it is inconceivable that they can be tolerated indefinitely. Under social pressures, they would eventually be disavowed and repudiated by peaceful or violent methods. If the state is ever to endure, its acts must conform, or give the impression that they have conformed, to an acknowledged standard of justice embodied in the public order.

Whether the public order is the outgrowth of positive law or considered to have been derived from an ultimate super-human power is a matter to be determined by the community. In Islam, the believers were committed to the doctrine that their public order was ultimately derived from a high divine source. In its earthly form, that source consisted of Revelation and Wisdom, the former embodied in the Qur'ān and the latter in the Prophet's Sunna (Traditions). These were often called the primary or textual sources of the Islamic public order.

Political Justice as the Expression of Divine Will

In conformity with its public order, political justice in Islam—indeed, all other aspects of justice—proceeds from God, the ultimate Sovereign, whose Will is not exercised directly upon His subjects (the community of believers), but through the Prophet and the Rulers (Imāms) who succeeded him. The believers are commanded to observe the Law and obey God's representatives who, "appointed . . . to judge among men with justice" (Q. XXXVIII, 25), are to exercise God's Sovereign Will on Earth. "O you who believe," it was decreed in the Revelation, "obey God and obey the Apostle and those in authority among you; if you quarrel about anything, refer it to God and to the Apostle" (Q. IV, 62). So the Prophet was granted the power to exercise God's Sovereign Will, and he was commanded to rule in accordance with the "truth" and the "path of God" (Q. II, 24).[3] The "truth" and "the path of God," according to most commentators, were equated with "righteousness" and "justice."[4] The Prophet's rulings, on all matters of public concern, were taken to conform to the right-

3. For further citations about entrusting divine power to the Prophet Muḥammad, see Q. IV, 62; V, 39 and 119; IX, 115; XII, 100; XX, 113; XXXVIII, 25.

4. See Bayḍāwī's *Tafsīr* [Commentaries] (Cairo, 1951), p. 601.

eousness and justice of God (Q. IV, 2).[5] If the Prophet ever erred or was faulted, his errors were at once corrected by Divine Command.[6] Small wonder that the Prophet's rulings and acts established precedents on the strength of which judges made decisions and the scholars ('ulamā') formulated their doctrines concerning all aspects of justice.

The Prophet, however, suddenly died before the structure of the political community was completed. There were fundamental questions as well as pending issues that had yet to be resolved. If the Prophet had considered them, he died before having attempted to solve them. The most immediate issue was, of course, the question of the "legitimacy" of the successor (Caliph) chosen after him. If legitimacy is taken to mean "the right to rule" in accordance with a recognized standard of political justice, it would in Islam have to be the true expression of the Divine Sovereign Will. Since legitimacy could no longer be confirmed by new prophecy,[7] it devolved upon the community to confirm it by consensus, provided the chosen successor would exercise his powers in accordance with the standard of justice set in the Revelation (Qur'ān) and Divine Wisdom (Traditions). Practice preceded the establishment of a rule, and the precedent set by the enthronement of the first Caliph provided the source on the basis of which the standard of political justice became acceptable to the political community, but this source was challenged later.

Three major schools of thought gradually began to emerge, each representing a political group claiming that its principle of legitimacy conformed more accurately than others—indeed, each claimed that its principle of legitimacy was the only valid one—in accordance with the

5. Although it was universally accepted that the Prophet was just, the question on the matter was once put to him and he answered, in no uncertain terms, that justice was always his aim. A case in point is illustrated by the following: "One day we were with the Apostle, who was distributing shares, when Dhū al-Khuwayṣira, a man from the tribe of Tamīm, came up to him and said, 'O Apostle, distribute in your tongue,' and the Apostle replied, 'Who would be just, if not I? I would be a poor thing if I were not just " (Muslim, *Ṣaḥīḥ*, under "Zakāt," trad. 148).

6. "No, my Lord, they do not believe until they make thee judge in their disputes and do not afterwards find difficulty in the decisions, but surrender in full submission" (Q. IV, 68). This Revelation, we are told, was communicated in connection with a case in which the Prophet exercised equity to correct a ruling in accordance with justice. See M. Khadduri, *Islamic Jurisprudence* (Baltimore, 1961), pp. 114–15, n. 9.

7. A few men, and one woman, claimed prophecy after Muḥammad's death, but none could persuade the community of believers to accept him (or her), and very soon they all vanished. The precedent was established that the Quranic injunction "seal of the prophets" (Q. XXXIII, 40), meant that Muḥammad was the last of the prophets (see Bayḍāwī, *op. cit.*, p. 559).

standard of political justice embodied in the Qur'ān and the Traditions. The elaborate theories of the Imamate (Caliphate) which the followers of the various sects and schools of thought advocated were not formulated by the early pretenders to the Caliphate but were the product of the events and developments that followed the *fait accompli*. The scholars of succeeding generations refined and articulated the principles of legitimacy and political justice of rival schools which had already been evolving.

Two of these schools—the Sunnī (Sunnite) and the Shī'ī (Shī'ite)—representing the major divisions of Islam, initially agreed on at least three fundamental principles: first, that the Imamate was necessary for the survival of the community and for putting the law into practice; second, that the Imamate, in order to be just, must be held by a member of the Prophet's family (according to Shī'ī doctrine) or by a member of Quraysh, the Prophet's tribe (according to the Sunnī doctrine), who claimed to have understood correctly how the Sovereign Will bequeathed by the Prophet was to be exercised; third, that the Imām should possess certain qualities of seniority and reputation (charisma, experience, and others) considered necessary for the discharge of his duties as commander of the believers and head of state.

Broadly speaking, these principles may be taken to provide the minimum standard of political justice, namely, that the Divine Sovereign Will must be exercised either by a member of the Prophet's family or a member of his tribe. The Shī'a, however, insisted that only a member of the Prophet's family could exercise the Divine Sovereign Will with justice, whereas the Sunnī argued that membership in the larger circle of the Prophet's tribe was quite adequate for the requirements of political justice. The Shī'a, arguing that legitimacy must be in accordance with the Sunna of the Prophet, invoked a Tradition which stated that 'Alī, the only candidate from the Prophet's family (he was the Prophet's cousin and son-in-law) had already been designated an Imām by the Prophet himself, and 'Alī, the first Imām, bequeathed the Imamate to his descendants in accordance with the rule of seniority.[8] No other Imām, according to the Shī'ī doctrine,

8. The text of the Tradition runs as follows: "Whoever recognizes me as his master (mawla)," said the Prophet, "will know 'Alī as his master." It is said that the Prophet made this declaration at Ghadīr Khum, on the way to Madīna, after he returned from Makka on the occasion of his farewell pilgrimage (10/632). Perhaps the earliest authority who gave an account of the event is al-Ya'qūbī, himself a follower of 'Alī (d. 277/891), in his *History*, ed. Houtsma (Leyden, 1883); text of the Tradition is reported in Ibn Ḥanbal's *Musnad*, ed. Shākir (Cairo, 1949), II, 644, 951, 963–64, 1310.

would be capable of exercising the Sovereign Will with justice in any other manner. The Sunnī, rejecting the authenticity of this Tradition, invoked another Tradition attributed to the Prophet in which he said that the Rulers of his community (al-umarā') should be from the tribe of Quraysh (the Prophet's tribe), but he laid down no rule specifying how the candidate from that tribe would become an Imām; therefore it was taken for granted that the choice of the Imām rested with the community as a whole.[9]

Other doctrinal principles ensued from disagreement on procedural justice, revealing with greater emphasis the deepening differences between the Sunnī and the Shī'ī communities. Since the first successor to the Prophet was chosen in accordance with a Sunnī precedent (and subsequently the Sunnī doctrine prevailed), the Shī'a (partisans of 'Alī) continued to assert the claim of 'Alī as the only legitimate one. Moreover, since the administration of justice under Umayyad rule was not always tolerant toward dissident groups, the leaders of heterodox sects were often persecuted and put to death on flimsy evidence of subversive activities. Small wonder that the Shī'a could with good reason denounce Sunnī rule as unjust and characterize the Sunnī Imamate as the Imamate of injustice (jawr). The Shī'ī criticism of Umayyad highhanded rule did not necessarily mean that the Sunnī Imamate was inherently unjust, since many Sunnī leaders and scholars who supported Sunnī Imāms deplored Umayyad repressive measures. Nevertheless, the Shī'a continued to assert that their principle of the Imamate was the only one which could insure justice. The legitimacy of the Shī'ī Imamate, claimed by its followers to rest on sound principles of political justice, may be summarized as follows:

1. The first Imām was designated by the Prophet who was empowered to exercise God's Sovereign Will. The Prophet, it is held, passed to the Imām an esoteric knowledge (al-ta'wīl) by virtue of which he could provide the explicit and implicit meaning of the Revelation and the Law.[10]

2. The Imām, a member of the Prophet's house, inherited by birth and upbringing special qualities and qualifications which rendered him immune to human failings. As a consequence, he is consid-

9. The Sunnī Tradition is based on the precedent of the election of Abū Bakr as first caliph in 10/632 (see Ibn Ḥanbal, *al-Musnad*, I, 323–27).

10. The Imām's power of ta'wīl can virtually lead in effect to the exercise of the power of legislating.

ered sinless (ma'ṣūm), a quality which enabled him to be not only infallible in decision-making, but also impeccable in character. In Shī'ī theory, the Imām is the most qualified man, after the Prophet, to exercise God's Sovereign Will by virtue of membership in the Prophet's house. No other person outside that house is capable of exercising God's Will with justice. He is the Imām al-Afḍal: the Imām *par excellence*.

3. Possessing such unique qualities, the Shī'ī Imām is the only Ruler who can command public respect; partly by the charisma inherent in his personality and partly by the allegiance and loyalty (walāya) which his followers owe to him as a religious duty. As the Imām al-Afḍal, he is the only one equal to the requirements of political justice and capable of providing effective leadership and achieving the ends of the state.[11]

The Sunnī doctrine of the Imamate, in contrast with the Shī'ī doctrine, is based on the assumption that the Prophet never really designated 'Alī or any other one to succeed him as the first Imām. The enthronement of an Imām, in the absence of any clear rule on the matter, must therefore rest with the community which would act on behalf of the Prophet, and ultimately on behalf of God. The choice of the Imām by the community (al-bay'a) is performed in accordance with the principle of ijmā' (consensus), based on the strength of a Tradition from the Prophet that the agreement of the community on public affairs is an expression of God's Sovereign Will. The voice of the community, according to this Tradition, is an echo of the voice of God: *vox populi vox Dei*.[12]

The choice of the Sunnī Imām by the community introduced a "popular" factor into the legitimacy of the Imamate. Under the Prophet, the Islamic state was a form of polity based on a single-contract arrangement, whereby the Prophet, appointed to rule by Divine Command, was accepted by the people in accordance with the principle of *pactum tacitum*. The Shī'ī doctrine of the Imamate,

11. For an exposition of the Shī'ī doctrine of the Imamate, see Shaykh Ṣadūq, *Risālatu'l I'tiqādāt*, trans. A.A.A. Fyzee, entitled *A Shī'ite Creed* (London, 1942); Qāḍī al-Nu'mān B. Muḥammad, *Da'ā'im al-Islām* [Pillars of Islām], ed. Fayḍī [Fyzee] (Cairo, 1951), I, 25–120; al-Ḥillī, *al-Bābu'l Ḥādī 'Ashar*, trans. Miller (London, 1928), pp. 62–81. For modern studies, see D. M. Donaldson, *Shī'ite Religion* (London, 1933); A.A.A. Fyzee, "Shī'ī Legal Theories," in Khadduri and Liebesay, eds., *Law in the Middle East* (Washington, D.C., 1955), chap. 5.

12. For the doctrine of the ijmā' as an expression of the Divine Will, see Shāfi'ī, *al-Risāla*, trans Khadduri, *Islamic Jurisprudence*, p. 38.

based on the principle of designation, sought to perpetuate such an arrangement. Thus the introduction of the consensus of the community as a principle of legitimacy changed the Islamic state from a single-contract to a two-contract arrangement. The double or two-contract theory is based on the assumption that once a political community is formed by one contract, the Ruler is enthroned by another contract, to govern in accordance with certain conditions and limitations on his authority. The Sunnī Imamate, based on a second-contract theory, provided that the Imām would carry out only the obligations which he and the community had accepted, in accordance with the Law laid down by the Prophet. Since the Prophetic legislation came to an end, the Imām's functions were reduced to the implementation of the Law and to "judge among men with justice" (Q. XXXVIII, 25). Nor was he necessarily the best (al-afḍal)—certainly not as infallible—as the Shī'ī doctrine stipulated.

Granting that such an arrangement was acceptable to the community, to whom would the Imām be responsible? Under the single-contract theory, the Imām owed his appointment to God and would be responsible only to Him. In accordance with the double-contract theory, the Imām was enthroned on the basis of certain constraints and limitations to his power. Since his power was derived from and limited by the Law, he owed only his enthronement to the community. Nor could he be removed after he had assumed power, according to most writers, but if he failed to fulfill or was incapacitated from fulfilling his duties, he had no right to remain an Imām. In contrast with the Shī'ī doctrine, the Sunnī doctrine has added an element of democracy (through the exercise of consensus) to its scale of political justice, notwithstanding that authority under both doctrines is derived from the Law (and ultimately from God)—not from the people. Before making decisions, however, the Sunnī Imām was under obligation to seek consultation (shūra) with the scholars on all matters concerning Law and Religion, a symbolic rule that public consent of the Imām's exercise of God's Sovereign Will was necessary.

Despite the virtual control of power by a Sunnī Imām, the Shī'a never really stopped to question the legitimacy of the Sunnī Imamate. After 'Alī (d. 60/661), al-Ḥusayn, his second son,[13] claimed the

13. Al-Ḥasan, 'Alī's first son, was in theory the titular Imām, although he surrendered his powers to Mu'āwiya, founder of the Umayyad line of caliphs. Upon Ḥasan's death (49/669), al-Ḥusayn became the third Imām.

Imamate and met his demise in an attempt to seize power in an encounter on the outskirts of Karbalā' (near the River Euphrates) on October 10, 680. That event, commemorated every year on the tenth of the month of Muḥarram, is an occasion of mourning with intent to display a feeling of repentance for the fall of Ḥusayn. The tragedy of Karbalā' is considered the *cause célèbre* of justice in the struggle against oppression under Sunnī rule. Ḥusayn's descendants, never giving up their claim to the legitimate Imamate, continued to challenge Sunnī rule until the Twelfth Imām suddenly disappeared in 260/874, when he was still an infant. In accordance with Shī'ī teachings, the Imām went into ghayba (absence)—he is not in evidence physically, but his spirit is considered still with the fold. He will eventually return in the capacity of al-Mahdī (Messiah) to reestablish Shī'ī rule. During his absence, the Shī'ī community is warned that it might suffer injustice under the Imām of Injustice (Imām al-Jawr) until the hidden Imām will return to reestablish legitimacy and justice.[14]

The Shī'ī doctrine of the Imamate can hardly be considered to have advanced the cause of political justice, since the Shī'ī Imām claimed monopoly of power without limitations, whereas the Sunnī doctrine, stressing the prerequisites of ijmā' (consensus) and consultation (shūra) with counsellors (the scholars), is inherently opposed to the concentration of power in the hands of one leader. The school of thought that stood in opposition to both Sunnī and Shī'ī doctrines and advocated a radical notion of political justice was the Khārijite (often called Khawārij), whose followers called themselves the partisans of justice (ahl al-'adl). Its doctrine of the Imamate represented a third scale of political justice.

The Khārijī Doctrine of Political Justice

Representing established houses and prominent clans, the Sunnī and the Shī'ī Imāms paid little or no attention to the cause of the common

14. The doctrine of ghayba and the return of the Imām as al-Mahdī prevails in the region of the Persian Gulf (in Iran and 'Iraq in particular), but there exist several other Shī'ī sub-divisions, like the Zaydīs in the Yaman, where the Imāmate survived to the middle of the present century. Smaller Shī'ī communities may be found in the Levant coast (Syria and Lebanon) and still others, whose spiritual head is the Agha Khān, are scattered in East Africa and the Indian sub-continent. For a brief account of Shī'ī sub-divisions, see Henri Lammens, *Islam: Beliefs and Institutions*, trans. Denison Ross (London, 1929), chap. 7.

man—let alone the subject races—and were preoccupied with a struggle for power under the guise of legitimacy, which led to the uprising of the tribes in the provinces and culminated in the murder of 'Uthmān, the third Caliph, in 35/656. Under the rule of the Caliph 'Alī, in whose name the Shī'ī doctrine of political justice was identified, the Khārijites organized a political party which advocated a revolutionary doctrine of justice—indeed, a doctrine touching almost all aspects of justice—challenging the scale of justice of other rival groups.

The Khārijites, rejecting both the Sunnī and Shī'ī doctrines of legitimacy, maintained that sovereignty belongs to God, and He alone is the Ruler and Judge among men ("lā ḥukm illa li-Allāh").[15] Its exercise, they held, is not the privilege of a few leaders but the responsibility of all men who should participate in the management of public affairs in accordance with the scale of justice laid down in the Qur'ān and the Traditions. In accordance with these textual sources, they added, no distinction among believers should be recognized save on the degree of their Godfearing (Q. XLX, 13)—otherwise all are equal in the eyes of God. Moreover, the Khārijites made a distinction between outward and inward belief and contended that only men who subscribed to inward belief (imān) and obeyed the Law and fulfilled their duties strictly were true and just believers who could live in peace and harmony.

In theory, no Imām was necessary to enforce the Law if everyone were to obey the Law and fulfill their duties. Most Khārijites, however, saw the need for an Imām to enforce the Law and achieve justice. Only the followers of Najdat B. 'Uwaymir, leader of a radical group, held that there was no need for an Imām.[16] The Najdites, considering religious and moral obligations an adequate substitute for government, may be regarded as the philosophical anarchists of Islam. They held that inward belief can possibly supersede discord and turn men into well-behaving individuals—therefore authority was not necessary for society.

Before men could become true believers, the Khārijites admitted that there was indeed the need for an Imām, but they reserved the right to remove him if he proved corrupt and inefficient, since God

15. Ash'arī, *Maqālāt*, I, 191.

16. Hishām al-Fuwaṭī, another radical leader, shared the opinion of Najdat and held that God alone is the Sovereign and no man should exercise a power on behalf of God (see Ash'arī, *Maqālāt*, I, 189–90; and Baghdādī, *Uṣūl al-Dīn*, I, 271).

would not possibly approve of such rulers. However, the legitimacy of the Imamate, they held, should rest not on empty claims of legitimacy, as Shī'ī and Sunnī maintained, but on sound principles of political justice derived from the textual sources. Since there is no evidence in the Qur'ān or the Traditions concerning the manner in which the Imām should be enthroned, he must therefore be chosen by the community from among the most highly qualified (al-afḍal) without distinction of tribe, race, color, or class.[17] In addition to the enforcement of the Law and the pursuit of justice, the Imām is also called upon to prosecute the jihād (just war)[18] which is individually and collectively binding on his followers, and stand against the unbelievers, presumably until they become true believers in Khārijī eyes. When such a goal is achieved, they held, there would no longer be a need for the Imamate and the state, both logically and doctrinally, will "wither away"—only the rule of Law would prevail.

The Khārijites, though preoccupied with political justice, talked about justice in its widest sense. As a tribal community, they led a simple and austere way of life and rejected the worldly ways and lax social habits of urban communities. The values they honored, especially freedom and a certain measure of equality, are still to be found in the tribal society of today; but to the Khārijites these values and traditions were interwoven with the creed and observed almost as religious duties.[19]

Owing to their extreme views, rejected by all other groups, the Khārijites found themselves completely isolated. It is true that not all Khārijites adhered to radical views; only one group, the followers of 'Abd-Allāh Ibn 'Ibād—now called the 'Ibāḍites—survived, whereas the others, who persisted in their struggle for justice, vanished in bloody wars with their neighbors.[20]

17. Some radicals, followers of Shabīb B. Yazīd al-Shaybānī (d. 77/697), acknowledged the Imāmate of women, provided they were able to discharge public duties. See Baghdādī, *al-Farq Bayn al-Firaq*, ed. Kawtharī (Cairo, 1948), pp. 65–66.

18. See chap. 7, section on The Jihād as Just War.

19. For an exposition of Khārijī doctrines, see Ash'arī, *Maqālāt,* I, 159–69; al-Malaṭī, *al-Tanbīh*, pp. 51–57; Baghdādī, *al-Farq Bayn al-Firaq,* pp. 45–67; al-Isfirāyīnī, *al-Tabṣīr fī Uṣūl al-Dīn*, pp. 46–59; Shahrastānī, *Kitāb al-Milal wa al-Nihal,* pp. 85–108. For modern studies, see A. J. Wensinck, *The Muslim Creed* (Cambridge, 1931), chap. 3; E. A. Salem, *Political Theory and Institutions of the Khawārij* (Baltimore, 1956); W. M. Watt, *Islamic Philosophy and Theology* (Edinburgh, 1962), pp. 10–19.

20. The Ibāḍī creed is the official faith in the Sultanate of 'Umān (Omān) and some of its followers may be found today in North Africa. See T. Lewicki, "al-Ibāḍiyya," *Encyclopaedia of Islam*, new ed., III, 648–60.

The significance of the Khārijī notion of justice is the comprehensive and pervasive meaning given to it. If "the believers are brothers" (Q. XLIX, 10), said the Khārijites, then all believers should participate in the exercise of God's Sovereign Will and gain the benefits of justice and other values of the Islamic brotherhood. They were the first group to confront the community of believers with basic issues concerning the relationship between authority and the individual—in a deeper sense they raised the question of fundamental human rights—and to demand a definition of its position on the central question of political justice. These and other unresolved issues became the subject of debate in the following generation, especially by the Mu'tazila, who, like the Khārijites, called themselves the partisans of justice.

Justice in Accordance with the Doctrines of Qadar and Jabr

Second only to the Imamate, no doctrinal question in early Islam stirred more emotions and political controversy among the believers than the question of whether human acts were predetermined—predicated by God—or produced by man's free will (ikhtiyār, *liberum arbitrium*). The first believer who raised the question may never be known; however, the Khārijites, denouncing unjust acts in all forms, were perhaps the earliest organized group who advocated the notion of qadar (power) and held man responsible for his unjust acts. We also know that a discussion about predestination and free will began shortly after Islamic rule had been established in centers where Christian monasteries existed in Syria, 'Iraq and Egypt, and Muslim theologians who came into contact with them began to discuss and refine their views about predestination and free will.[21]

The doctrine of qadar is based on the premise that man, upon his creation by God, was granted the capacity or will-power—hence the term qadar (power)—to produce his own acts, and therefore must be held responsible for them. By contrast, the doctrine of jabr, which literally means compulsion, is based on the assumption that both man and his acts were created by God and therefore the question of human responsibility is irrelevant. The debate between the two schools of

21. For a brief account of the disputations among early Muslim and Christian theologians, see William Thomson, "al-Ash'arī and His al-Ibānah," *Muslim World*, XXXII (1942), 242–60; and M. S. Seale, *Muslim Theology* (London, 1964).

qadar and jabr, beginning as a controversy over political issues, gradually shifted to an inquiry into the nature of human responsibility and the broader philosophical question of voluntarism and involuntarism.[22]

The political aspect of justice was at the outset central in the controversy between the advocates of qadar and jabr. For this reason, the Khārijites, opposed to the Umayyad caliphate, talked about human responsibility and faulted its repressive measures—denouncing them as unjust and illegal, on the grounds that they were contrary to God's Sovereign Will and Justice. The Umayyads, on the other hand, finding in jabr a legitimizing doctrine of the *status quo* (and consequently of their claim to the Imamate) as an act of God, repudiated the doctrine of qadar and persecuted its advocates. Meanwhile, the Shī'a, considering Umayyad rule unjust and devoid of legitimacy, found in the qadarite doctrine of voluntarism justification for their opposition first to the Umayyad and then the 'Abbāsid regimes, and adopted it as part and parcel in their teachings. The Qadarites held that all human acts were the product of a will-power granted to men by God, and that each man was free to choose between the paths of justice and injustice. Since the Umayyad caliphs had by their free will, according to the Quadarites, chosen to exercise God's Sovereignty contrary to the scale of justice laid down in the Law, they had forefeited their right to rule; therefore, their claim to the legitimacy of the Imamate was null and void.

The Umayyads rejected both the Khārijī and the Shī'ī claims to legitimacy with equally strong arguments. They reiterated the well-known Sunnī position on the question of the Imamate that in the absence of a clear rule in the Qur'ān and the Traditions, the choice of a successor to the Prophet was a matter necessarily delegated to the community of believers, who were called upon to exercise it on the basis of ijmā'. It was in accordance with this principle that the first four caliphs were elected and confirmed by the bay'a (public delegation), including the election of 'Alī (the fourth Caliph), despite the claim of his followers that his enthronement as Imām rested on the grounds of designation by the Prophet. Upon his assassination in 40/661, Mu'āwiya, the first of the Umayyad caliphs, was elected caliph in

22. For a brief account of the meaning and origins of the terms qadar and jabr, see Sharīf 'Alī al-Jurjānī, *Kitāb al-Ta'rīfāt*, ed. G. L. Flügel (Leipzig, 1845), pp. 77 and 181; J. Van Ess, "Kadariyya," *Encyclopaedia of Islam*, new ed., pp. 868–72.

accordance with the same rule as his predecessors. This rule, the basis of Umayyad legitimacy, became the familiar Sunnī claim to political justice for succeeding regimes.[23]

But this was not all. The Umayyads tried to defend their position against allegations of injustice by theological arguments. They invoked the doctrine of jabr, which stated that human acts were not created by man but were predicated by God, and sought by such an argument to validate their policies and actions. Mu'āwiya, founder of the Umayyad house, was perhaps the first who argued that his claim to the caliphate was confirmed by God. As evidence of this confirmation, he cited his historic appeal to the community of believers for arbitration over his conflict with 'Alī on the basis of the Qur'ān, and claimed that God granted him support for his assumption of power as the first Umayyad caliph.[24] It is true that Mu'āwiya introduced certain modifications in the scale of political justice, such as the nomination of his son as a successor (which compromised the principle of choice by the community of believers) and his emphasis on a temporal outlook of the Imamate.[25] But Mu'āwiya and his successors, finding their opponents invoking Qadarite doctrines to undermine their position, sought to rationalize their legitimacy on jabarite grounds. The doctrine of jabr, presuming that the drama of history is an expression of the Divine Will, became the official doctrine of the Umayyad court, because it called for obedience to and acceptance of the status quo. Perhaps in no other document had that official position been made more clear than in a letter issued by the Caliph Walid II to his governors (in 'Iraq and other provinces) on the occasion of the nomination of his two sons, al-Ḥakam and 'Uthmān, to become successors after him, in the year 125/743. This was not the first official statement on the subject, but it was perhaps the most remarkable expression of the Umayyad doctrine of political justice, intended to be a reply to Qadarite critics of the Umayyad regime. The relevant parts are as follows:

23. For a discussion of the legitimacy of the Imamate under the dynasties that succeeded the Umayyads, see chap. 2, section on Political Justice as the Expression of Divine Will.

24. See Qāḍī 'Abd al-Jabbār, *al-Mughnī* (Cairo, 1960), VIII, 4. For a discussion of the background and process of arbitration between 'Alī, the fourth caliph, and Mu'āwiya, then governor of Syria, see M. Khadduri, *War and Peace in the Law of Islam* (New York, 1979), chap. 20.

25. For the view that Mu'āwiya sought to transform the caliphate into temporal kingship, see al-Ya'qūbī, *Ta'rīkh*, ed. Houtsma (Leiden, 1883), II, 176.

> The Prophet's successors as Caliphs were appointed by God and charged with the execution of His commands. . . . The Caliphs who came afte. the Prophet followed the law and justice as it had been established (by Him). . . . Each Caliph followed one another in accordance with God's commands which caused them to inherit all the affairs of the Prophet. He appointed them his successors and no one can oppose their right to rule without being thrown down by God, nor forsake the community without inviting destruction. . . . God has always made it possible for the Caliphs to overcome those who rebelled and has made them an example and an admonition to the rest of the community. . . . When God said to the angels: "Verily, I am about to appoint a caliph on earth," they said: "Will you appoint one who will be evil and shed blood while we proclaim thy praise and call thee holy?"; He said: "Verily, I know what you know not (Q. II, 28)."
>
> And so by the Caliphate God makes remain whom he makes remain . . . and He knows that there is no support or benefit for anything except by his obedience. . . . Whoever accepts what has commanded receives his rewards. . . . and whoever turns his face from God's commands forfeits his shares and disobeys the Lord and loses this world and the hereafter. . . . Obedience to God is the key to all these matters; by obedience to God men attain happiness and receive reward, but in disobedience is the revenge and anger and torture of the Almighty. . . . Therefore, adhere to obedience of God in whatever befalls you, for you have seen the evidence of God's judgement on his Caliphs by enhancing them and by making their arguments prevail and by repelling the falsehood of those who compete or take issue with them. . . .
>
> To put an end to bloodshed and disunity, God has instituted the Caliphate as a means to insure security and maintain harmony and solidarity. . . . The Caliphate is a safeguard against evil and destruction. . . . And the Caliph, praying for God's help, has seen fit to present to you a covenant, subject to your acceptance, that al-Ḥakam, his son, and after him 'Uthmān, shall rule and hope that they will serve the office with the best virtues that God has given them.[26]

In reply to its critics, the Umayyad Imamate is represented in the Caliph Walīd's letter as a divine institution, designed to enforce the Law, maintain unity of the community, and administer justice. To achieve these ends, the caliph was entitled to obedience; those who opposed him would incur God's displeasure in life and perdition in

26. This letter is an abridgement taken from an almost full translation from D. C. Dennett, *Marwān Ibn Muḥammad: The Passing of the Umayyad Caliphate* (Harvard University, unpublished thesis, 1939), pp. 169–71. I have checked the translation with the original text in the new edition of Abū Ja'far B. Jarīr al-Tabarī, *Ta'rīkh al-Rusul wa al-Mulūk*, ed. Abū al-Faḍl Ibrāhīm (Cairo, 1965), VII, 218–24.

the hereafter. All the events that had taken place in the past, the letter stated, were in accordance with God's Will, and the caliphs were to maintain unity against dissension with God's assistance and hence with His approval. Needless to say, the aim of Walīd's letter was to identify Umayyad political justice with the doctrine of predestination, seeking support of the advocates of jabr for the regime against their opponents who invoked the doctrine of qadar.[27] But it was not only the doctrine of jabr that provided validation for Umayyad political justice. The doctrine of the suspension of judgement, advocated by the Murji'ites, provided a convenient justification for all who wished to dissociate themselves from heterodox controversies. They tried to divert the debate on justice from political to other aspects, and they seem to have directly or indirectly supported the Umayyad position.

Political Justice in Accordance with the Doctrine of the Suspension of Judgement

The deepening controversy over legitimacy and political justice among rival groups led to accusations and counter-accusations of kufr (heresy or unbelief) and the possible consequent disqualification of membership in the community of believers by one another. Were the believer ever accused of kufr, he would be liable for punishment with eternal fire in Hell. Some Khārijites went so far as to declare that he who is accused of kufr would be punished both in the hereafter as well as while still alive. Others held that he should be punished with death only if he failed to repent.[28] The doctrine of kufr, so often invoked in political controversies, aroused the concerns of conscientious believers who objected to religious sanctions against innocent believers for differing political opinions. They urged moderation and called for the separation of religious and moral questions from political controversies.

Under these circumstances, there was a widespread feeling that an end should be put to accusations of kufr and several groups, individually and collectively, sought to discuss questions of faith irrespective of

27. It is said that Ibn 'Abbās, a great supporter of 'Alī, dispatched to Syria messages to leading Jabarites in which he repudiated Umayyad rule as devoid of political justice. See Ibn al-Murtaḍa, *Kitāb al-Munya wa al-Amal*, p. 8.

28. See Ash'arī, *Maqālāt*, I, 181; Baghdādī, *Uṣūl al-Dīn*, I, 248–49.

political opinions. Such groups were called the Murji'a (Murji'ites)—men who advocated the doctrine of suspension of judgement (irjā') on political issues of the day. They were the first to initiate a discussion on the question of the destiny of man in terms of moral and religious responsibility, apart from differences on questions of political justice. They came into prominence early in the Umayyad period at a time when conflict between Orthodox and heterodox leaders had inflamed emotions to a high pitch and the need to diffuse tensions was widely felt. Because they tried to divert the discussion from political to moral questions, most Murji'ites were on good terms with the authorities, although some, holding qadarite views construed to be dangerous to the state, were looked upon with suspicion and disfavor. They continued to influence opinion until the latter part of the Umayyad and the early 'Abbāsid periods and laid the ground for thinkers of the following generation—Mu'tazilites, Ash'arites and others—to discuss justice primarily from theological and philosophical perspectives.

The Murji'ites maintained that rival political leaders, whether they belonged to Orthodox or heterodox sects, must be considered true believers, regardless of the accusations of kufr by one party or another, so long as they affirmed their belief in Islam in word and deed. On the central question of legitimacy, they held that no believer really knew which party was right or wrong. Only on the Day of Judgement (the Last Day), will the truth be known when God will pronounce the final word. And He, "the Merciful and Compassionate" (Q. I, 1), might on that Day forgive the party that was wrong. If God were to forgive even the party that was wrong, "who are we," the Murji'ites might well say, "to condemn the believer with unbelief before God declares His final judgement." Therefore, the Murji'ites argued, one is bound to suspend judgement on questions involving different political opinions.

The doctrine of "the suspension of judgement," though seemingly an expediency in favor of the authorities, led to religious and moral debate on the meaning of irjā' (literally deferment). Broadly speaking, it was construed to imply that believers were under no obligation to take sides on questions of political justice. In a deeper sense irjā' meant that each believer had an inherent right to hold his own opinion on controversial issues, immune to accusations of kufr, so long as he believed in the existence of One God, and in the message of His Apostle. "Imān" (inward belief), said Jahm B. Ṣafwān, "is the acknowledgement of God and His Apostle"; nothing else was required, not even prayer to God or other ritualistic performances, although others held that "the love of God" and the acknowledgement of His existence by tongue was necessary for inward belief.[29] Everyone—Muslim, Christian and Jew—who believed in God and in an Apostle of God was a "believer," according to some Murji'ites, since knowledge of God was shared by all believers, not only by Muslims. Abū Shimr, an early Murji'ite, talked about justice irrespective of its political implications and held that man is inherently "free" to choose between the paths of justice and injustice.[30]

The Murji'ites did not form a well-defined school of thought, since many of them held differing views about human responsibility and the destiny of man. They claimed to include among their early adherents such men as al-Ḥasan al-Baṣrī (though he did not consider himself a Murji'ite), the jurist Abū Ḥanīfa, founder of the school of law bearing his name, and others. It is outside the scope of this study to discuss the origins of the idea of irjā' and its theological implications, since our concern is mainly to discuss the relevance of the doctrine of irjā' to one of the major questions of the day—whether the destiny of man was to be decided on the scale of political justice or by other moral or religious standards.[31] The significance of the Murji'ite movement as a whole may be summarized as follows: First, its emphasis on the idea that political justice was not necessarily the determining factor in the destiny of man; second, its diversion of the debate on justice from an almost exclusively political angle to other aspects. It provided the ground for the rise of other schools which discussed justice from different perspectives.[32]

Political Justice as Righteousness

The Umayyad authorities, considering qadar as a doctrine opposed to their scale of political justice, were not prepared to tolerate subjects,

29. Ash'arī, *Maqālāt*, I, 197–98; Baghdādī, *al-Farq Bayn al-Firaq*, p. 128.

30. Ash'arī, *Maqālāt*, I, 199.

31. For a discussion of the origins and meanings of irjā', see J. Van Ess, "Skepticism in Islamic Religious Thought," *al-Abḥāth*, 21 (1968), 1–14; Michael Cook, *Early Muslim Dogma* (London, 1981), chap. 7.

32. For Murji'ite doctrines, see Ash'arī, *Maqālāt*, I, 197–215; Abū al-Ḥusayn al-Malaṭī, *al-Tanbīh wa al-Radd* (Cairo, 1949), pp. 139–48; Baghdādī, *al-Farq Bayn al-Firaq*, pp. 122–25; Abū al-Muzaffar al-Isfirāyīnī, *al-Tabṣīr fī al-Dīn* (Cairo, 1955), pp. 90–92.

whether in Orthodox (Sunnī) or heterodox circles, who expressed views in favor of qadar. It was taken for granted that heterodox groups—Khārijites, Shī'ites and others—sought, by upholding the Qadarite notion of voluntarism (ikhtiyār), to undermine the position of the Umayyad caliphs by holding them responsible for the injustices committed under their regime. But the acceptance of Qadarite notions by the adherents of Orthodoxy aroused the concern of the authorities on the grounds that qadar was opposed to jabr, the official doctrine of the Umayyad Imamate, even though Sunnī Qadarites may have been on good terms with the authorities. For this reason, the authorities often censored the activities of Sunnī Qadarites and entered into debate with some on theological questions which may not have direct bearing on political justice. The caliphs 'Abd al-Malik B. Marwān (d. 86/705) and 'Umar B. 'Abd al-'Azīz (d. 101/720) seem to have exchanged letters with men reputed to have held or entertained Qadarite ideas. The authorship of those letters has been questioned by modern scholarship on the grounds that they were either interpolated or composed by later writers, although the subject-matter was quite relevant to the theological controversies in which their authors have been involved.[33]

The first letter, sent by order of the Caliph 'Abd al-Malik to al-Ḥasan al-Baṣrī, is more directly concerned with qadar and political justice. The name of Abū Sa'īd al-Ḥasan al-Baṣrī (21/642–110/728), an almost legendary figure known for piety and uprightness, was reported to the authorities as having expressed seemingly unorthodox views in favor of qadar.[34] Respected by many political leaders and on good terms with the authorities, he is reputed to have spoken his mind openly at the great Mosque of Baṣra, where he met with his disciples and discussed moral and religious questions that had political implications. He was claimed by rival theologians to have been the

33. Michael Cook questions the authenticity of both the letters of 'Abd al-Malik and 'Umar, especially the latter, which Van Ess has reproduced from Abū Nu'aym's *Ḥilyat al-Awliyā'*, V, 346–53. See J. Van Ess, *Anfänge Muslimischer Theologie* (Beirut, 1977), pp. 113–76 (Arabic text of the letter, pp. 43–54); and Michael Cook, *op. cit.*, pp. 124–36. 'Umar wrote several other letters on political and theological matters which neither Van Ess nor Cook mention; they may be found in Ibn 'Abd al-Ḥakam's *Sīrat 'Umar Ibn 'Abd al-'Azīz*, ed. Aḥmad 'Ubayd (Cairo, 1954); the letter which Van Ess reproduced from Abū Nu'aym (d. 430/1039) is not to be found in the earlier work of Ibn 'Abd al-Ḥakam (d. 214/830).

34. For life of al-Ḥasan al-Baṣrī, see 'Abd al-Raḥmān B. al-Jawzī, *al-Ḥasan al-Baṣrī*, ed. al-Sandūbī (Cairo, 1931); Ibn Khallikān, *Wafayāt al-A'yān*, I, 354–57.

fountain of their conflicting views, as each tried to influence opinion by invoking the authority of a man held in high esteem. The Caliph 'Abd al-Malik was naturally interested to find out where al-Ḥasan stood in the controversy between the Jabarites and Qadarites, since southern 'Iraq, where he was preaching his doctrines, was the center of active heterodox activities, and rival political leaders might have derived support from his teachings in favor of their political doctrines.

Was Abū Sa'īd al-Ḥasan a Qadarite or a Jabarite? Were his views in favor of Umayyad legitimacy and political justice or their opponents?

Al-Ḥasan's ideas, orally transmitted, have often been cited by some in favor of qadar and by others in favor of jabr, but no work from his pen has been preserved to reveal his position clearly. An epistle attributed to him and reputed to have been an answer to a letter from the Caliph 'Abd al-Malik, has come to light in recent years, although references to it may be found in several works without a clear indication of al-Ḥasan's stand on qadar and jabr. From this exchange of letters, even though its authenticity is not without doubt, we are able to know at least the general trend of his thought, especially concerning justice. However, his views about voluntarism and involuntarism are not, strictly speaking, stated with clear commitment to either one, perhaps either because he held independent views or because he was *persona grata* to the authorities and did not want to appear opposed to the doctrine of jabr. Nor was he in favor of the notion of qadar as expressed by some of the heterodox opponents to the Umayyad regime on political grounds.[35]

In his Epistle, al-Ḥasan appears to have taken an independent position on jabr and qadar. He did not say that all human acts were the product of free will. Nor did he speak of evil and unjust acts as predicated by God in the same terms as expressed by the advocates of jabr. Moreover, his views about qadar were derived not from Reason, as the Qadarites maintained, but from the Revelation, such as the following:

35. For the text of the letters, see H. Ritter, "Studien zur Geschichte der Islamischen Frömmigkeit: Ḥasan al-Baṣrī," *Der Islam*, XXI (1933), 67–93; Muḥammad 'Umāra, ed., *Rasā' il al-'Adl wa al-Tawḥīd* (Cairo, 1971), I, 82–93; M. Fakhry, *al-Fikr al-Akhlāqī al-'Arabī* (Beirut, 1978), I, 20–28. For a critical study of the authenticity and the contents of al-Ḥasan's *Epistle*, see Julian Obermann, "Political Theory in Early Islam: Ḥasan al-Baṣrī's Treatise on Qadar," *Journal of the American Oriental Society*, LV (1935), 138–62; J. Van Ess, *Anfänge Muslimischer Theologie*, p. 18ff.; M. Cook, *op. cit.*, p. 117ff.

> Say: God does not command indecency; what do you say concerning God such things as you do not know? Say: God commands justice. (Q. VII, 27–28)
>
> To whoever of you desires to go forward or lag behind, every soul shall be pledged for what it has acquired. (Q. LXXIV, 40)
>
> God charges no soul save to its capacity; standing to its account is what it has acquired, and against its account what it has merited. (Q. II, 286)

From these texts, al-Ḥasan concluded, God has not created all human acts—He commanded men only to do good in accordance with justice and prohibited indecency and injustice. Unwilling to commit himself to the doctrine of qadar as understood by the authorities, al-Ḥasan talked about "the qadar of God," in which the destiny of man was described as having been generally dependent on God but specific acts involving moral and religious responsibility were considered the product of man's free will. "Guidance flows from God," he said, "but wrong-doing comes from man."[36] In these terse words, he summarized his notions of qadar and jabr in a nutshell. God commands mankind as a whole, he said, and every man is expected to obey. But each man is personally responsible for all acts involving wrong-doing. It is hardly necessary to say that the doctrine of "the qadar of God" is neither equivalent to the doctrine of complete voluntarism nor involuntarism, since he disclaimed the view of the qadar of God as a determinative factor of acts for which men are held responsible. In other words, he accepted some aspects of qadar, rendering man responsible for injustice, but he did not reject jabr without reservations.

However, al-Ḥasan warned the Qadarites about free will, as they seem to have taken the duties prescribed in the Qur'ān lightly. He denounced the extremists, in harsh words as "the ignorants," "the wrong-doers," and "the misleaders," and condemned their views as false and their acts of violence as tyranny. Their acts, he said, were not acts prescribed by God. This was his answer to all the opponents of the authorities—Khārijite, Shī'ite, and others—who questioned the Sunnī claim to legitimacy, and he in no uncertain terms supported their standard of political justice and affirmed his loyalty to the Umayyad House.

Ḥasan al-Baṣrī, essentially pious and moralist by nature, tried to

36. Ḥasan's *Epistle* (Ritter, *op. cit.*, pp. 71 and 79; 'Umāra, *op. cit.*, pp. 86 and 87); Fakhry, *op. cit.*, I, 22.

draw a line between political and ethical justice. He equated the latter with righteousness and conformity to Law and Religion. Opposed to violence, he asserted order and quietude. His teachings were in favor of the status quo; but his support of the established authority was unquestionably justified in accordance with the Revelation which states: "Obey God and the Apostle and those in authority among you" (Q. IV, 62). However, his concept of political justice, though bordering on jabr, was not without qualifications, since he urged the authorities in no uncertain terms to pursue justice and warned against oppression and injustice. For this reason, he did not consider himself a Murji'ite, although he came very near to sharing their views and accepted tacitly the doctrine of the suspension of judgement. Small wonder that several scholars claimed to have received inspiration from his teachings and ascribed to him ideas that they had put forth and circulated.

Some of the Qadarites seem to have been in touch with al-Ḥasan, although they held a notion of qadar entirely different from his which brought them into conflict with the authorities. Perhaps some of the most outspoken, reputed to have been the earliest Qadarites, were Ma'bad al-Juhanī (d. 80/699) and Ghaylān al-Dimashqī (d. 125/743). Ma'bad had indeed attended al-Ḥasan's circle at the Baṣra Mosque, but Ghaylān, a disciple of Ma'bad, had only indirectly known al-Ḥasan. Little is known about Ma'bad's life; he seems to have held some broad notions of qadar, though his views were on the whole moderate (perhaps under the influence of al-Ḥasan). Ghaylān, however, held extreme views, especially about political justice, which were almost as revolutionary as Khārijī doctrines. For instance, he asserted, with the Khārijites, that the legitimacy of the Imamate should not be dependent on the Qurayshi qualifications, as God's Sovereign Will can be exercised by any believer worthy of the office without distinction. But he disagreed with the Khārijites on the question of rituals as a necessary part of "imān" (inward belief).[37] Both he and Ma'bad were put to death for political and conspiratorial activities (the first in 80/699 under the Caliph 'Abd al-Malik and the other in 125/743 under the Caliph Hishām), although the reason given for their execution was their qadarite views.[38]

37. See Ash'arī, *Maqālāt*, I, 200.

38. Ghaylān was interrogated by the jurist al-Awzā'ī (d. 157/774) who gave his verdict in favor of execution on the grounds of qadarite heresy (see *Maḥāsin al-Masa'ī fī Manāqib al-Imām Abī 'Amr al-Awzā'ī*, ed. Shakīb Arslān [Cairo, 1352/1933], pp.

If Ma'bad and Ghaylan were forerunners of the doctrine of qadar, Jahm B. Ṣafwān (d. 128/746) was perhaps the first to express extreme and abstract views about jabr. Both Ma'bad and Jahm shared al-Ḥasan's views by making a distinction between political justice and other aspects of justice, and they seem to have been interested not in political but in theological and ethical questions. Jahm preceded the Mu'tazilites in advocating the doctrine that God possesses no attributes other than Oneness and Omnipotence, which distinguish Him from mankind. God, said Jahm, is unique—"nothing can be like him," as He is described in the Revelation (Q. XLII, 9). In accordance with this doctrine, Jahm argued that everything, including the Quranic Revelation (considered written in God's own words), was created by God. The idea that the Qur'ān was created, advocated later by the Mu'tazilites, was perhaps the only one he held in common with the Qadarites, for he was adamantly opposed to voluntarism and maintained that the Qadarite position on the question of free will and human responsibility qualifies God's attribute of Omnipotence. Nor was Jahm interested in the notion of justice, for in a world dominated by God's Will the concept of justice is irrelevant and his preoccupation with God's absolute power and unique qualities diverted his thought from man to God.[39] Small wonder that Jahm was denounced by the advocates of both qadar and jabr, who were primarily concerned with political justice, although long after his death there was an increasing interest in his ideas when the Ḥanbalites and other advocates of jabr stood in opposition to Qadarites and attacked his ideas to discredit the Mu'tazilites for holding identical views with Jahm.[40]

106–11). For the views of Ma'bad and Ghaylān, see Ash'arī, *op. cit.*, I, 200; Baghdādī, *op. cit.*, pp. 70 and 125; Aḥmad B. Yaḥya B. al-Murtaḍa, *Kitāb Ṭabaqāt al-Mu'tazila*, ed. S. Diwald-Wilzer (Beirut and Wiesbaden, 1961), pp. 25–27. See also W. M. Watt, *Free Will and Predestination in Early Islam*, pp. 40–48, 53–54; Albert N. Nadir, *Les Principales Sects Musulmanes* (Beirut, n.d.), pp. 42–43.

39. For Jahm's ideas, see Ash'arī, *op. cit.*, I, pp. 197–98; Abū al-Ḥusayn al-Malaṭī, *op. cit.*, pp. 93–139; Baghdādī, *op. cit.*, pp. 128–29; al-Isfirāyīnī, *al-Tabṣīr fī al-Dīn*, pp. 96–97. For modern studies, see W. M. Watt, *Free Will and Predestination in Early Islam*, pp. 96–104; Albert Nādir, *op. cit.*, pp. 40–42.

40. 'Abd al-Qāhir al-Baghdādī states that the school of thought to which he belonged (the Ash'arites) approved of Jahm's views about jabr, but disagreed with him only on the question that the Qur'ān was created, a doctrine which they repudiated and for which Jahm was executed (see Baghdādī, *Kitāb Uṣūl al-Dīn*, I, 333).

Political Justice as Retribution

Moderate in temper and constantly calling for peace and tranquility, al-Ḥasan displayed tolerance even to iconoclasts toward the end of his life. Like the Murji'ites, he was prepared to postpone judgement on questions of political justice to the hereafter. But his views aroused criticism from among some of his disciples who held either Qadarite or Jabarite views, although most of his followers remained loyal to him out of deference to his seniority, integrity, and reputation for piety.

The disciple who more openly disagreed with al-Ḥasan, especially on questions of political justice, was Wāṣil B. 'Aṭā' (80/699–131/749), who seceded to form a dissident group and became a forerunner of Mu'tazilite thought. Born in Madīna, Wāṣil came under the influence of some of the descendants of the Caliph 'Alī, especially 'Abd-Allāh B. Muḥammad B. al-Ḥanafīya (an offspring from 'Alī's second wife), before he left Madīna for Baṣra and sat at the feet of al-Ḥasan al-Baṣrī. Though he was at the outset a loyal disciple of al-Ḥasan, Wāṣil attended other circles and participated in discourses with such men as Ma'bad al-Juhanī, Jahm B. Ṣafwān, and others who held conflicting theological views. He also became closely associated with 'Amr B. 'Ubayd, another disciple of al-Ḥasan, and married his sister.[41]

Under the influence of these diverse streams of thought, Wāṣil was not unnaturally inclined to develop views about justice and qadar, not altogether in agreement with al-Ḥasan's line of thought. Like al-Ḥasan, he equated justice with righteousness, but his scale of justice differed considerably from that of his master. On good terms with the authorities, al-Ḥasan took a position almost identical to the Murji'ites and refused to be drawn into a debate on political justice; but Wāṣil, though rejecting Khārijī revolutionary doctrines, showed an interest in political justice and shared some of their ideas about it. He held that the believer who denounces allegiance to the Imām must bear a certain measure of responsibility.[42] To the Khārijites, the believer who

41. For the life of Wāṣil, see al-Murtaḍa, *op. cit.*, pp. 28–35; and Ibn Khallikān, *Wafayāt al-A'yān*, V, 60–64.

42. See al-Murtaḍa, *op. cit.*, pp. 33–34. Wāṣil seems to have been sympathetic with Shī'ī views of political justice and supported them in their claim to the Imāmate. For the possibility that he was engaged in an active role in 'Abbāsid propaganda when Shī'ī and 'Abbāsid leaders joined hands against the Umayyad caliphate, see W. M. Watt, *Islamic Philosophy and Theology*, p. 61.

denounced allegiance to the Imām was considered to have committed a grave sin (al-kabīra) and was equated with the unbelievers. But Wāṣil, taking a middle position between Khārijites and Murji'ites, developed his own doctrine of the intermediate position (al-manzila bayn al-manzilatayn); therefore, he disagreed with both as well as with his master. He maintained that the believer who denounced allegiance to the Imām was neither an unbeliever nor entirely innocent of infidelity (kufr), and assigned for him an intermediate position which he called "fāsiq"—an impious who commits a venial sin. He would be liable for certain punishment, he asserted, but should not be denounced as an unbeliever.[43]

A traditional story about how master and disciple were separated might not be out of place, as it reveals certain intellectual concern among those who felt that the Murji'ite position on political justice disguised hypocrisy under the guise of the doctrine of irjā'. Wāṣil, it is said, arrived with his brother-in-law 'Amr B. 'Ubayd at al-Ḥasan's circle one day and, having taken his usual place, put forth a question to his master on the destiny of the grave sinner. Before waiting for al-Ḥasan's reply, Wāṣil volunteered his own answer by saying that the so-called grave sinner should be considered in an intermediate position. Wāṣil then abruptly moved to another pillar of the Mosque, followed by 'Amr B. 'Ubayd, to form his own circle. Al-Ḥasan reportedly remarked that Wāṣil "separated himself" (i'tazal) from us (al-Ḥasan's circle)—a remark which earned Wāṣil and his new followers the nickname of "al-Mu'tazila," later to be applied to a new school of thought, claiming Wāṣil as its founder.[44]

The story of Wāṣil's separation from his master must be taken as symbolic and not necessarily as a historic event. For the form in which it was reported indicated that a sudden break had taken place between Wāṣil and his master, whereas in reality the debate on political justice had been going on uninterrupted for a long time in several circles, including al-Ḥasan's, and the question of the punishment of the fāsiq must have been discussed and resolved in Wāṣil's mind (and

43. The idea of dividing sinners into grave sinners (murtakib al-kabīra) and venial sinners (fāsiq) coincides with the Catholic doctrine which divides sins into two classes: *peccatum mortale* and *peccatum veniale*. The first represents the Khārijī position on the infringement of political justice; the other is equivalent to Wāṣil's doctrine of the "intermediate position."

44. For the story of Wāṣil's separation from al-Ḥasan, see Shahrastānī, *op. cit.*, p. 33; cf. Abū al-Ḥasayn al-Malaṭī, *op. cit.*, p. 41.

perhaps in the minds of several others) in accordance with the dictum of "the intermediate position" long before Wāṣil suddenly brought it up before his master in a confrontational manner. Wāṣil's sudden move to another pillar is indicative of his desire to form a circle of his own which would make public its stand for retribution against those who failed to express an opinion on a question in flagrant violation of political justice. It was known that al-Ḥasan himself had denounced those who refused to express an opinion on the question of grave sin as hypocrites.[45] If a believer were a hypocrite, it was then asked, should he be forgiven without blame? The Khārijites, who insisted that the grave sinner was an unbeliever (kāfir), cited a Tradition from the Prophet to the effect that the hypocrite was indeed a grave sinner. The Tradition runs as follows: "There are four features which give a man the stamp of a hypocrite: when he speaks, he lies; when he makes a contract, he deceives; when he promises, he fails to fulfill his promise; and when he litigates, he is dishonest."[46] On the strength of this Tradition the Khārijites argued that a hypocrite was one who possessed an immoral character and therefore had no faith, but only hypocritical belief.[47] Since al-Ḥasan failed to express an opinion on the destiny of the grave sinner, Wāṣil and other disciples declared their separation from his circle and made public their own position on that question.

What prompted Wāṣil to take a firm stand on the question of the grave sinner and not merely to brand him as a hypocrite was the notion of retributive justice, which was overlooked by al-Ḥasan. By failure to pronounce judgement on the matter, al-Ḥasan and the Murji'ites appeared in Wāṣil's eyes to have relieved the fāsiq from responsibility and to have set a principle of political justice aside; consequently, the spirit of the Revelation and the Law were undermined.

The significance of Wāṣil's contribution to the debate on justice is that he called attention to an important aspect of justice—retributive justice—which had been inadvertently ignored by his master and the

45. See al-Jawzī, *op. cit.*, pp. 25 and 42–43.

46. Muslim, *Saphīḥ* (see under Imān, trad. 106); Wensinck's rendering of the Tradition in the *Muslim Creed*, p. 45.

47. This Tradition, raising questions on the relationship between faith and works, has been the subject of controversy among theologians and therefore doubt has been raised about its authenticity (see Nawawī, *Saḥīḥ*, I, 149; and Wensinck, *op. cit.*, p. 45).

Murji'ites. Perhaps no less important, he offered a more convincing solution for a question of political justice than his contemporaries, and thus prepared the ground for the scholars of the generation that followed him for a more thorough examination of the whole meaning of justice than where he and others had left it. Since Wāṣil's doctrine of "the intermediate position" was later adopted by the Rationalist Mu'tazila as one of their basic principles, he deserves indeed more credit than had yet been accorded to him by modern writers.[48]

48. Cf. W. M. Watt, *Free Will and Predestination*, pp. 63–64.

3

Theological Justice

God can only do that which is salutary (al-aṣlaḥ) and just unto His servants.

—Abū al-Hudhayl al-'Allāf

God created everything. . . . He created justice and injustice in the world; [but] He did not create injustice as His injustice; He created it as another's injustice.

—Ash'arī

Theological justice is justice in accordance with the doctrines laid down by the theologians concerning God's attributes of Will and Essence. While the theologians were in agreement that theological Justice—the *jus divinum*—flows from God and that He is the final Judge, they disagreed on whether it is an expression of His will and Power or an expression of His Essence and Perfection. The ramification of these differences proved so important that Muslim theologians were divided into two major schools—the school of Revelation and the school of Reason—each stressing one of God's attributes as overriding, resulting in a continuing debate on the nature of justice and on man's capacity to realize it on Earth as well as on the destiny of man in the hereafter (life after death).

The forerunners of the two schools of Revelation and Reason were the Qadarites and the Jabarites, who were engaged from the early Umayyad period in a debate which was outwardly on man's capacity to be the author of his acts; but in reality their primary concern was essentially political and not theological in the strict sense of the term. The debate between the neo-Qadarites and the neo-Jabarites of the following generation revealed a higher level of sophistication, and it began to concentrate on the nature of justice, whether as an expression of God's omnipotence or His inherent justice—and on how it is realized on Earth. Although the debate on political justice was by no means over, its other aspects—theological or others—stirred greater excitement, reflecting public concern about the impact of new streams of thought that began to influence Islamic society. The passing of the Imamate from Umayyad to 'Abbāsid hands in 132/750 ushered in a new era in which a relatively stable and more enduring regime was re-established. Khārijī agitation against 'Abbāsid legitimacy subsided and eventually disappeared, notwithstanding that political justice continued to be reasserted by other opponents. The Shī'ī claim to the Imamate on the grounds of membership in the Prophet's house lost much of its meaning, since the 'Abbāsids also claimed legitimacy on the grounds of kin relationship to the Prophet, and both had initially cooperated in the destruction of the Umayyad dynasty and the re-establishment of authority in the Prophet's household.[1] However, since the 'Abbāsids took direct control of authority without Shī'ī participation, the Shī'ī theologians continued to speak about legitimacy and justice which, they claimed, was possessed by their Imāms alone.

The 'Abbāsid house was not slow in seeking to identify the legitimacy of their Imamate with Sunnīsm and in becoming involved in the debate on justice in opposition to Shī'īsm and to heterodox doctrines of justice. From the time when the 'Abbāsid regime was established, the spiritual and temporal powers were reunited and theologians and jurists—indeed, all men of learning—began to frequent the Court and offer counsel to the Caliphs. 'Abbāsid patronage of men of learning stirred an intellectual revival that was already in progress from Umayyad time—stemming from ancient and classical streams of thought—which might be called the Islamic Renaissance. One of the striking aspects of that revival was the continuing debate on justice by a vigilant group of theologians known as the Mu'tazila (Mu'tazilites), who tried to win over their opponents with the sword of Reason. This group, beginning first in Baṣra in the latter part of the second/eighth century, spread to the capital of Islam and to other centers of learning. Under the Caliph al-Ma'mūn (d. 218/833), their doctrines were recognized as official and were imposed on their opponents by state acts. The triumph of the Mu'tazila, however, was short-lived, as it came to an abrupt end during the reign of Caliph al-Mutawakkil (d. 247/

1. The 'Abbāsids claimed descent from the Prophet's uncle, al-'Abbās; the Shī'ī Imāms claimed descent from 'Alī, the Prophet's cousin and son-in-law.

847). The Caliph, under popular pressure, repudiated their teachings and confirmed the doctrines of their opponents as official. Nonetheless, the impact of the Mu'tazilite rational method remained permanent as it eventually compelled its opponents to adopt, in the defense and the refinement of their doctrines, both the Mu'tazilite method and some of their notions of justice.[2]

Justice as the Expression of Reason

The Mu'tazila, calling themselves the Partisans of Justice and Oneness (ahl al-'adl wa al-tawḥīd), carried the tradition of the Khārijites and the Qadarites who held that man is the author of his acts, both just and unjust, for which he will be rewarded or punished in the hereafter. The early Qadarites and Jabarites agreed on the premise that justice was Divine and God is its fountain, but there was a difference of opinion on how Divine Justice would be realized on Earth. Before the Mu'tazila entered the debate, three answers had already been offered to this question. The first, to recapitulate, was the Jabarite answer embodied in the doctrine of predestination, for which evidence may be found in the textual sources (the Qur'ān and Traditions) stating that man and his acts have been created by God and that man's life on Earth was the unfolding of Divine Will. The second, offered by the Qadarites and equally supported by texts, stated that man was the author of his acts for which he alone was responsible. The third, a *via media* represented in the teachings of al-Ḥasan al-Baṣrī, stated that "the good flows from God but wrongdoing comes from man." The Mu'tazila, rejecting both the Jabarite doctrine of predestination and al-Ḥasan's partial acceptance of human responsibility, proposed a new theory of justice by presuming the existence of two levels of justice—Divine and human—the one laid down by God and the other determined by Reason.

All theologians were agreed on the premise that Divine Justice is perfect, eternal, and ideal. To the Jabarites, justice is an expression of God's Will and all human acts, irrespective of justice, are predicated

2. For an account of the rise and development of the Mu'tazilite movement, see Zuhdī Ḥasan Jār-Allāh, *al-Mu'tazila* (Cairo, 1947); A. J. Wensinck, *The Muslim Creed* (Cambridge, 1932); Albert N. Nader, *Le système philosophique des Mu'tazila* (Beirut, 1956); W. M. Watt, *Islamic Philosophy and Theology* (Edinburgh, 1962), pp. 58–71; R. M. Frank, *Beings and Their Attributes* (Albany, N.Y., 1978).

by Him. The Mu'tazila, however, held that Divine Justice is an expression of God's Essence and that He can only do what is salutary (al-aṣlaḥ) to man. God by nature can do no injustice. Man always endeavors to realize Divine Justice on Earth, but he can do so only by means of Reason—a level of justice which is an approximation to and a reflection of Divine Justice and is translated into human acts by a free will (ikhtiyār) for which man is responsible. This kind of justice may be called Rational Justice. It may coincide with natural justice, consisting of general principles and maxims of justice determined by Reason, but it is theistic in character and comprehended only by those who believe in the One God.

Three underlying principles may be said to determine the scope and character of the Mu'tazila's doctrine of Rational Justice: (1) the principle of rationalism—that justice is determined by Reason, (2) the principle of voluntarism—that man's acts are the product of free will (ikhtiyār), and (3) the principle of responsibility—that man would ultimately be rewarded or punished in accordance with his choice between justice and injustice. The Mu'tazila held fast to these principles on the grounds that if all human acts were predicated by God, as the Jabarites maintained, how could man be held responsible for acts over which he had no control? The inescapable conclusion, they argued, is that God would be committing an injustice, were He to punish man devoid of responsibility, since such act is inconceivable according to Reason and contrary to Revelation in which it is stated that "God is never unjust unto His servants" (Q. VIII, 53).

But certain difficulties may arise which call for clarification. First, Rational Justice, defined and determined by Reason, and voluntarism (ikhtiyār), granting man control over his acts, have been found by Sunnī theologians to be contrary to Revelational texts which state that God has created everything on Earth and all motions in the Universe (Q. IV, 80; VI, 73; XIII, 2; LIV, 49; LXIV, 2–4). Second, the Mu'tazila's premise that Divine Justice is realized on Earth by Reason necessarily presupposes the existence of two scales of justice—Rational and Revelational—which may or may not be in harmony. In case of a conflict between the two, which one should the believer follow? These and other matters, leading to controversies and endless disputation, prompted both the Mu'tazila and their opponents to reconsider and refine their doctrines, to the mutual advantage of both; but what hurt the Mu'tazila's movement and discredited its teachings was the occasional resort of its founding father to compulsion rather than to persuasion.

It is true that the Mu'tazila assigned an important role to Reason in human affairs, and held that if there were any discrepancy between Reason and Revelation, the latter must be construed to conform to the former. But, as true believers, they really never questioned the authority of Revelation and have, like their opponents, taken the validity of the textual sources for granted. They made it clear that Reason and Revelation are always in harmony—the first to guide man in accordance with general principles of justice, and the other on particular acts.

Some of the leading Mu'tazila—Abū al-Hudhayl al-'Allāf (d. circa 235/846), founder of the group in Baṣra, Bishr Ibn al-Mu'tamir (d. 210/826), head of the Baghdad group, Abū 'Alī al-Jubba'ī (d. 303/933), and others[3]—may have over-emphasized the role of Reason in human affairs, but others conceded that Reason cannot always lead to sound judgement. However, they were all in agreement that Reason is the power by virtue of which man acquires knowledge and distinguishes between just and unjust acts.[4] Abū al-Hudhayl conceded that on certain matters of details or on matters concerning which Reason is in doubt, man should be guided by Revelation, but he insisted that Reason cannot be faulted on matters of general principles. However, if any discrepancy should arise between judgement made in accordance with Reason and judgement in accordance with Revelation, the latter should be construed in a manner to conform to the former. For this reason, the Mu'tazila rejected the literal meaning of certain Revelational texts which may be inconsistent with the explicit meaning of others, and proposed to apply the metaphorical method of interpretation (al-ta'wīl) which would provide consistency for the meaning of the Revelational texts as a whole. In other words, Reason becomes, in the final analysis, the arbiter in deciding the meaning between conflicting texts. For instance, references to God

3. For the life and thought of al-'Allāf and al-Mu'tamir, see *Wafayāt al-A'yān*, III, 396–97; Ibn al-Murtaḍa, *Kitāb Tabaqāt al-Mu'tazila*, ed. Diwald-Wilzer (Wiesbaden, 1961), pp. 44–49, 52–54. For modern studies, see Jamīl Ṣalība, *al-Dirāsāt al-Falsafīya* (Damascus, 1964), I, 75–109; and R. M. Frank, *The Metaphysics of Created Being According to Abū al-Hudhayl al-'Allāf* (Istānbūl, 1966).

4. See Shahrastānī, *Kitāb al-Milal wa al-Niḥal*, ed. Cureton (Leipzig, 1923), I, 29; Qāḍī 'Abd al-Jabbār, *al-Mughnī*, ed. Madkūr (Cairo, n.d.), XII, 4–6; 77ff.; A. N. Nādir, *Falsafat al-Mu'tazila* [Philosophy of the Mu'tazila] (Baghdad, 1950), II, chap. 2.

denoting that He is in possession of hands, sight, hearing and that He sits on a throne and possesses other anthropomorphic qualities, are abundant in the Qur'ān. These references, the literal meaning of which may vary from one verse to another, cannot be taken out of context according to the Mu'tazila, and must therefore be interpreted by a Rational allegorical (ta'wīl) method.[5]

Rejecting all references to God implying human and imperfect qualities, the Mu'tazila accepted only a general Quranic description denoting that He is unique—"nothing can be like Him" (Q. XLII, 9)—as consistent with Reason. All other adjectives, which the theologians call "attributes," are unacceptable to them on the grounds that they ascribe human qualities to God. The Mu'tazila have accepted only two: Oneness and Justice (al-tawḥīd and al-'adl) which are unique; but other qualities, like human virtues, are considered implied in the attributes of Oneness and Justice.[6] Only His essence and His perfection are recognized by the Mu'tazila, which they consider to supersede all other qualities attributed to Him by other theologians.[7]

From the two qualities of Oneness and Justice, the Mu'tazila derived their name, "ahl al-'adl wa al-tawḥīd" (the Partisans of Justice and Oneness), although the name "ahl al-'adl" (Partisans of Justice) had been claimed earlier by the Khārijites. Justice in Mu'tazilite thought, however, is more central, for if Oneness describes God's existence as One, Justice is His very essence. It is His unique nature—"nothing can be like Him" (Q. XLII, 9)—that distinguishes Him

5. The term ta'wīl, or the metaphorical interpretation of the Qur'ān, must be distinguished from the Shī'ī doctrine of ta'wīl empowering the Imām to provide an esoteric meaning which may depart not only from the explicit but also from the implicit meaning of a text. For the term "ta'wīl," see Jurjānī, *al-Ta'rīfāt*, ed. G. L. Flügel (Leipzig, 1845), p. 52; Nu'mān B. Ḥayyūn al-Tamīmī, *Kitāb Asās al-Ta'wīl* [Treatise on the Foundation of Ta'wīl], ed. Tāmir (Beirut, 1960).

6. Abū al-Hudhayl argued that the mere fact that God exists implies that his existence means that He is living and He is knowledgeable and powerful. Other Mu'tazilites, like al-Nazzām and Ḍirār, said that God's essence implies knowledge and power, as it is inconceivable that God is ignorant and powerless (see Ash'arī, *Maqālāt*, I, 218–23; and al-Khayyāṭ, *op. cit.*, pp. 59–60).

7. It is deemed outside the scope of this study to discuss the theological implications of the doctrines of attributes and essence, save in so far as they relate to the concept of justice. For an exposition of the differences between the Mu'tazilites and other theologians, see Wensinck, *Muslim Creed*, pp. 58–82; W. M. Watt, *Free Will and Predestination in Early Islam* (London, 1953), pp. 61–88; and Nader, *Le système philosophique des Mu'tazila*, pp. 48–129; and Frank, *Beings and Their Attributes*.

from everything else. It is, in short, the embodiment of His Perfection and Justice. Not only is He just, the Mu'tazila held; He can do no injustice. For, in accordance with Reason, it is contrary to His perfection to associate His name with injustice. Nor is it conceivable that He will ever do injustice.[8] Just as the Revelation has it, "God will not do injustice to anyone" (Q. X, 45; XVII, 47).[9]

But to deny the capacity to do injustice, some of the Mu'tazila argued, might reflect on God's Omnipotence. Abū al-Hudhayl, leader of the Baṣra group, expressed the opinion of his followers when he said: God has indeed the capacity to do injustice, but will never do what He knows would be injustice, as it is contrary to His nature.[10] But al-Iswārī, a member of the Baghdad group, pointed out that "to state that God does no injustice but has the capacity to do what He will never do" is a contradiction in terms.[11] Nazzām and Jāḥiz, in agreement with al-Iswārī, went so far as to say that were God to have the capacity to do injustice, such capacity would detract from His capacity to do justice, and it is contrary to His essence and perfection.[12] Qāḍī 'Abd al-Jabbār and other later Mu'tazila, who reformulated and refined the views of their forerunners, pointed out that it is inconsistent with God's Omnipotence and Justice to confuse His capacity to do justice with His capacity to do injustice.[13]

But then other difficulties were raised. What about the children of unbelievers who die in infancy and who God knows would become believers had they been given the opportunity? Would it not be injustice that He would let them die before they became believers? In answer to this question some said that the suffering of children was intended to be an example to parents who persisted in disbelief;

8. Qāḍī 'Abd al-Jabbār, *al-Mughnī*, VI, 48.

9. There are several other Quranic injunctions to this effect: "God will not be unjust to anyone the weight of a note" (Q. IV, 44).

10. Ibrāhīm al-Nazzām (d. 231/845), one of the early Mu'tazila of Baṣra, had his own followers known as the Nazzāmīya; 'Alī al-Iswārī, a disciple of Abū al-Hudhayl, and a contemporary of al-Nazzām; 'Umar al-Jāḥiz (d. 256/869), a well-known literary figure and a member of the Baṣra circle.

11. 'Abd al-Jabbār, *al-Mughnī*, VI, 127 and 141; *Kitāb al-Majmū' fī al-Muḥīṭ*, p. 246.

12. Some raised an objection to this doctrine on the grounds that the ascription of such a capacity to God might imply that He will exercise it (see Ash'arī, *Maqālāt*, I, 252–53; 'Abd al-Jabbār, *al-Mughnī*, VI, 127–28).

13. 'Abd al-Jabbār, *al-Mughnī*, VI, 127–34, 145–54; XIII, 298–311; *al-Majmū' fī al-Muḥīṭ*, p. 246–50 and *Sharḥ al-Uṣūl al-Khamsa*, pp. 345–54.

others said that they would be compensated in the hereafter.[14] But the later Mu'tazila rejected the view that the suffering of children was intended to be an example, on the grounds that punishment for the guilt of parents is an injustice and contrary to the principle embodied in the Revelation that "Every soul earns only to its own account, and no laden soul bears the burden of another" (Q. VI, 164). The majority, however, seems to have accepted the solution of compensation (al-'awaḍ) in the hereafter.[15]

The doctrine of compensation, accepted as an answer to the problem of suffering of children, proved a satisfactory solution for other kinds of sufferings caused by accidents (al-a'rāḍ) and natural phenomena such as plagues and other similar events as well as for the pains of animals. Qāḍī 'Abd al-Jabbār (d. 415/1025), however, said that he and his master Abū Hāshim al-Jubbā'ī were not quite convinced that the doctrine of compensation was a satisfactory answer to the question of suffering children.[16] But, he pointed out, acts which are seemingly unjust and are committed by men upon themselves, such as self-inflicted injuries or suicide, do not fall into the category of accidents, and the person who commits them is not eligible for compensation.[17] The doctrine of compensation, offered as a solution to the problem of injustice done to innocent men, was intended to be a refutation of the doctrine of predestination (that human acts are predicated by God) and not an answer to the question of whether self-inflicted acts are just or unjust in themselves.[18]

The Mu'tazila, indeed all Qadarites, were in agreement with other theologians on the concept of Retribution. The application of this concept, however, led to differing theological views. If all human acts were created by God, said the Mu'tazila, why should men be punished at all? The Jabarites provided the seemingly simple answer that man's destiny has already been predicated by God (although the doctrine of predestination is by no means so simple, as we shall see later) and the question of distinguishing just from unjust acts

14. Ash'arī, *Maqālāt*, I, 292–93.

15. Qāḍī 'Abd al-Jabbār, *Sharḥ al-Uṣūl al-Khamsa*, pp. 477–83; and *al-Mughnī*, XIII, 226–97.

16. Qāḍī 'Abd al-Jabbār, *al-Mughnī*, VI, 26. For discussion of the problem of the pains of animals, see Ash'arī, *Maqālāt*, I, 293–94; Qāḍī 'Abd al-Jabbār, *Sharḥ al-Uṣūl al-Khamsa*, pp. 483–93.

17. Qāḍī 'Abd al-Jabbār, *Sharḥ al-Uṣūl al-Khamsa*, pp. 501–3.

18. *Ibid.*, pp. 493–509.

becomes irrelevant. But to the Mu'tazila, this doctrine is contradictory to God's essence (that by His very nature God can do no injustice) and leads to the inescapable conclusion that He is capable not only of committing injustice but also of inflicting it indiscriminately on the innocent and guilty. Not only is such an act contrary to Reason, but also to Revelation (Q. III, 173).

In an attempted solution, as noted before, the Mu'tazila advanced the doctrine of voluntarism. In accordance with this doctrine, man exercises his free will (ikhtiyār) to choose between just and unjust acts, for which he would be rewarded or punished in accordance with the scale of *jus divinum*. But what is that scale? The Law indicates only what man's obligations are, stating the permitted acts and those acts that are prohibited, but it provides no rule for distinguishing the one from the other. Man, accordingly, is bound to fall back on Reason for guidance in order to distinguish just from unjust acts. The Mu'tazila said that, even before the Revelation had been received by the Prophet, men were not unaware of the notion of justice and were able to distinguish between just and unjust acts by Reason.

The Mu'tazila held with other theologians that the ideal justice is the *jus divinum*. But they argued that, apart from the justice embodied in the Revelation, man can comprehend the concept of justice by Reason.[19] The two concepts of Justice are not unrelated; the Rational is intended to illuminate for man the path to do justice in accordance with the Revelational. The Mu'tazila's doctrine of justice thus presupposes the existence of two standards of justice—a Divine (Retributive) Justice, weighed by the scale provided under the Law (reward and punishment on the Day of Judgement), and Rational, weighed on the scale laid down for human conduct on Earth. The two-level concept of justice is the Mu'tazila's attempted solution for the problem of responsibility for human acts; one is designed for Retribution in accordance with the scale of Divine or Revelational Justice[20] and the other—Rational Justice—in accordance with the scale of God's essence and perfection arrived at by Reason.

19. For the notion that man is by nature inclined to do good, see Shahrastānī, *al-Milal wa la-Niḥal*, p. 58; *Nihāyat al-Iqdām*, p. 371; Qāḍī 'Abd al-Jabbār, *al-Mughnī*, VI, 18.

20. This may answer the query raised by Goodman about the duality of the Mu'tazila's Rationalism and theism concerning the proposition of the synthetic nature of God's goodness (see L. E. Goodman's review of George Hourani's *Islamic Rationalism* in the *Middle East Journal*, XXV [1971], pp. 543–45).

The Mu'tazila held that man is by nature inclined to pursue the path of justice. This justice, in harmony with God's essence and perfection, is Rational Justice. But if man were to pursue such a path, what would be its scale?

The writings of the early Mu'tazila have failed to reach us. Only in the works of their later followers do we find a more detailed account of their doctrines and concepts of justice. The works of Qāḍī 'Abd al-Jabbār (d. 415/1025), which have recently come to light, are particularly important, as they contain a wealth of material about Mu'tazilite teachings.[21]

Qāḍī 'Abd al-Jabbār opens his discussion of justice with a definition of what just and unjust acts are. A just act, he says, is an act performed by man, not necessarily for his own advantage but for the advantage of another man (or men) for whom the act is intended. For instance, strictly speaking, eating and drinking and performing of a religious duty are not considered just acts, since the beneficiary of such acts is none other than the man who performs them and not other men. The fulfillment of a religious or legal duty is an act for which man is to be judged (rewarded or punished) in accordance with the Law (Revelational Justice). Nor should the judge be called "just" simply because he performs his functions as a judge; rather, he would be considered just only if he were fair and made the right decision in favor of one party against another. Just acts may, generally speaking, be defined as those acts which promote the welfare of other men, and the man who performs them would be called a just man.[22]

The Mu'tazila are agreed on the premise that all God's acts are just acts, for everything done by God, including punishment for wrongdoing, is for the welfare of mankind and not for His own advantage. Perhaps the only act that might not be called, strictly speaking, a just act, Qāḍī 'Abd al-Jabbār held, is God's Creation of mankind, notwithstanding that all of God's acts are described as "wise and just."[23] It may seem strange indeed that Qāḍī 'Abd al-Jabbār, contrary to the

21. The major works of Qāḍī 'Abd al-Jabbār that have been published are the following: (1) *al-Mughnī* (to which references have been made earlier); (2) *Sharḥ al-Uṣūl al-Khamsa*, ed. 'Uthmān (Cairo, 1965); (3) *Kitāb al-Majmū' fī al-Muḥīṭ bi al-Taklīf*, ed. Houben (Beirut, 1962). For modern studies of 'Abd al-Jabbār's Rationalism, see George F. Hourani, *Islamic Rationalism* (Oxford, 1970); and Ḥusnī Zaina, *al-'Aql 'Ind al-Mu'tazila* (Beirut, 1978).

22. Qāḍī 'Abd al-Jabbār, *al-Mughnī*, VI, 48–51; *Sharḥ al-Uṣūl al-Khamsa*, p. 132.

23. Qāḍī 'Abd al-Jabbār, *al-Mughnī*, VI, 48–49.

prevailing view, did not consider Creation as a just act, although his viewpoint seems strictly in conformity with the definition of a just act since God might be considered the beneficiary of Creation by obliging men to worship Him and never to associate other gods with Him. For God himself said, "I have not created jinn and mankind except to worship Me" (Q. LI, 56), although this Revelation must be qualified by another which states, "I desire of them no provision, neither do I desire that they should feed Me" (Q. LI, 56). It is also possible to argue that men who deserve the reward of Paradise might prompt the sinners who will be punished with the fires of Hell to wish that they would have preferred not to have been created. It is in this particular sense that one may argue that Creation—God's greatest act—is not necessarily a just act, and the believer who is rewarded with Paradise and often called a just man is only symbolically called so for his piety and uprightness and not because he has performed beneficial acts for other men.[24] Thus, on balance, Creation is not necessarily advantageous to all men, although scholars have generally considered it as a favor from God.

Just and unjust acts are weighed on the scale of a set of fundamental principles called "al-uṣūl al-khamsa" (the five principles), arrived at by Reason in which the substantive elements of Justice are embodied. These principles, however, were not all laid down by one particular theologian on a special occasion, but they seem to have evolved ever since the Qadarite movement came into prominence in the Umayyad period. For instance, the principle of the intermediate position, identified with the name of Wāṣil B. 'Aṭa', providing a penalty for the impious (fāsiq), became popular among the Qadarites of Baṣra from the time of al-Ḥasan al-Baṣrī. Others, like the principle of commanding the good and prohibiting indecency, in which some of the moral values were enshrined in the textual sources, had already been known to the community of believers from early Islam. The other principles, especially those stressing human conduct, have been laid down by leading members of the Mu'tazila. The five principles are as follows:

1. the Principle of the Oneness of God (al-tawḥīd)
2. the Principle of Justice (al-'adl)
3. the Principle of the Promise and Warning (al-wa'd wa al-wa'īd)

24. *Ibid.*, p. 49.

4. the Principle of the Intermediate Position (al-manzila byan al-manzilatayn)
5. the Principle of Commanding the Good and Prohibiting Indecency (al-amr bi al-ma 'rūf wa al-nahī 'an al-munkar).

The first two principles relating to the attributes and essence of God, generated the most intense controversy between the Mu'tazila and their opponents because they formed the very basis on which the scope and method of Mu'tazilite thought was founded. Reason as a method in theological discourse was not new, since it had already been used by the Qadarites, and the Mu'tazila have only re-emphasized it. It was, however, the concepts of Oneness and Justice, considered central in Mu'tazilite thought, which stirred controversy and high emotions.

The third and fourth principles, dealing with Retributive justice, are essentially legal and may be said to fall in the domain of the Law (Sharī'a). The Mu'tazila had indeed made it crystal clear that on all legal matters they accepted the rule of the Sharī'a (Law).

The fifth principle stirred no great controversy, as it may be considered a declaration of the moral values enshrined in the textual sources. The Mu'tazila, however, held that Reason urges men to adhere to this principle, especially its second part, since the inflicting of an unjust act might cause distress to men who witness the act and would be inclined to prohibit it. It is taken for granted that the state is under obligation to enforce such a principle, as it is closely connected with the maintenance of public order; but acts relating to the welfare of the individual are essentially moral and may be said to fall under the category of commendable acts. The Mu'tazila, however, were not unaware of the fact that opinion could vary from one society to another on the question of where to draw the line between acts relating to the welfare of the individual and the community and the extent to which the state should be involved.[25]

The five principles, providing a comprehensive standard of justice, are obviously not exclusive. Man is urged to use Reason in the pursuit of justice, but in matters of detail (furū') he may follow the Law. By virtue of Reason, man would be able to distinguish between the general good (al-ḥasan) and the general evil (al-qabīḥ), whereas by

25. On these intricate questions, see Qāḍī 'Abd al-Jabbār, *Sharḥ al-Uṣūl al-Khamsa*, pp. 148, 742–73.

the Law he can distinguish between particular good and particular evil expressed in the acts that are either commanded or forbidden. In accordance with Reason, an act which merits praise (madḥ) and brings about an advantage (naf') or prevents a harm (ḍarar) is considered good; but an act which merits blame (dhamm) and brings little or no advantage (it may even bring a harm in its train) is considered evil.[26] For the distinction between good and evil, the telling of the truth (ṣudq) and lying (kadhb) may be cited as cases in point.

Which one would be just—the truth or the lie? Everything being equal, man is by nature inclined to tell the truth rather than the lie. Even if one were to be hurt by telling the truth, he knows that to tell the truth is right and to lie is wrong. In accordance with Reason, the Mu'tazila maintained, there is an inward feeling, a moral obligation, urging man to tell the truth rather than to lie.[27] If one ever chose not to tell the truth, said the Mu'tazila, he must be either under a threat or expecting to gain an advantage; therefore, he must bear responsibility for the injustice resulting from not telling the truth.[28]

With regard to their attitude towards the unbelievers, the Mu'tazila have taken a special position on the matter. According to theological doctrines, the unbelievers do not merit salvation and the reward of Paradise because they do not believe in Islam, even though some (like Jews and Christians) do believe in the existence of God.[29] The Mu'tazila maintained that the unbelievers, by virtue of the fact that they possess Reason and have the capacity to exercise voluntarism (ikhtiyār) should be able to know of the existence of One God and to distinguish between just and unjust acts. However, since they have failed to become believers either because they had not received the message of Islam or, having received it, failed to respond to it, they do not merit salvation and the reward of Paradise.

But what about the possibility of extending taklīf (the obligation of observing the Sharī'a) or bestowing luṭf (Divine Grace) on a man who God knows will not believe; will he become a believer and merit salvation? Most theologians held that the unbelievers were under no

26. For definitions of al-ḥasan and al-qabīḥ, see Qāḍī 'Abd al-Jabbār, *al-Mughnī*, VI, 18–30, 31–36; *Kitāb al-Majmū ' fī al-Muḥīṭ*, pp. 232–36.

27. Shahrastānī, *Kitāb Nihāyat al-Iqdām*, p. 371; Qāḍī 'Abd al-Jabbār, *al-Mughnī*, VI, 199.

28. Qāḍī 'Abd al-Jabbār, *al-Mughnī*, VI, 18.

29. See my *War and Peace in the Law of Islam*, chap. 17.

obligation of taklīf nor were they entitled to the favor of luṭf until they became believers. Most of the Mu'tazila, however, seem to have looked at the matter from a different perspective. Abū al-Hudhayl and al-Nazzām held that God is under no obligation to bestow luṭf on unbelievers who will merit reward if they become believers, because they are in possession of Reason and must make their own choices on matters of faith.[30] Bishr B. al-Mu'tamir, however, maintained that if God bestows luṭf on a man even though He knows he does not believe, the man will believe and will merit the reward of the faith.[31] Abū Hāshim al-Jubbā'ī held that God is capable of bestowing luṭf to men who might voluntarily become believers and merit reward, but He bestows luṭf not as an obligation but as a manifestation of His Perfection.[32] Qāḍī 'Abd al-Jabbār and the later Mu'tazila accepted the doctrine of luṭf as stated by al-Jubbā'ī and held that an exposure to taklīf is an opportunity for the unbeliever to avail himself of it and achieve salvation and reward in the hereafter. An exposure to taklīf and luṭf, Qāḍī 'Abd al-Jabbār said, is consistent with Reason and not contrary to the Law. It is like an opportunity offered to a drowning man in dire need to save his life. If he were offered such an opportunity, would he turn it down? Needless to say, if he were to avail himself of it, he should do so by his own free will (ikhtiyār) in order to merit reward like other believers. If he missed the chance, the unbeliever would have failed to respond to Reason and exercise the right of choice between justice and injustice.[33]

Belief in Islam, in accordance with the Mu'tazilite theory of justice, is a matter of Reason and a manifestation of voluntarism. If a man wishes to be rewarded in accordance with the Mu'tazilite standard of justice, he must become a believer by his own free will, since Reason enables all mature men to know about the existence of One God. But if the unbelievers held fast to their belief, should they be tempted by God's luṭf to become believers? Although only a few held that luṭf is inconsistent with the principle of voluntarism, the majority seem to have accepted the doctrine of extending luṭf to unbelievers on the grounds that it is not a personal offer of grace but a general Divine

30. Ash'arī, *Maqālāt*, I, 288.

31. *Ibid.*, p. 287.

32. *Ibid.*, p. 287–88; Qāḍī 'Abd al-Jabbār, *Sharḥ al-Uṣūl al-Khamsa*, pp. 519–20.

33. Qāḍī 'Abd al-Jabbār, *Sharḥ al-Uṣūl al-Khamsa*, pp. 509–18; and *al-Mughnī*, XIII, 9ff.

Grace radiating from God to illuminate the path of justice for mankind. However, not all men are expected to avail themselves of it to merit reward, and the fate of those who failed to respond would be decided in accordance with the scale of Retributive justice.

Justice as the Expression of God's Will

The Mu'tazila incurred the wrath and antagonism of almost all other groups through their enthusiasm in search of a coherent and rational doctrine of Justice. They were in agreement with other theologians on the doctrine of Oneness—Oneness and Justice being the two primary Mu'tazilite doctrines—but they disagreed with them on several other matters.

First, their heavy dependence on Reason appeared in the eyes of their opponents to have subordinated Revelation to Reason.

Second, by entrusting the pursuit of justice to free will (ikhtiyār), the Mu'tazila necessarily altered the meaning and scope of God's attributes of Justice and Will, subordinating the latter to the former, and granting man the power to decide all matters affecting his destiny by Reason. This may not have been their purpose, but, by attempting to view justice from two perspectives—Divine and human—they appeared to limit God's concern with human affairs to the role of Judge who weighs man's acts on the scale of Retributive justice—reward and punishment on the Day of Judgement. Did God, the Merciful and Compassionate, create man only to leave him alone without Divine care (e.g., luṭf, taklīf, and others) until the Last Day—the Day of Judgement? Even the Qur'ān, the embodiment of the Revelation, appeared to be equated to a created object and no longer clothed with the halo of divinity and eternity as the Book of God.[34]

Finally, the Mu'tazila, claiming to use Reason as a method of inquiry, tried to enforce their doctrines not by persuasion but by coercion through the state, contrary to the spirit of their teachings. An inquisition was set up by the Caliph al-Ma'mūn (d. 218/833) which compelled judges and theologians in public service to testify publicly

34. For the controversy over the doctrine of the creation of the Qur'ān and its implications, see Qāḍī 'Abd al-Jabbār, *Sharḥ al-Uṣūl al-Khamsa*, pp. 527–608.

to their acceptance of Mu'tazilite doctrines. Aḥmad B. Ḥanbal (d. 241/855), a noted scholar in Traditions and the future founder of a school of law, emerged as the most forceful opponent of Mu'tazilite teachings and the champion of what came to be called the creed of the Partisans of Sunna (ahl al-Sunna) or Sunnīsm.[35] More specifically, he refused to accept the doctrine of the creation of the Qur'ān, arguing that there was no evidence in the texts that it was created, and he rejected Reason as a method of interpretation despite imprisonment and persecution. The Qur'ān and the Sunna, Ibn Ḥanbal insisted, had to be taken in their explicit or literal sense without asking questions (bila kayfa); for, he went on to say, questions are unnecessary on matters of faith. Upon the accession of the Caliph al-Mutawwakil (232/847), the Mu'tazilite doctrines were repudiated. By the time Ibn Ḥanbal died eight years later, there was no question that Sunnīsm had become the acknowledged creed, not only by Ḥanbalī followers but also by the state.

The Ḥanbalī reaction, however, was negative in nature; it was extremely conservative and failed to provide a rationale for Sunnīsm. Meanwhile some of the Mu'tazila, like Abū 'Alī al-Jubbā'ī and his son, Abū Hāshim, appeared more flexible and were prepared to accept some of the Sunnī concepts (like taklīf and luṭf). If Sunnīsm were to stand the test, the need for a more constructive approach which would maintain a balance between Revelation and Reason was necessary. The need for such a positive approach was felt at several centers of learning where a number of theologians suggested formulas to bridge the chasm between the two extreme trends. Abū Ja'far al-Ṭaḥāwī of Egypt (d. 321/933) and Abū Manṣūr al-Māturīdī of Samarqand (d. 323/935) offered formulations which found local support, but the compromise that Abū al-Ḥasan B. Ismā'īl al-Ash'arī of Baghdad (d. 324/935) proposed in the very center where the controversy had occurred commanded wider public appeal.

Ash'arī was a disciple of al-Jubbā'ī, head of the Mu'tazila group of Baṣra after Abū al-Hudhayl. As a vigilant and inquisitive student of

35. The followers of Ibn Ḥanbal, called the Ḥanbalites (who founded a school of law and theology after his name) were able to arouse public concern about Mu'tazilite teachings and induced the authorities to abandon their doctrines. For the life of Ibn Ḥanbal and the Ḥanbalī movement, see Abū al-Faraj 'Abd al-Raḥmān B. al-Jawzī, *Manāqib al-Imām Aḥmad Ibn Ḥanbal* (Cairo, 1947); W. M. Patton, *Aḥmad B. Ḥanbal and the Miḥna* (Leiden, 1897); M. Abū Zahra, *Ibn Ḥanbal* (Cairo, 1947).

theology, Ash'arī frequented several other centers of learning and was exposed to different streams of thought which brought him into conflict with his master. Since the Ḥanbalī position was too rigid and lacking in depth to be acceptable to all Sunnī students of theology, Ash'arī proved more capable and well-equipped to lead a movement which would reassert Sunnīsm on a more sound and defensible basis. His movement, as one modern scholar observed, may well be considered as the logical development of Mu'tazilite thought, since Ash'arī's master, al-Jubbā'ī, had himself already pointed out some of the limitations of the rational method on a number of points.[36]

Ash'arī's dramatic renouncement of Mu'tazilite doctrines and his conversion to Sunnīsm was announced in the great Mosque of Baṣra, on the first day after the fast of Ramaḍan was over in 299/912. Before the assembled public in the Mosque, he stood on the steps of the pulpit and, throwing away his garment cried aloud, "As I cast away this garment, so do I renounce all that I formerly believed." The event, however, must be considered symbolic, since Ash'arī's reservations and doubt about some of the Mu'tazilite premises had already been evolving in his mind long before his break with his master, al-Jubbā'ī. The traditional story that brought about the break may be summarized as follows:

In one of the discourses, Ash'arī asked al-Jubbā'ī a question about the destiny of three brothers. One of these was pious, the second, wicked, and the third died in infancy. Jubbā'ī is reported to have answered that the first would be among the glorified, the second among those who would perish and the third among those who were safe. Dissatisfied with the answer, al-Ash'arī said that since God knew that, had the infant been allowed to live, he would either have been pious or wicked, then taking his life at infancy therefore betrayed an injustice. The master, it is said, demurred. The purpose of this discourse was to demonstrate the inadequacy of Reason to provide a convincing answer, and Ash'arī sought to prove his point that one had to fall back on Revelation.[37] This event was the rationale given for

36. See W. M. Watt, *Free Will and Predestination*, p. 137.

37. In another traditional story, Ash'arī is reported to have seen the Prophet in three dreams during the fasting month of Ramaḍān, in which the Prophet urged, in the first and second, to support the Sunna, and in the third, not to give up theological speculation. See Ibn 'Asākir's *Apology*, in Ash'arī, *Kitāb al-Luma'* [A Treatise on Aphorisms], trans. McCarthy (Beirut, 1953), pp. 152–55.

Ash'arī's conversion to Sunnīsm. Obviously this and other stories were merely popular accounts of deeper discourses about justice and other matters that had long been taking place among theologians within the walls of learned circles.

After his conversion, Ash'arī began with enthusiasm and intellectual vigor to fulfill the promise of his burden—the exposition of Sunnīsm in accordance with the authoritative texts. He demonstrated by example, with considerable success, that Reason is in conformity with the explicit meaning of the texts, and he made it clear that Reason was subordinate to Revelation. In one of the most influential though not necessarily major work entitled *Kitāb al-Ibāna,* composed soon after his conversion, Ash'arī summarized his fundamental theological ideas and supported the Ḥanbalī position on several questions, such as that the Qur'ān is eternal and uncreated, and other matters.[38]

While Ibn Ḥanbal reaffirmed the doctrine of the overriding Will of God on the evidence of the literal meaning of the texts, in his *Kitāb al-Ibāna* and other works, Ash'arī had no hesitation in using Reason as a method, which he learned as a former Mu'tazilite, to support Ibn Ḥanbal's position and to provide a rationale for the doctrine of Divine Justice within the framework of God's Will. He made it clear that God's power is supreme, by stating that God's Will is embodied in the totality of things and embraces "everything which can be willed," but the doctrine should not be construed to mean that God's Will is individually imposed on men. God created human acts generally—as part of the totality of things in society—but He did not assign them to particular individuals. In their conduct, men encounter these acts and do them as they come to pass.

Justice, however, is not subject to man's free will according to the Ash'arī doctrine, because God is the creator of "everything" and there is no room for human or Rational Justice (Q. II, 19 and 27; XIII, 17). Justice is an expression of God's Will and man is commanded to do that which has been predicated to be just, because God knows what is good for man as a whole. In other words, the principle of public good by virtue of which the good of the individual is realized is implied in this doctrine, but evil and injustice will arise if the individual good should come into conflict with the general good.

38. See Abū al-Ḥasan 'Ali B. Ismā'īl al-Ash'arī, *Kitāb al-Ibāna 'An Uṣūl al-Diyāna* [Treatise on the Exposition of the Fundamentals of Religion], 2nd ed. (Hyderabad, 1367/1948). English translation, by W. C. Klein, *al-Ibāna 'An Uṣūl Al-Diyānah: The Elucidation of Islam's Foundation* (New Haven, 1940).

But if both justice and injustice are mere expressions of God's Will, how can man distinguish between justice and injustice? One of the questions that remained unclarified in the Mu'tazilite doctrine of justice was the relationship between Justice and the Law, although some of the Mu'tazila did express an opinion on the matter. According to Ibn Ḥanbal, all questions relating to justice must be decided in accordance with the Law. Indeed, all jurists, including Abū Ḥanīfa (who advocated the use of Reason through analogy) were generally in agreement that justice is defined in accordance with the Law. Shāfi'ī, who worked out an elaborate system of jurisprudence, summed up the position of the scholars by defining justice strictly as "acting in obedience to God."[39] As follower of the Shāfi'ī school of law, Ash'arī accepted Shāfi'ī's position on legal justice, but he was quite aware that the question was more complex from a theological point of view. Since God has created "everything," Ash'arī asked, did he not likewise create human injustice? In the *Ibāna*, he pointed out that, although the Revelational texts state that "God does not will injustice to men" (Q. III, 104), these texts do not necessarily mean that He did not create injustice. Ash'arī went on to explain that they mean:

> He wills not to do them injustice, because He said "God does not will injustice to men," but He did not say "He does not will their injustice to each other," and therefore He does not will to them injustice, even if He wills their injustice to each other, that is, He does not will to them injustice, even if He wills that they do each other injustice.[40]

In other words, Ash'arī held that God did create injustice as He created justice, but in an encounter between one man and another, man may do injustice to the other as he may also do it to himself. In the *Kitāb al-Luma'*, he gave a direct answer to this question which was put to him by an interlocuter (presumably a Mu'tazilite), who asked, "Has not God created the injustice of creatures?" "He created it," Ash'arī replied, "as their injustice, not as His."[41] In answer to another question, as to whether God, in creating injustice, has Himself become unjust, Ash'arī replied:

> One who is unjust is not unjust because he makes injustice as another's injustice and not as his. If he were unjust for this reason, no creature

39. Shāfi'ī, *al-Risāla*, ed. Shākir (Cairo, 1940), p. 25; trans. M. Khadduri, *Islamic Jurisprudence* (Baltimore, 1961), p. 70.
40. Ash'arī, *Kitāb al-Ibāna*, p. 58; trans. Klein, *op. cit.*, p. 109.
41. Ash'arī, *Kitāb al-Luma'*, trans. McCarthy, p. 63.

> would be unjust. Hence, since one who is unjust is not unjust because he makes injustice as another's injustice, God is not necessarily unjust because He created injustice as another's and not as His.[42]

However, critics of the doctrine of predestination, whether Mu'tazilites or others, continued to hold that the question of responsibility for injustice remained still unresolved. The Mu'tazila proposed the doctrine of voluntarism (ikhtiyār) in order to hold man responsible for his acts, but this doctrine was unacceptable to Sunnī theologians because it compromised the attribute of God's Will. Ash'arī, aware of the implications of the doctrine of God's Will, tried to make a distinction between injustice created for mankind generally and injustice created for the individual. Both were created by God, said Ash'arī, but while the individual has nothing to do with the former, he is able to play a certain limited role in the latter by personal initiative. This initiative is a form of human responsibility called "kasb" (acquisition), by virtue of which man endeavors to pursue justice and avoid injustice, for which he merits reward. Ash'arī's concept of acquisition, though a corollary of the doctrine of predestination, came under the attack by the advocates of voluntarism, as it conceals an element of human will.

Justice as the Expression of Human Endeavor: The Doctrine of Acquisition

Owing to the extreme positions taken by Rationalists and Revelationists, no fully satisfactory answer to the question of human responsibility for justice and injustice was found. But if Sunnīsm were ever to endure, a positive approach to demonstrate the strength of Sunnī dependence on Revelation had become necessary. The doctrine of acquisition (kasb), though still vague and controversial, attracted the attention of many Revelationist theologians. In accordance with this doctrine, man can acquire (yaktasib), by his own endeavors, certain acts created by God for him and for which he (man) would be held responsible. By this subtle distinction between creation and acquisition—presumably the latter implying some form of contingent capac-

42. *Ibid.*, p. 63. Similarly, in answer to the question of whether evil is from God, Ash'arī replied, "I maintain that evil is from God in the sense that He creates it as evil for another, not for himself" (*ibid.*, pp. 67–68).

ity—a correlation between God's Omnipotence and human capacity became possible. By virtue of this distinction, man is not considered an entirely passive agent for whom the question of justice is irrelevant, but an active one who can play a part for which he would be responsible. Thus justice, though created by God, would in effect become a human affair in which a limited responsible role is assigned to man. By virtue of this doctrine, it became possible for Ash'arī's followers to reintroduce Reason as a factor in the realization of justice.

As a concept, acquisition was not new. It was used by earlier theologians to denote a variety of meanings, but as a doctrine attributed to Ash'arī, it merely meant that man had been assigned a certain responsible role to play within the framework of God's ordering of human affairs.[43] But Ash'arī was quite careful not to over-emphasize the human factor. In the *Ibāna*, composed shortly after his conversion, he had not yet begun to talk about the concept of acquisition (kasb) though he used the term "iktisāb al'-Ibād" (the acquisition of men), and he insisted that "there cannot be within the framework of God's authority any acquisition on the part of man which God does not will."[44] But in the *Kitāb al-Luma'*, written later when his ideas about acquisition had matured, he used the doctrine of acquisition against the Ḥanbalites. He insisted that man, in the pursuit of justice, could indeed play a certain limited role in human affairs. However, he rejected the Mu'tazila's retort that kasb (acquisition) was nothing other than man's qadar (capacity), implied in the doctrine of voluntarism (ikhtiyār). In answer to an interlocutor (a Mu'tazilite), who asked, "If man's acquisition be a creation, then why do you deny that he (man) is its creator?" Ash'arī replied:

> I did not say that my acquisition is a creation of mine in such ways that I am compelled to say that I am its creator. I said only that it is another's creation. How, then, if it be the creation of another, am I compelled to say that I am its creator? If I were the creator of my acquisition, when it is really a creation of God, then God Himself would be moving by the necessary motion which He creates in one who moves thereby. Since that is impossible, because God creates it as the motion of another, we are not constrained by what they say, because our acquisition is a creation of another.[45]

43. For the various meanings of kasb and iktisāb before Ash'arī, see W. M. Watt, "The Origin of the Islamic Doctrine of Acquisition," *Journal of the Royal Asiatic Society* (1943), pts. 3 and 5, pp. 234–47.

44. Ash'arī, *Kitāb al-Ibāna*, p. 52; trans. Klein, *op. cit.*, p. 103.

45. Ash'arī, *Kitāb al-Luma'*, p. 62.

In other words, Ash'arī stopped short of saying that man possesses the capacity of acting, because acting might imply creation; he preferred to describe man's role as a "doer" rather than as a "creator."[46] It is perhaps hardly necessary to say that Ash'arī's insistence on the difference between creation and acquisition was essentially verbal, leaving the larger problem of the relationship between the doctrines of omnipotence and acquisition unresolved. No matter how deep an impression he had made on the public, who acclaimed his defense of Sunnīsm, his tasks had not been fully accomplished. It therefore fell upon his successors to redefine the concept of acquisition and to work out a more constructive correlation between Revelation and Reason.

From among his contemporaries, Ash'arī was challenged by three leading scholars: al-Ṭaḥāwī (d. 321/933), al-Māturīdī (d. 333/944) and al-Bāqillānī (d. 403/1012). The first, although essentially traditional in outlook, criticized Ash'arī's position on the relationship between human capacity and justice. In his theological treatise, often called the Ṭaḥāwī Creed (al-Ṭaḥāwīya),[47] Ṭaḥāwī rejected Ash'arī's doctrine that God created injustice for men, since God could not be described as unjust, nor could He impose a duty beyond man's capacity. In explaining his position, he said:

> The acts of man are God's creation and man's acquisition. God does not impose on man any duties which he is unable to perform, and men have the capacity to perform the duties imposed.[48]

In the form in which he stated his doctrine, Ṭaḥāwī sought to define and correlate man's capacity within the framework of God's Will. In brief, his doctrine may be summarized as follows: The acquisition of human acts, originally created by God, became a reality on Earth as the product of man's capacity.[49]

Ṭaḥāwī's brief exposition of the doctrine of human capacity was more elaborately elucidated by two other theologians—Abū Manṣūr al-Māturīdī and Abū Bakr al-Bāqillānī[50]—who asserted, in no uncer-

46. *Ibid.*, pp. 39–40; trans. 57–58.

47. Abū Ja'far Aḥmad B. Muḥammad al-Ṭaḥāwī, *Bayān al-Sunna wa al-Jamā'a* [Creed of the Partisans of Sunna], ed. al-Ṭabbākh (Aleppo, 1344). See commentary on the Ṭaḥāwī Creed, entitled *Sharḥ al-Ṭaḥāwīya fī al-'Aqīda al-Salafīya*, ed. Shākir (Cairo, 1373/1953).

48. Ṭaḥāwī, *Bayān*, p. 9 (translation with literal alterations from W. M. Watt, *op. cit.*, p. 151).

49. Ṭaḥāwī, *Sharḥ al-Ṭaḥāwīya*, pp. 368–79.

50. For the life of Bāqillānī, see Ibn Khallikān, *Wafayāt al-'Ayān*, III, 400–401.

tain terms, the necessity of Reason for the interpretation of Revelation. In his *Sharḥ al-Fiqh al-Akbar,*[51] Māturīdī set forth the Sunnī creed with a certain rational overtone which may be considered as the *via media* between the doctrines of Ash'arī and the Mu'tazila. In the *Fiqh Akbar II*, attributed to Abū Ḥanīfa, the doctrine of kasb is stated as follows:

> All the acts of man—his moving as well as his resting—are truly his own acquisition (kasb), but God creates them and they are caused by His Will, His knowledge, His decision and His decree.[52]

It is not clear in the Abū Ḥanīfa text whether man's acts are "truly his own acquisition" in the sense that they are the product of his own capacity or his acquisition, denoting that they are acquired within God's creation, as Ash'arī meant in his doctrine of acquisition. At any rate, the controversy over the meaning of kasb (acquisition) had not arisen in Abū Ḥanīfa's time and its insertion in the text suggests a later amendation of the text. In his commentary on the *Fiqh al-Akbar*, Māturīdī made his position on the doctrine of acquisition crystal clear—that man produces his own acts by a capacity implanted in him by God. He said:

> Creation is the act of God, consisting in the originating of capacity in man, but in the use of the originated capacity is truly the act of man and not metaphorically.[53]

One of the implications of Māturīdī's doctrine of acquisition is that man would be responsible for his acts and consequently would merit reward or punishment. However, he did not indicate in the commentary its relevance to justice; instead he dealt with the matter as man's moral obligations in general. Nor did his two distinguished disciples, Abū al-Yusr al-Bazdawī (d. 493/1099), and al-Nasafī (d. 537/1143),

51. Apart from Māturīdī's *Sharḥ*, the *Fiqh Akbar* is an exposition of the Sunnī Creed attributed to Abū Ḥanīfa (d. 150/768), founder of the Ḥanafī school of law. While the main substance of both *Fiqh Akbar I* and *Fiqh Akbar II* may have genuinely come from Abū Ḥanīfa's time, the extant literary forms have been considerably altered. For a critical study of these treatises, see A. J. Wensinck, *The Muslim Creed* (Cambridge, 1932), chaps. 6 and 8.

52. See Art. 6; for translation of the whole text, see Wensinck, *op. cit.*, pp. 189–97.

53. Abū Manṣūr al-Māturīdī, *Kitāb Sharḥ al-Fiqh al-Akbar*, 2nd ed. (Hyderabad, 1946), p. 10. For translation of a portion of the Sharḥ, see W. M. Watt, *op. cit.*, p. 155. See also Māturīdī, *Kitāb al-Tawḥīd*, ed. Khulayf (Beirut, 1970), pp. 256–62.

add any significant clarification of their master's doctrines.[54] This task devolved upon another skillful theologian who came into prominence half a century after Ash'arī—Abū Bakr al-Bāqillānī (d. 403/1012).[55] Ash'arī, it will be recalled, was able to criticize the Mu'tazilite doctrines by indicating the shortcomings of the Rationalist method, but he left the task of providing a constructive rationale for Sunnīsm unfinished. It was indeed al-Bāqillānī who established it on a firm foundation and prepared the way for Abū Ḥāmid al-Ghazzālī (d. 504/1111) to reconstruct from the works of his predecessors an elaborate structure of the Sunnī creed which might be regarded as a happy compromise between Rationalists and Revelationists.

In his theological inquiry,[56] Bāqillānī proposed a method of answering questions by first making a distinction between divine and human knowledge. The latter, he said, is derived from both Revelation and Reason, whereas the former is necessarily dependent on Revelation, because Reason is inadequate for man's comprehension of divine knowledge and the method applied to human affairs, with whose nature man is acquainted, cannot be applied with the same rigor to divine matters whose nature is entirely unknown to man.[57] In the use of Reason, he proposed applying the method of istidlāl (deduction) by virtue of which man derives knowledge about the unknown from the known (al-ghā'ib min al-shāhid); but al-Bāqillānī pointed out that transcendental questions belong to an entirely different world, in which the rational method is inapplicable.[58]

By his acceptance of the dual method of Revelation and Reason, al-Bāqillānī sought to combine the Ash'arī and Mu'tazilite theological concepts and defended Sunnīsm against the rising tide of Shī'ī opposition.[59] He supported Ash'arī on the relationship between Law and

54. See Abū al-Yusr al-Bazdawī, *Kitāb Uṣūl al-Dīn*, ed. Linss (Cairo, 1383/1963), pp. 42–43, 99–110.

55. For his life, see Qāḍī 'Iyāḍ B. Mūsa, *Tartīb al-Madārik wa Taqrīb al-Masālik*; manuscript reprinted in M. M. al-Khuḍayrī and M. A. Abū Rīda, *Bāqillānī's al-Tamhīd* (Cairo, 1946), pp. 241–56.

56. See Bāqillānī, *Kitāb al-Tamhīd*, ed. McCarthy (Beirut, 1956); and *Kitāb al-Inṣāf*, ed. Kawtharī (Cairo, 1382/1963).

57. Bāqillānī, *al-Tamhīd*, p. 61ff.; *al-Inṣāf*, p. 13ff.

58. Bāqillānī, *al-Tamhīd*, pp. 8–9. See also al-Jurjānī, *Kitāb al-Ta'rifāt* [Treatise on Definitions], ed. G. L. Flügel (Leipzig, 1845), p. 17.

59. Bāqillānī's successors—Fakhr al-Dīn al-Rāzī (d. 606/1210), 'Adud al-Dīn al-Ijī (d. 756/1355) and others—carried this tradition a step further and prepared the ground for modern religious reformers like Afghānī, 'Abduh and Rāziq to take it for

Justice—both derived from the Revelation—but he disagreed with him on the doctrine of acquisition. He maintained that acts "acquired" by man fall in the province of human knowledge, although acts seemingly done by man may not necessarily fall into the same category. Some acts over which man has no control, such as shivering and accidents, are obviously involuntary (iḍtirārīya), but others, such as praying and fasting, over which man can exercise control, are voluntary (ikhtiyārīya) and should fall into the category of human knowledge. Therefore, they are subject to Reason. While the involuntary acts are predicated by God, the voluntary acts are the product of free will, for which man is held responsible.[60] The latter, acquired by man's endeavor (kasb), would be partly determined by Revelation and partly by Reason.[61] It is taken for granted that all the acts created by God are just, including sickness, the suffering of children, and others, as it is inconceivable that God would inflict an injustice, and it is impossible to know from the Revelation the underlying reason for them.[62]

What about the telling of lies and acts of disobedience?, asked an interlocutor. Bāqillānī said in reply that it is inconceivable that God will tell a lie, not because the lie is an evil in itself, but because He is described in the Revelation as truthful, and therefore it is inconceivable to describe Him as a liar.[63] As to whether it is possible for God to command men to lie or disobey the Law, Bāqillānī seems to have held that it is possible wherever they had been predicated by Him and not as commandable lies or disobediences.[64] For instance, God has decreed that lies are permissible in certain extraordinary circumstances, such as when the believer is concerned about his safety in the dār al-Ḥarb (the territory of war), but in normal circumstances the believer is expected to conduct himself in accordance with the princi-

---

granted that Reason is an indispensable source for religious knowledge. See Rāzī, *Kitāb al-Muḥaṣṣal* (Cairo, 1323/1906), p. 2ff.; al-Ijī, *al-Mawāqif* (Istānbūl, 1286/1870), p. 11ff.

60. Bāqillānī, *al-Tamhīd*, p. 286. But, perhaps as a concession to Ash'arī, Bāqillānī held that capacity coincides with human acts and does not precede the act (*ibid.*, p. 287).

61. Bāqillānī, *al-Tamhīd*, chap. 35.

62. *Ibid.*, pp. 342–43.

63. *Ibid.*, p. 343.

64. *Ibid.*, pp. 325–27.

ple of good faith (the nīya).[65] It is remarkable that not long after Ash'arī had violently reacted against the Mu'tazila's Rationalism, Bāqillānī consciously sought to reconcile Revelation with Reason, thus preparing the ground first for Gazzālī and later for modern reformers to advocate Reason as a method in the contemporary round of debate over justice and other measures of reform.[66]

Heterodox Doctrines of Justice

The re-establishment of Sunnīsm as the official creed under 'Abbāsid rule not unnaturally induced Shī'ī followers to sympathize with Mu'tazilite thought (especially in its emphasis on justice) in which they found justification for their claim to legitimacy. From the time of the disappearance of the twelfth Imām in 260/874, the Shī'ī scholars began to realize that their claims to political justice would be enhanced if they rested on Mu'tazilite doctrines and the rational method. Their participation in the debate about justice in Mu'tazilite circles aroused sympathy with Shī'ī pretenders to the Imamate of Justice. After the establishment of Buwayhid rule in 'Iraq and Persia (from the fourth/tenth to the fifth/eleventh centuries) and Faṭimid rule in Egypt (from the fourth/tenth to the sixth/twelfth centuries), the Shī'ī creed and jurisprudence were refined and reformulated on rationalist grounds, and a widespread propaganda campaign was set in motion for the reassertion of Shī'īsm. The movement, though not lacking in vigor, was divided into three major subdivisions, each advocating a different standard of justice, which ultimately weakened them as a whole.

First, the Ithna 'Asharī or the Twelvers, also called the Ja'farī (after the name of Ja'far al-Ṣādiq, who died in 148/765), is the earliest and perhaps the most active sect in Islamic lands. Its followers spread from southern 'Irāq into Persia and beyond. Gradually it came to prevail over Sunnīsm in Persia, where it became the official creed at the opening of the tenth/sixteenth century. From the time of Buwayhid rule, especially under the enlightened Vizir al-Ṣāḥib B. 'Abbād (326/841–385/996), a man of letters in his own right, Mu'tazilite scholars

65. *Ibid.*, pp. 343–44. For the meaning of dār al-ḥarb, see chap. 7, section on Justice and the Islamic Public Order.

66. See chap. 9.

were appointed to public offices and the Mu'tazila movement was given an impetus.[67] It was owing to such scholars as Ibn Bābawayh (d. 381/991), Muṭṭahar al-Ḥillī (d. 726/1326) and al-Majlisī (d. 1112/1700) that the Shī'ī doctrines of justice and legitimacy were reformulated and the creed established on a firm basis. The fundamental principles, perhaps more clearly and succinctly set forth by al-Ḥillī, may be summarized as follows:

1. The Shī'a maintain that human knowledge ('ilm) about God's attributes and other doctrines are derived from both Revelation and Reason. But while the Sunnīs claim to use Reason through consensus (ijmā'), the Shī'a prefer to use Reason through deduction (istidlāl).[68] If deduction were a prerogative of the Imām, after his disappearance (ghayba), the scholars (mujtahids) claimed to exercise it collectively on all matters of Law and Religion.[69]

2. Like the Mu'tazila, the Shī'a maintain that justice is a divine quality second only to God's Essence and Oneness. Likewise, they set forth two levels of justice: Divine and Rational; the first flows from God and the other from Reason. By virtue of Reason, man can distinguish between good and evil and is inclined to pursue the path of justice rather than injustice.[70] Long before Ḥillī, Bābawayh stated that God "commanded us to be just; He Himself treats us with something even better—Divine Grace (tafaḍḍul)."[71] Both are agreed that Rational justice is not predicated by God.

3. Man is a free agent (fā'il bi al-ikhtiyār) and the author of his acts, whether just or unjust, for which he is solely responsible. For, were God to create injustice, He would be "the most unjust of unjust beings."[72] The Ash'arī doctrine, according to Ḥillī, which describes God as "the doer of everything," is inconsistent with the concepts of Prophecy and Imāmate, since the Prophet and the Imām, who exer-

67. For the life and literary works of Ibn 'Abbād, see Ibn 'Abbād, *al-Ibāna 'an Madhhab Ahl al-'Adl* [Elucidation of the Doctrines of the Partisans of Justice] *in Nafā'-is al-Makhṭūṭāt*, ed. Yāsīn (Najaf, 1372/1953), pp. 5–28.

68. In the Sunnī practice, ijmā' is the agreement of the community exercised by the scholars who may or may not arrive at a decision by Reason, but istidlal is a form of individual reasoning.

69. Ḥasan Ibn al-Muṭahhar al-Ḥillī, *al-Bābu'l Ḥādī 'Ashar*, trans. W. W. Miller, *A Treatise on the Principles of Shī'ite Theology* (London, 1928), pp. 3–8.

70. *Ibid.*, p. 40.

71. Ibn Bābawayh, *A Shī'ite Creed*, trans. Fyzee (London, 1942), p. 70.

72. Ḥillī, *op. cit.*, p. 44.

cise God's Sovereignty, are by nature sinless (ma'ṣūm) and infallible and therefore can do no wrong. They are indeed the just rulers.[73]

4. Since justice is inherent in the Imāmate, it is taken for granted that as long as the Imām is in evidence, justice would be realized on Earth; but after his disappearance, the Shī'ī community became a flock without a shepherd when it passed under the domination of Sunnī tyrants (the Imāms of injustice). No matter how careful a Shī'ī may be to escape evil, he cannot avoid persecution and injustice unless he resorts to dissimulation (taqīya), a form of a defense mechanism by virtue of which he declares his allegiance to the Sunnī Caliph, but inwardly he should remain loyal to the Shī'ī Imām and his teachings. The practice of taqīya, though implying repudiation of Shī'īsm, is not considered an act of injustice on the grounds that "imān" (belief) is considered essentially an inward and not an outward act of commitment, and therefore the practice of taqīya does not necessarily compromise the Shī'ī standard of justice. Under the Sunnī creed, the taqīya is considered inconsistent with the principle of the nīya (good faith) without which the concept of justice is reduced to personal convenience.

The second major Shī'ī subdivision is the Ismā'īlī sect. Taking its name from Ismā'īl, son of the sixth Imām of the Twelvers, Ja'far al-Ṣādiq, the sect formed the second largest Shī'ī community in Islamic lands. The split took place over a difference of opinion on the specific meaning of legitimacy. While Ja'far al-Ṣādiq was still alive, his oldest son Ismā'īl died in 146/762. The majority was in favor of the succession of Mūsa, second son of Imām Ja'far, but others held that the Imamate should be bequeathed to Muḥammad, Ismā'īl's son, and they considered both Ismā'īl's and his son together as the seventh Imām, as legitimacy would be questionable were succession to pass from brother to brother rather than from father to the elder son. Thus those who insisted on the Imamate of Ismā'īl came to be known as the Ismā'īlis or Seveners (followers of the seventh Imām).

From a split on legitimacy—a basic concept of political justice—other credal variants ensued. The Ismā'īlī Imām is considered in possession of an esoteric knowledge of ta'līm (teachings), derived from a Divine source, and therefore such teachings are taken to be the embodiment of Divine Justice. Since the Imām is clothed with sinless-

73. Ḥillī, *op. cit.*, pp. 44–45; Ibn Bābawayh, *op. cit.*, pp. 99–100.

ness ('iṣma), a quality stressed by the Ismā'īlīs more than others, his decisions should be accepted without question as the final word on justice. The ta'līm includes the ta'wīl (metaphorism), which indeed all Shī'a accept, but the Ismā'īlīs considered it a higher science—the science of bāṭin (inward knowledge)—for an understanding of the concealed meaning of the Quranic Revelation. So abstract and different from other allegorical interpretation, this method has earned for them still another name—the Bāṭinīya.

The establishment of Fāṭimid rule, first in Northwest Africa and then in Egypt and Syria (297–567/909–1171), set in motion an active Shī'ī propaganda in eastern Islamic lands against Sunnī legitimacy in the name of "'Alīd legitimacy," a Shī'ī concept of political justice. This concept is considered the embodiment of a higher level of justice, consisting of neo-Platonic ideas reminiscent of Mu'tazilite notions of Rational Justice, free will (ikhtiyār), and human responsibility which rendered Ta'līmism an appealing set of doctrines in Sunnī circles.[74] An avalanche of literature on Sunnī legitimacy and political justice, written by Sunnī scholars, was initially started as a response to Ta'līmism and Ismā'īlī propaganda against the 'Abbāsid Caliphate. Only after the downfall of Fāṭimī rule did the controversy subside. The Fāṭimī challenge, however, prompted, first such great theologians as al-Bāqillānī and al-Ghazzālī and later Ibn Rushd and Ibn Khaldūn, to refine and reformulate Sunnīsm and Sunnī concepts of justice on a higher level of sophistication than before.

The third major Shī'ī subdivision is the Zaydī sect. The Zaydīs are the most moderate in their claims to legitimacy and the nearest to Sunnīsm. As a movement, it had its origin with Zayd, grandson of al-Ḥusayn, second son of 'Alī, who considered himself the depository of Shī'ī legitimacy after the death of al-Ḥusayn. He sought to re-establish the Imamate of Justice by force of arms. Like his grandfather, he perished in 'Iraq where he declared his uprising against the Umayyad authorities in 122/740. Some of his followers, led by al-Qāsim al-Rassī

74. The political assassinations for which the Ismā'ilīs owe the reputation of assassins in Europe do not form part of their teachings (ta'līm). An offshoot of Fāṭimism, a subdivision called neo-Ismā'īlism, led by Ḥasan B. Ṣabāḥ (d. 519/1124) and one faction of his followers, called the partisans of Shaykh al-Jabal (Old Man of the Mountain) became notorious as the Assassins (Hashshāshīn). Engaged in the time of the Crusades in political assassinations, they were nicknamed the Assassins. See M. G. S. Hodgson, *The Order of the Assassins* (The Hague, 1963), p. 37ff.

(d. 246/860), resumed the struggle after him and were able to establish an independent 'Alid dynasty in the Yaman, claiming Zayd as their first Imām.

The Zaydī standard of political justice is based partly on the principle of membership in the Prophet's House but mainly on the personal qualities and qualifications of the candidate for the Imamate. According to this standard, 'Alī's claim to legitimacy, though stemming from his membership in the Prophet's House, rested above all on his superior qualities—courage, wisdom and knowledge of Religion and Law—which he is considered to have possessed. Nor do the Zaydīs ascribe to the Imām any esoteric knowledge or super-human qualities such as sinlessness ('iṣma) and infallibility. Indeed, the Imām may be chosen from among any worthy member of the 'Alid house, notwithstanding direct descent. The Zaydī principle of legitimacy is obviously a combination of the Sunnī principle of election and the Shī'ī requirements of membership in the 'Alīd's house. Above all, the candidate must be a person of good character and able to administer justice in accordance with the Law. Moreover, the Zaydīs rejected the taqīya (dissimulation) and other practices, as they are inconsistent with the notion of justice, which led to the isolation of the Shī'a from the larger Sunnī community. No major barrier to dealing with other believers exists in the creed, but the inaccessability of the region in which it spread kept its followers in isolation from others and helped maintain their independence.[75]

The Zaydī concept of justice seems to have been derived mainly from Mu'tazilite sources. Zayd, to whom the Zaydīs traditionally ascribe most of their teachings, is said to have met Wāṣil Ibn 'Atā', a forerunner of the Mu'tazilite movement, and adopted from him the doctrine of the intermediate position as a penalty for the grave sinner.[76] But Zayd seems to have been opposed to taqīya and called for an open rebellion (khurūj) against the Umayyad Caliph Hishām (d. 125/742), on the grounds of his alleged injustices against Zaydī followers. Zayd also rejected the doctrine of predestination, which the Umayyad house had advocated as justification of its legitimacy, and he supported the doctrines of qadar and free will.[77]

75. For an early account of the Zaydī creed, see Ash'arī, *Maqālāt*, I, 129–32; Shahrastānī, *al-Milal wa al-Niḥal*, I, 115–18. For a modern study, see Aḥmad M. Ṣubḥī, *al-Zaydīya* (Cairo, 1980).

76. See chap. 2, section on Political Justice as Retribution.

77. Ibn al-Murtaḍa, *al-Munya wa al-Amal*, p. 8.

The real founders of the Zaydī movement, however, were the descendants of Zayd, who maintained a close touch with Mu'tazilite scholars. Perhaps the most influential were al-Qāsim al-Rassī (d. 246/801) and Yaḥya Ibn al-Ḥusayn (d. 298/911). Rassī, who claimed to have succeeded Zayd, laid down the fundamental teachings of Zaydīsm. The sources of the creed, according to him, are three: Reason, Revelation (Qur'ān) and the Prophets' Traditions. But Reason, he added, is the basis of all other sources. By virtue of Reason, implanted in man by God, man is able to comprehend the meaning of Revelation and other textual sources. Perhaps no other founding father had stressed the primacy of Reason in the Zaydī Creed more than Rassī. Moreover, Rassī adopted the Mu'tazilite "five principles,"[78] however, not without certain alterations. The doctrines of Oneness (tawḥīd) and justice, which were in particular stressed, became the most commonly acceptable to his followers.[79]

Second only to Rassī, Yaḥya Ibn al-Ḥusayn may be regarded as the scholar who provided the Zaydī creed with a firm foundation. Born in Madīna in 245/858, he spent most of his life in study and scholarly pursuit until the death of his father, Imām al-Ḥusayn, in 280/893. No sooner was Yaḥya proclaimed Imām than he proceeded to Ṣan'ā', seat of the government, and began at once to govern the country strictly in accordance with the Law. He met resistance in rural areas which prompted him to engage in bloody battles before the country was pacified. In 298/910 he suddenly died, probably by poison administered at the instigation of rival factions.

Imām Yaḥya was a righteous and pious man in thought and action, adhering to the basic Mu'tazilite teachings, with an emphasis on legal justice. He tried to interpret Revelation by Reason, but in reality the textual sources (Qur'ān and Traditions) were to him overriding. He accepted the doctrine that "God is the Creator of everything" (Q. XIII, 16); but, he said, God did not say that He created man's acts. On the contrary, he warned in another Revelation, "you (men) create a calumny" (Q. XXIX, 16), which means, according to Reason, that God did not create injustice. While there is nothing new in Yaḥya's method of interpretation, it affirmed the Zaydī commitment to Reason for an understanding of Revelation.

78. See pp. 49–50.

79. For texts of Rassī's treatises on the Zaydī creed, see Muḥammad 'Umāra, *Rasā'il al-'Adl wa al-Tawḥīd* [Treatises on Justice and Oneness] (Cairo, 1971), I, 96–100, 102–40, 144–56, 158–59.

Zaydī principles, according to Imām Yaḥya, are binding not only on individual believers but, above all, on the Imām himself. If the Imām misapplies the Law, or fails to observe it, he can no longer be considered as a Just Imām and should be removed. In contrast with the doctrines of other Shī'ī sects, the Zaydī doctrine relegates ultimate responsibility to the community and deprives the Imām of sinlessness. He is liable to err and inflict injustice, for which he would be responsible.[80]

Scholars who followed the Imāms Rassī and Yaḥya may be divided into two categories: some were inclined to pursue more closely Mu'tazilite doctrines and emphasized Reason; others proved more conservative and tended to stress the Revelation. Both, however, were in agreement that Revelation and Reason were indispensable, regardless of which one depended on the other.

The significance of the Zaydī interest in Reason and in particular in Mu'tazilite thought is not so much in the originality of Zaydī doctrines as in Zaydī concern to perpetuate the Mu'tazilite thought, the original sources of which had been destroyed in other Islamic lands. Had such works as those of Qāḍī 'Abd al-Jabbār and others not been preserved and recently brought to light, our knowledge of Mu'tazilite thought would have been completely dependent on the inadequate summaries provided in the works of their critics.[81]

Justice as the Expression of the Beauty and Love of God

No less concerned about Divine Justice were the Ṣūfīs (mystics), who developed their own notions of justice and tried to achieve it by an entirely different method from all other believers. They rejected both the form and substance of theological justice and tried by direct contact with God to realize Divine Justice by meditation and spiritual exercises without an intermediary. Thus, whereas theological justice is defined in terms of human acts created by God (the Ash'arites) or

80. For Imām Yaḥya's major works, see 'Umāra, *op. cit.*, II, 34ff.; for a summary of his doctrines, see Ṣubḥī, *op. cit.*, pp. 150–211.

81. For the discovery and compilation of the works of Qāḍī 'Abd al-Jabbār on Mu'tazilite thought, see G. Anawati, et al., "Une Somme inedite de théologie Mu'tazilite: le Moghnī du qāḍī 'Abd al-Jabbār," *Mélange de l'institut Dominicain des Études Orientales*, IV (1957), 281–316; V (1958), 417–24.

determined by Reason (the Mu'tazila), Ṣūfī justice is a manifestation of "spiritual experience" gained directly from union with God and not from ordinary human action.

The Ṣūfī notion of justice is different from other notions of justice, partly because God's attributes are described not in theological concepts like Will and Wisdom, nor indeed in anthropomorphic terms, but in highly abstract and poetic symbols like Light, Beauty, and Love. Even those vague words which the Ṣūfīs are fond of using are not intended to describe, but rather to manifest an ultimate reality summed up in the concept of al-ḥaqq (Truth), in which the highest values are embodied. For this reason, they call themselves "ahl al-ḥaqq," depositories of the Truth, and their notion of Divine Justice is an emanation from, or a manifestation of, the Truth. The Ṣūfīs do not say where God may be found in order for His Justice to be sought; rather, they posit three channels of spiritual communication: the "qalb" (heart), which knows God; the "rūḥ" (spirit), which loves Him; and the "sirr" (inward secret), which contemplates Him. Vague and intangible, these means of communication are different from others, whether Rational or otherwise, and belong to the realm of divine illumination. "Look in your own heart," says the Ṣūfī, "for the Kingdom of God is within you."[82]

Nonetheless, not all men can gain Divine Justice by mentioning the name of God or by praying to Him, because not everyone is able to seek Him—only a true Ṣūfī. To become a Ṣūfī, one must possess certain qualities which only some can attain, such as piety, purity of heart, poverty, and renunciation of every worldly aspiration, even the desire to find reward in the next world. Only after a long "journey" along the "path" to the goal of union with the ultimate Reality does the "traveler" (the would-be mystic) become a Ṣūfī. It is an austere discipline requiring patience and indifference to hardship which few can endure. Writers on Ṣūfism enumerate several "stages" called maqāmāt (such as meditation, nearness to God, love, fear, longing, intimacy, and others), which must be achieved. While the "stages" can be acquired with relative mastery, the "states" (al-aḥwāl) are spiritual dispositions over which full control is rarely achieved. "They descend from God into his heart," says the Ṣūfī, "without his being

82. For the meaning of Sūfī terms, see Ḥujwīrī, *The Kashf al-Maḥjūb*, trans. Nicholson (Leiden and London, 1911), chap. 24.

able to repel them when they come or to retain them when they go."[83] Only after having attended to all "stages" and having become experienced in the "states," which God may or may not grant, does the person reach one or more of the levels of mystic consciousness. These levels are "al-ma'rifa" (knowledge), and al-ḥaqīqa (Truth), where one realizes that "knowledge," "knower" and "known" are but One.

The goal of the Ṣūfī is said to be the "apprehension of al-ḥaqq (truth)";[84] but the intent lies deeper in the inner desire to achieve perfection by spiritual exercises in search of the Divine. The culmination of the process is the threshold where the soul becomes isolated from everything foreign to itself, from all that is not Divine. When the soul is finally united with the Divine, the Ṣūfī is transformed from the state of "al-fanā'" (literally: extinction), the reality of existence to the state of "al-ḥaqq," the ultimate reality or the reality of union with the Divine. One of the Ṣūfīs, Ḥusayn B. Manṣūr al-Ḥallāj (d. 309/922), who declared to have achieved union with God, used to say, "Anā al-Ḥaqq" (I am the Truth). For this declaration he was accused of heresy and brought to trial. He was condemned to death and executed by beheading and crucifixion.[85]

The Ṣūfīs were men of piety and uprightness who despaired in finding evil, corruption and injustice in society; they tried to urge like-minded men to pursue the Ṣūfī way of life and to give an example of how to seek justice in the Kingdom of God.[86] Divine Justice, however, in the eyes of the Ṣūfī, is not the reward in the hereafter, but the possession of the light, beauty, and love of God. By possessing these qualities, the Ṣūfī attains an inward satisfaction for having pursued the path of the Truth, the path of purity and justice. His mind is constantly preoccupied with the name of God and his soul is often tormented with an admixture of passion and love. Perhaps the most outspoken about the love of God, al-Ḥallāj cried:

About God's Love I hover
While I have breath,

83. R. A. Nicholson, *The Mystics of Islam* (London, 1963), p. 29.

84. This saying is attributed to Ma'rūf al-Karkhī (d. 198/812). He is considered one of the founders of the earliest of the Ṣūfī orders. See R. A. Nicholson, *Literary History of the Arabs* (Cambridge, 1953), pp. 385–86.

85. For the life and mystical philosophy of al-Ḥallāj, see Louis Massignon, *La Passion de Ḥusayn Ibn Manṣūr Ḥallāj* (Paris, n. ed., 1975); trans. Herbert Mason, *The Passion of al-Ḥallāj* (Princeton, 1982), 4 vols.

86. Some may have found in the Ṣūfī way of life an escape from existence in sin in a society full of evil and injustice.

> To be His perfect lover
> Until my death.[87]

The Ṣūfī, al-Ḥujwīrī (d. circa 450/1057), expressed love in terms of the perfection of God which all men seek as the universal law. He said:

> Man's love toward God is a quality which manifests itself, in the heart of the pious believer, in the form of veneration and magnification, so that he seeks to satisfy his Beloved and becomes impatient and restless in his desire for vision of Him, and cannot rest with anyone except Him, and grows familiar with the remembrance (dhikr) of Him, and abjures the remembrance of everything besides. Repose becomes unlawful to him, and rest flees from him. He is cut off from all habits and associations, and renounces sensual passion, and turns towards the court of love, and submits to the law of love and knows God by His attributes of perfection.[88]

Rabī'a al-'Adawīya (d. 185/801), a female mystic, identified her love for God as love for man. She said:

> O God! Whatever share of this world Thou hast allotted to me, bestow it on Thine enemies; and whatever share of the next world Thou hast allotted me, bestow it on Thy friends. Thou art enough for me.
>
> O God! If I worship Thee in fear of Hell, burn me in Hell; and if I worship Thee in hope of Paradise, exclude me from Paradise; but if I worship Thee for Thine own sake, withhold not Thine everlasting beauty.[89]

The love and beauty of God, always expressed in poetic words (for most Ṣūfīs sang the praise of God in poetry) are symbolic, denoting the love of mankind as a whole, since the Kingdom of God is not open only for the few, but for all men. Only in the Kingdom of God is the *jus divinum* realized; it is in the light, beauty, and love bestowed on man.

What about justice and injustice? Can they possibly exist in God's Kingdom where only love and beauty are sought?

Before they began to fall under theological and philosophical influences, the question did not arise among the Ṣūfīs who were looked upon with suspicion and disfavor by theologians and jurists and were

87. Abū Nu'aym, *Ḥilyat al-Awlīyā'*, X, 61 (trans. in A. J. Arberry, *Sufism* [London, 1950] p. 62).

88. Ḥujwīrī, *op. cit.*, pp. 307–8.

89. Nicholson, *Mystics of Islam*, p. 115; Arberry, *Sufism*, pp. 42–43. For a study of the life and ideas of Rabī'a, see Margaret Smith, *Rabī'a the Mystic* (Cambridge, 1928).

considered to have strayed from the fundamental teachings of Islam. Nor were the Ṣūfīs concerned about theological and philosophical questions, as they considered their pathway by direct union with God to be a surer way to the Truth than theological and philosophical speculation. But Ṣūfīsm began to fall under theological and philosophical influences toward the turn of the fifth/eleventh century, and the ostracism from which the Ṣūfīs had suffered in theological and philosophical circles began to change. The theologian Abū Ḥāmid al-Ghazzālī (d. 504/1111), himself a Ṣūfī in his own right, was perhaps the most instrumental in reconciling Ṣūfīsm with other Islamic disciplines, making it crystal clear that despite the limitation of each discipline, all had the same goal of seeking the Truth in one's own way.[90] The most illustrious figures after Ghazzālī who contributed to this marriage between Ṣūfīsm and the other disciplines were Suhrawardī (d. 587/1191), Muḥyī al-Dīn B. al-'Arabī (d. 638/1240) and Ṣadr al-Dīn al-Shīrāzī (d. 1050/1640). Of these, only two—Ghazzālī and Ibn 'Arabī—were interested directly or indirectly in justice, while the interest of the others lay in highly abstract theological doctrines that had little or no relevance to justice. Although Ghazzālī wrote more extensively than Ibn'Arabī on justice, especially about its philosophical and ethical aspects,[91] Ibn'Arabī dealt with justice from a strictly Ṣūfī perspective.[92]

Perhaps more than any other Ṣūfī, Ibn 'Arabī expressed a pantheistic view of religion, a view which is universal and not necessarily exclusive in nature. All religions, he maintained, from idolatry to the highest form, are pathways leading to one general and straightforward path (al-ṭarīq al-amām), which ultimately leads to the One God (ṭarīq al-āḥadīya).[93] He talked about waḥdat a-wujūd (oneness of being) as a universal manifestation, and considered that his spiritual experiences

90. For Ghazzālī's conversion to mysticism, see his intellectual autobiography, *al-Munqidh Min al-Ḍalāl*, ed. Jabr (Beirut, 1959) and a French translation by the editor. For an English translation, see W. M. Watt, *The Faith and Practice of al-Ghazzali* (London, 1953).

91. See chap. 5, section on Ethical Justice as the Expression of Divine Virtue.

92. For the life of Ibn al-'Arabī, see Ibrāhīm B. 'Abd-Allāh al-Qārī, *Manāqib Ibn 'Arabī*, ed. Munajjid (Beirut, 1959), with a bibliography consisting of the works of Ibn al-'Arabī as well as the original sources about his life, pp. 9–12. For a modern critique of Ibn 'Arabī's Ṣūfī philosophy, see A. E. Affifi, *The Mystical Philosophy of Muhyid Din Ibnu'l 'Arabi* (Cambridge, 1933).

93. Ibn 'Arabī, *Fuṣūṣ al-Hikam* [Bezels of Wisdom] (Cairo, 1309/1892), p. 405 and passim.

were confined not only to believers—his co-religionists—but were equally applicable to all other believers and unbelievers. In verse, he summed up his view of religions as follows:

> People have formed different beliefs about God,
> And I behold all that they believe.[94]

Divine Justice, an expression of the essence of God, is obviously not intended for believers only, but for all who seek justice, each one in his own spiritual pathway.[95] To Ṣūfīs generally, Divine Justice is the object of God's love, but to Ibn 'Arabī the object of all religions is love, which binds them together and expresses their inward urge for love. He said:

> I swear by the reality of Love that Love is the cause of all Love; Were it not for love (residing) in the heart, Love (God) would not be worshipped.[96]

Moreover, Ibn 'Arabī held that God's Beauty is the ultimate basis of Love. His beauty is the source of all forms of beauty and the expression of His perfection. It is also the cause of creation and the cause of man's worship of God. All Ṣūfīs are agreed on the premise that Love and Beauty are the expression of God's essence and perfection; but Ibn 'Arabī is the only one who considered Beauty the basis of Love. Since, to the Ṣūfīs, Divine Justice is an expression of Love and Beauty, to Ibn 'Arabī its ultimate source must be Beauty.

As a thinker who dealt with Ṣūfī as well as theological questions, Ibn 'Arabī tried to give a Ṣūfī view of the doctrine of voluntarism and

94. Ibn 'Arabī, *al-Futūḥāt al-Makkīya* [Makkan Revelations], III, 175 (trans. 'Affīfī, *p. cit.*, p. 151).

95. In verse, Ibn 'Arabī says:

> My heart is capable of every form,
> A cloister for the monk, a fan for idols,
> A posture for gazelles, the pilgrim's Ka'ba,
> The Tables of the Torah, the Qur'ān.

See Ibn 'Arabī's *Tarjumānu'l Ashwāq*, ed. Nicholson, p. 19.

96. Ibn 'Arabī, *Fuṣūṣ*, pp. 387 and 390, trans. 'Affīfī, *op. cit.*, p. 151. He also says:

> Love is the faith I hold: Whenever turn
> His camels come, still the true faith is mine.

Ibn 'Arabī's *Tarjumānu'l Ashwāq*, ed. Nicholson, p. 19.—He maintains that the Revelation in Q. XXV, 45 embodies this meaning of God's love (see 'Affīfī, *op. cit.*, p. 151, n. 4).

involuntarism which had long occupied the minds of believers and for which neither the Mu'tazilites nor Ash'arites had given a final answer. In his comment on the Revelation, "God is not unjust to His servants" (Q. III, 178), Ibn 'Arabī gives his answer as follows:

> I (God) did not ordain polytheism which dooms them to misery, and then demand of them what lay not in their power to perform. No, I dealt with them only according as I knew them, and I knew them only by what they "gave" me from themselves, of what they themselves really are. Hence if there is any wrong, they are the wrongdoers. I said to them nothing except what my Essence decreed that I should say to them, and my Essence is known to me as it is. . . . It is mine to say and it is for them to obey or not to obey.[97]

However, although Ibn 'Arabī concedes a larger margin of free choice (ikhtiyār) to the believer, he still maintains that in the broader sense of the term man's circle of voluntary acts must by necessity fall within the larger circle of involuntary acts predicated by God. Thus, in the Kingdom of God, where man is in a union with Him, the Ṣūfī answer to the problem of predestination versus free will has not carried it beyond where the later Ash'arites—Bāqillānī and Ghazzālī—had left it. God, said Ghazzālī, created all human acts and gave man the capacity (qadar) to act through Reason.[98]

Ibn 'Arabī sought to express himself in abstract philosophical terms without reference to the familiar theological doctrines. Above all, he felt the compulsion to free himself from all conventional concepts of value—good and evil, right and wrong, justice and injustice—considering them subjective and relative to human knowledge. The only objective good is the good of God, which is His existence and being. Everything else, indeed all values—good and evil, justice and injustice—come from God; they are the unfolding of His acts, and man calls them right and wrong, or just and unjust acts. But the goodness of God and His Will stand supreme as an expression of His absolute and pure being.[99]

The Ṣūfī movement, having certain objectives in common with

97. Ibn 'Arabī, *Fuṣūṣ*, p. 237 trans. 'Affīfī, *op. cit.*, p. 152.

98. Abū Ḥāmid al-Ghazzālī, *Kitāb al-Iqtiṣād fī al-I'tiqād* (Cairo, n.d.), pp. 42–47.

99. The doctrine of Being as an overriding attribute of God has been elucidated by Ṣadr al-Dīn Shīrāzī (d. 1050/1642). For Ibn 'Arabī's view of Being, see 'Affīfī, *op. cit.*, chap. 1; for Shīrāzī's views, see F. Raḥmān, *The Philosophy of Mulla Sadra* [Ṣadr al-Dīn al-Shīrāzī] (Albany, N.Y., 1975).

utopian movements, may be regarded, at least in part, as a protest by men of piety and uprightness against the prevailing evil and injustice, and an attempt to set an example for other believers of how to overcome evil and injustice. It may also be regarded as a reaction to theological and other forms of intellectual discourse, which failed to resolve fundamental questions about the destiny of man and the realization of the *jus divinum* on Earth. However, by pursuing a style of spiritual experiences different from the conventional, the Ṣūfīs incurred the wrath of all credal groups as well as the authorities, and brought disaster and death upon several of their followers before their endeavors were finally tolerated and accepted as orthodox.

The significance of the Ṣūfī movement lies in its freedom from the conventional limitations, set by both Revelationists and Rationalists, on the nature and components of Divine Justice. The Ṣūfī notion of justice is that of perfection. Unlike the Mu'tazila, who also talked about Divine Justice in terms of perfection, the Ṣūfīs did not only raise it to a higher level of religiosity, but also extended it to all mankind. In seeking justice, man is not expected merely to pray and hope for it; he must achieve it through rigorous spiritual experiences. But once man is admitted to the house of justice—the House of God—he would surely be in the presence of the Perfect Judge—the Judge of Love, Beauty, and Truth. This kind of justice is not intended only for believers: God's justice, embodied in all Eternal Laws, is for all men. In the words of the Ṣūfī:

He makes the Law His upper garment
And the mystic path His inner garment.

4

Philosophical Justice

All men have some natural inclination to justice.

—Aristotle

He who pursues the pathway of justice would be in possession of the most fortified garden.

—al-Kindī

Philosophical justice, unlike theological justice, is justice defined and determined by philosophers not in accordance with Revelation, but with Reason, although Muslim philosophers consciously tried to harmonize Reason with Revelation. Like the *jus naturale,* philosophical justice is Rational Justice and essentially naturalistic in character; and therefore it is eternal and unchangeable irrespective of time and place.

Muslim philosophers, under the impact of Greek philosophy, made another attempt to enter the debate on justice with an appeal to Reason to provide a rationale for the *jus divinum.* Earlier, it will be recalled, the Mu'tazila tried in earnest to use Reason as a method to provide a rationale for the *jus divinum*, but failed. The violent reaction with which they were met was not necessarily against Reason itself (indeed, some theologians, including Ash'arī, themselves used Reason in their discourses); it is mainly because they gave the impression that they assigned a higher authority to Reason than to Revelation.

The aim of Muslim philosophers, often called the falāsifa, was not to question the authrority of Revelation, as the Mu'tazila seemed to have attempted, but to seek an understanding of justice as presented in the works of Greek philosophers and to make it intelligible to believers without necessarily compromising the creed. Indeed, whenever Muslim philosophers touched upon theological questions in the course of their studies, they tried to demonstrate its harmony with

Reason. In the pursuit of such a harmony, they were not always spared the criticism and even the attack of theologians; but whether they succeeded in achieving a synthesis of the two—Reason and Revelation—or they merely paid lip service to Revelation and concealed their primary loyalty to Reason is still an open question. Only from the perspective of their discourse on justice shall we be able to provide an answer to that question. The theories of justice of four major philosophers—al-Kindī, al-Fārābī, Ibn Sīna and Ibn Rushd—will be scrutinized, though reference to others connected with our discussion will also be made.

Rational Justice as the Harmony between Divine and Natural Justice

The first Muslim philosopher to discuss justice within the framework of both Greek and Islamic concepts was al-Kindī.[1] Although al-Kindī's main concern was not essentially with justice, he did indeed lay the ground for his successors to discuss justice as a rational concept and set the precedent for how it could be in harmony with Divine Justice. It is true that Greek philosophy, especially in its neo-Platonic garb, had long been discussed in Christian theological circles with which Muslim scholars were acquainted, but it was unacceptable to them. Kindī was perhaps the first Muslim philosopher who sought to interpret it in a style of thought acceptable to believers.

Owing to his family background and personal qualifications, al-Kindī found an opportunity to present his philosophical views in the highest circles of society. He served as a Court philosopher under two Caliphs—al-Ma'mūn and al-Mu'taṣim—at a time when the Mu'ta-

1. Abū Yūsuf Ya'qūb B. Isḥāq al-Kindī, often called the philosopher of the Arabs (because he was of Arab descent), was born in al-Kūfa and studied in Baṣra and Baghdad, then the principal centers of learning. The date of his birth is not known, but there is evidence that he was probably born around the year 185/801 and died in the middle of the third/ninth century. He is reputed to have been a descendant from the royal family of Kinda which ruled southern Arabia before Islam, and his father was governor of al-Kūfa under the caliphs al-Mahdī and Harūn al-Rashīd. He served at the Court and came into prominence under two caliphs—al-Ma'mūn (d. 218/833) and al-Mu'taṣim (d. 227/842)—and acted as a tutor to al-Mu'taṣīm's son. For his life, see *Fihrist of al-Nadīm*, ed. Dodge (New York, 1970), II, 25–26; Ibn Juljul, *Ṭabaqāt al-Aṭibbā'*, ed. Sayyid (Cairo, 1955), pp. 73–74; Qifṭī, *Ta'rīkh al-Ḥukamā'* (Leipzig, 1903), pp. 366–78; Ibn Abī Uṣaybi'a, *'Uyūn al-Anbā'* (Beirut, 1965), pp. 285–93; George Atiyeh, *al-Kindī: The Philosopher of the Arabs* (Karachi, 1966), chap. 1.

zila reached the height of their influence. It was therefore neither expected nor indeed appropriate for him to disagree with Mu'tazilite teachings. As a philosopher, he was, of course, in favor of the use of Reason as a method. But contrary to allegations that he was a Mu'tazilite, his philosophical studies give no evidence to such allegations; they rather indicate that he pursued an independent line of thought, and he even had some differences of opinion with them.[2]

In his philosophical inquiry, al-Kindī covered a wide range of subjects (not all his works have yet been recovered) but his primary concern was to seek the truth (al-ḥaqq) in its theoretical and practical settings. As a philosopher, he naturally sought the truth through Reason. But to believers, there was another channel to it. Reason, he maintained, is the instrument with which man can comprehend the truth; but in deference to religion, he conceded that there existed another pathway—the Revelation—by virtue of which prophets were able to promulgate the truth. Since he considered the ultimate truth is One, whether embodied in the Revelation or obtained through Reason, the two pathways must be in harmony.[3] His method thus stated, he tried to demonstrate his fidelity to both Islam and philosophy. Since Greek philosophy was translated into Arabic by Christian scholars in the tradition of neo-Platonism (indeed, the so-called Aristotle's theology [ūthūlūjiya] was mistakenly taken to represent Aristotle's own rather than Plotinus's views) it is possible to accept al-Kindī's position on the question of the One Truth (al-ḥaqq), implying God, as a genuine conviction.[4]

Perhaps a more convincing argument in favor of his attempted solution for the harmony of Reason and Revelation is his distinction between the ultimate truth and the practical truth. The ultimate truth is One, but it may be different in practice. It is not enough to know the ultimate truth, he said, on which Reason and Revelation are in agreement; one must know the truth in practice. The latter—the

2. See M. A. Abū Rīda, *Rasā'il al-Kindī al-Falsafīya* (Cairo, 1950), I, 27–31; and A. L. Ivry, *al-Kindī's Metaphysics* (Albany, N.Y., 1974), chap. 3.

3. See al-Kindī's "On First Philosophy," in Abū Rīda, *op. cit.*, I, 96ff., trans. Ivry, *op. cit.*, pt. 2, p. 55ff.

4. For the impact of Greek philosophy on Muslim philosophers, stressing a naturalistic viewpoint, see F. R. Walzer, *Greek into Arabic* (Oxford, 1926); F. E. Peters, *Aristotle and the Arabs* (New York, 1968). For the opposite approach, stressing the Islamic viewpoint, see Abū Rīda, *op. cit.*, I, 52–58; Jamīl Ṣalība, *al-Dirāsāt al-Falsafīya* (Damascus, 1964), I, 110–31.

practical truth—is the primary concern of the philosopher. In taking this position, he dealt with justice on two levels, one Divine on which Reason and Revelation are in agreement, and the other a form of natural justice, the product of Reason, is Rational Justice. Rational Justice, according to al-Kindī, is the form of justice with which the philosopher is primarily concerned. Although he accepted the two pathways to the truth, al-Kindī revealed Aristotelian naturalism by an emphasis on the practical pathway as the philosopher's primary object. Since our concern is with justice, perhaps a discussion of al-Kindī's notions of justice might be a clue to whether he accepted the two pathways as separate or as one united method.

In his extant published works, al-Kindī did not directly discuss the concept of justice. But a work of al-Sijistānī, consisting of aphorisms attributed to al-Kindī, deals with justice and some other related notions which seem to be consistent with al-Kindī's other extant works, as listed in his bibliography.[5] The sections relating to al-Kindī's conception of justice are as follows:

> 26. He [al-Kindī] said: Justice, which may be found in all things, is a quality of the innate instinct; accidental acts contrary to true [i.e., Rational] justice (al-aṣl al-ḥaqqī) are extremities which go either beyond or fall behind [justice]. Thus, justice according to the discriminating faculty [Wisdom] means that one should neither retreat from the most gainful truth nor lean toward a wrong, such as fraud, deception and others. Justice of the concupiscence (al-shahwa) means that one should neither abstain from doing anything which is necessary for the survival of man nor from that which may afflict the body and the soul with injuries and prevent them from doing noble acts. Justice of wrath (or ghaḍab) means that one should not be wanting in fortitude, that is, not to overlook possible physical harms nor to spare an effort to offset adversities, provided that he does not exceed the bounds of wrath, outrage or oppression. Therefore, the natural things [i.e., virtues] in ourselves, are wisdom, justice, temperance, and fortitude, since their opposites, though deeply rooted in ourselves, are unnatural and accidental. We should, therefore, exert all our efforts to cultivate these noble [qualities].
>
> 102 . . . . And he [al-Kindī] was once asked: who is the most just man? "He is the one who sticks to the truth, never to depart from it nor to shrink from acting in accordance with the obligations imposed by it," he replied. "And who is the most temperate among men?" he

5. For a bibliography of al-Kindī's works, see Atiyeh, *op. cit.*, pp. 148–210 (Appendix).

> was asked. "He who maintains a just balance over his desires (shahawātih): he will never satisfy them beyond that which is indispensable for the preservation of himself in accordance with the rules of Reason and the requirements of existence," he replied.
>
> 104 . . . . . And he was asked: What are the human virtues? "They are wisdom, justice, temperance and fortitude in all [actions]," he replied.
>
> 108. And he was asked: Who is the one most praiseworthy in the eyes of wisemen? "The Creator of everything, may His praise be glorified, Who made it the evidence for the vindication of His Creation and Existence, may His praise be glorified," he replied. And he was asked: What is the evidence for the vindication of His Creation? "Justice," he replied, "for everything which is upright (al mu'tadil) is enduring and any departure from uprightness is liable to vanish and decay. By virtue of His existence, may His praise be glorified, Reason came into being and through it we realized that we have been created. Thus [we realized that] there must exist a Creator."[6]

From these as well as from other passages, a general outline of Kindī's theory of justice might be drawn. It is clear from the foregoing passages that a sense of justice is a quality inherent in man which prompts him to do the right thing, guided and determined by Reason. Injustice, said al-Kindī, is accidental. Like evil—to him injustice is indeed an evil—it is produced by rage or fury whenever Reason fails to control intemperate impulses (wrath, rage, and others). But in the absence of wrath or fury, man is ordinarily under the control of Reason which urges him to do the right thing.

Justice, however, is not merely a counterpart of evil; it is a virtue which man may cultivate and improve by his own initiative in the light of his comprehension of the truth. Since the aim of philosophy is not only to know the truth but to act truthfully, man is urged not only to know and comprehend justice, but also to act in accordance with it. For this reason, al-Kindī insists that philosophy teaches us to relate theory to practice and to act in accordance with the truth arrived at by Reason.[7]

Of all virtues—wisdom, courage, temperance, and others—al-Kindī considers justice as central, because it is not just one of the noble virtues, but because it is, above all, the balancing and coordinating instrument whenever the other virtues come into operation. In

6. See *Muntakhab Ṣiwān al-Ḥikma* [Selections from the Preserve of Wisdom] of al-Sijistānī (Arabic text in Atiyeh, *op. cit.*, Appendix 3).

7. See al-Sijistānī's *Ṣiwān*, in Atiyeh, *op. cit.*, pp. 219, 230–35; and note 3, above.

a treatise on sorrow,[8] al-Kindī discusses the material and psychological causes of sorrow, and he points out the ways and means by which man can overcome sorrow, such as material possessions and other worldly deeds; but nothing, he says, could give greater satisfaction to overcome man's sorrow than the cultivation of virtues. Wisdom and justice, he added, are the highest virtues; but justice stands above all.

This naturalistic aspect of al-Kindī's theory of justice is not stated without qualification by his concession to Revelation. True, justice is the product of Reason, said al-Kindī, but it may also be taken as "the vindication of His [God's] Creation." "By virtue of His existence," he went on to say, "Reason came into being and through it we realized that we have been created." Thus although justice is the direct product of Reason, it is ultimately inspired by God who implanted Reason in man. In accordance with al-Kindī's two-pathways, the aim of Rational Justice is the attainment of happiness in this world (the natural good) and happiness in the hereafter (a form of moral good). The latter is a theistic notion of justice, since he maintained that the soul will survive after death and will be in eternal happiness.[9] These views are on the whole consistent with Islamic teachings, but they raise the problem of whether the truth is One, as he held, or exists on two levels. It is possible to assume, as he tacitly seems to admit, that the truth in practice is not necessarily the same as the ultimate truth, which is One; but then the practical truth, the primary concern of the philosopher, seems to be relegated to a secondary level in deference to Revelation. Kindī provided us with no convincing rationale for the relationship between the two levels of justice. This problem was left for his successors to grapple with.

Rational Justice as the Ideal Justice

Rational justice in its ideal form as theistic justice was only vaguely discussed by al-Kindī; it was not really developed as a philosophical concept. It appeared more clearly in the philosophy of al-Fārābī, who tried to harmonize it with religion—thus he sought to provide an answer to theological objections—and it came into prominence in the

8. See al-Kindī's bibliography in *al-Fihrist of al-Nadīm*, *op. cit.*, II, 623.

9. See al-Kindī's "Treatise on the Soul," in Abū Rīda, *op. cit.*, I, pp. 272–82; and al-Sijistānī's "Ṣiwūn," in Atiyeh, *op. cit.*, pp. 19–20.

writings of Miskawayh and Rāzī.[10] Whereas al-Kindī stresses the naturalistic aspect of rational justice, giving the impression that he pays only lip service to religion, al-Fārābī reveals his indebtedness to Platonic and neo-Platonic influences, which are vigorously theistic, and his personal inclination towards mystical speculation on the assumption that Plato and Aristotle were in full agreement on metaphysical questions.

A few facts about al-Fārābī's character and his early upbringing may illuminate the nature and scope of his theory of justice.[11] From early life, he was known to have been withdrawn, and his ascetic propensities became more pronounced as he grew older. He seems to have had little or no regard for material possessions, and this spiritual outlook on life may well have been the reason to seek the patronage of Sayf al-Dawla (d. 356/967), founder of the Shī'ī Arab branch of the Hamdānī dynasty of Syria, where he could live in relative quietude and devote all his time to contemplation and learning.[12]

Fārābī was a prolific writer whose interest in the human faculties (rational and psychic) and in social relationships induced him to write innumerable philosophical treatises, several of which have failed to reach us. Of the extant works dealing with the public order and justice, three are most useful for our study: the first entitled the *Political Regime,*[13] the second the *Virtuous City,*[14] and the third the

10. See chap. 5.

11. Abū Naṣr al-Fārābī was born in Fārāb (a small town in Transoxiana) in 259/870 to a family of mixed parentage—the father, who married a Turkish woman, is said to have been of Persian and Turkish descent—but both professed the Shī'ī heterodox faith. He spoke Persian and Turkish fluently and learned the Arabic language before he went to Baghdad. The date of his departure to Baghdad is not known. We know, however, that he went to study logic and philosophy under two well-known Christian scholars, Abū Bishr Matta (d. 328/949) and Yuḥanna B. Ḥaylān (died under the caliph al-Muqtadir, who died in 339/944). In 330/941 al-Fārābī went to Damascus and finally, after a short visit to Egypt, he settled in Ḥalab (Allepo). In 339/950 he died on the way to Damascus, in the company of Sayf al-Dawla, while on an expedition to put down a rebellion. For his life, see Ibn Khallikān, *Wafayāt,* IV, 239–43; Ibn Abī Uṣaybi'a, *op. cit.,* pp. 603–9. For a summary of his political philosophy, see M. Mahdi, "Alfarabi," in *History of Political Philosophy,* ed. L. Strauss and J. Cropsey (Chicago, 1963), pp. 160–80.

12. As a philosopher, al-Fārābī's mysticism, unlike his contemporary mystics (ṣufīs), was not to seek union with God through spiritual exercises; it was a personal preoccupation with metaphysical questions by contemplation and contact (ittiṣāl) with the highest possible intellect for an understanding of the ultimate truth. See Ibrāhīm Madkūr, *Fī al-Falsafa al-Islāmīya* (Cairo, 3rd ed., 1976), I, 39–60, 42–49).

13. Abū Naṣr al-Fārābī, *Kitāb al-Siyāsa al-Madanīya,* ed. F. M. Najjar (Beirut, 1964).

14. Fārābī, *Kitāb Arā' Ahl al-Madīna al-Fāḍila,* ed. A. N. Nādir (Beirut, 1959).

Aphorisms of the Statesman.[15] The latter two treatises seem to have been written toward the end of his life, and therefore can be taken to reflect his mature thought on the subject. In the formulation of his theories, he was influenced by Plato's *Republic* and the *Laws,* on the one hand, and by Aristotle's *Ethics* and a book on theology attributed to Aristotle on the other. But al-Fārābī did not merely summarize the ideas of Plato and Aristotle; he provided us with his own theory of justice based on the harmony of Reason and Religion.

Fārābī's theory of justice is intimately linked with his theories of the political order (al-siyāsa al-madanīya), which he discusses in several parts of his major works. In agreement with Plato and Aristotle, he maintained that no political order can possibly endure unless it is founded on the qualities of excellence and perfection (to which he refers as the virtues) and on justice. Whereas the Greek philosophers maintained that the perfect community can be attained only in the *polis,* al-Fārābī held that man may attain his perfection in three kinds of political communities—the large, composed of the inhabited regions of the world, presumably to form a world-state; the intermediate, consisting of one people or one nation, forming a nation-state; and the small, confined to the city, forming a city-state.

In his departure from the Greek ideal political order, al-Fārābī set forth his theory to conform to the Islamic political order. He pointed out that the "virtuous city" is the minimum unit for the attainment of human perfection; he explained how the aggregate of virtuous cities belonging to one nation forms the "virtuous nation"; and he discussed how cooperation among nations of differing languages and other characteristics who submit to one supreme Ruler (the Imām, often called the Just Imām) constitutes the "virtuous World-State."[16] Justice, said al-Fārābī, is the highest of the virtues which man endeavors to cultivate and is the foundation on which the political order is erected.[17] But how is justice achieved in the Virtuous City, the minimum political unit?

The Virtuous City possesses a unique system of public order presided over by a Ruler. The Ruler is no ordinary person; he must be a man who is endowed with the highest qualities which enable him to assume his functions naturally, just as the body assumes control over

15. Fārābī, *al-Fuṣūl al-Madanī,* ed. and trans. D. M. Dunlop (Cambridge, 1961).

16. See al-Fārābī, *al-Siyāsa al-Madanīya,* pp. 69–70; *al-Madīna al-Fāḍila,* pp. 96–97.

17. Fārābī, *al-Fuṣūl al-Madanī,* pp. 120–21 (trans. pp. 39–40).

its organs by natural processes. Above all, he must possess the highest of all qualities—Reason.[18] The function of the Ruler is not just to preside over the City. He must combine all powers in his hands—executive, legislative, and judiciary—and, moreover, he must be endowed with a sense of justice which would enable him to operate the public order in accordance with the standard of justice embodied in the Law.[19]

In theory, according to al-Fārābī, the best Ruler is the man who combines the qualities of a wise man and a prophet. In the *Republic,* Plato calls him the philosopher-king. Combining the qualities of the philosopher-king with prophecy, rulership of the Virtuous City is not equated with the office of the Imām (called by al-Fārābī the First Ruler) who presides over the virtuous nation, as he did not think that such an office was necessary for the Virtuous City.[20] The Imām is the supreme Ruler and the source of all power of the virtuous nation (and potentially of the virtuous World-State). He holds the scale of justice in his hands, because he alone has the power to enact, interpret, and apply the Law. Indeed, the Imām governs virtually as an authoritarian Ruler.[21] He is the equivalent of the Imām al-āfḍal (the best) and the Imām al-'ādil (the just) seemingly in accordance with the Shī'ī creed.[22]

Under such a public order, what is the standard of justice? Justice, according to al-Fārābī, is realized "first in the division of the good things shared by the people of the city among them all, and then in the preservation of what is divided among them."[23] The good things

18. In the exercise of Reason, according to al-Fārābī, men are divided into three classes: first, the wise men or philosophers, who understand the nature of things by the qualities of the mind; second, the followers who have confidence in wise men and comprehend the nature of things as presented to them by the wise men; third, the masses, or the general public, who comprehend the nature of things in parables. See al-Fārābī, *al-Madīna al-Fāḍila,* pp. 82–84; *al-Siyāsa al-Madanīya,* pp. 77–78.

19. Fārābī, *al-Madīna al Fāḍila,* pp. 99–104; *al-Siyāsa al-Madanīya,* pp. 79–80.

20. Fārābī, *al-Madīna al-Fāḍila,* p. 105ff.

21. For the powers of the Imām, see al-Fārābī, *al-Madīna al-Fāḍila,* pp. 99–104, 105–8; *al-Siyāsa al-Madanīya,* pp. 79–80.

22. In accordance with the Sunnī creed, only the Prophet can claim such qualities; but in accordance with the Shī'ī doctrine, the Imām combines temporal as well as divine powers. Since al-Fārābī was a Shī'ī by birth, his concept of the Imamate might have been used to influence opinion in favor of the Shī'ī doctrine; but as a philosopher, it is doubtful that al-Fārābī formulated his concept for political reasons. See F. M. Najjar, "Farabi's Political Philosophy and Shī'ism." *Studia Islamica,* XIV (1961), 57–72.

23. Fārābī, *al-Fuṣūl al-Madanī,* pp. 141–42; trans. pp. 53–54.

which constitute justice are: security, wealth, honor, dignity, and all other things in which the people can share. Each one is entitled to a share (qisṭ) or a portion of these good things, equal to his deserts. Any increase or decrease in the individuals' share is an injustice (jawr)—the excess over any fair share is an injustice against the people of the city, and the difference must be returned to the party (the individual or the people) to whom it should belong. In other words, each one is entitled to his due, since any encroachment might lead to injustice.[24]

Rational Justice, according to al-Fārābī, is a quality of perfection. It can be realized only in a Virtuous City. In all other cities, called by al-Fārābī the ignorant cities, where the goal of happiness degenerates into pleasure, acquisition of worldly objects, lust for glory and power, and conquest of foreign lands, justice cannot possibly be realized. Fārābī expatiates in describing the kinds of ignorant cities, ranging from those not unaware of the significance of virtues to others whose rulers and people are in complete ignorance of them, where injustice (jawr) prevails in varying degree.[25] For this reason, justice acquires an entirely different meaning in such cities. Its scale is determined not by the qualities of virtues but by the men who possess power, and those who are oppressed seek a kind of "justice" equated with the maintenance of survival and relative security. Only when two equally powerful men fail to overpower one another do they agree to divide the advantages, each taking his share (qisṭ) in the deal. This kind of justice is obviously not Rational Justice, which al-Fārābī exalts, but injustice (jawr).[26]

Fārābī's Rational Justice is ultimately connected with the destiny of man. For the men who comprehend justice in the Virtuous City, their souls realize Divine Justice in the hereafter. The souls of men who do not comprehend the justice of the Virtuous City (Rational Justice) and pursue the standard of justice of ignorant cities disappear when their bodies vanish; the souls which comprehend Rational Justice yet do not accept them continue to live in eternity but live in sorrow, whereas the souls of men in the Virtuous City which comprehend justice and accept it will live in eternal happiness in the hereafter—the realm of the Truth (the active intellect)—where Divine Justice prevails. In contrast with al-Kindī, who revealed in his concept of Rational Justice a

24. *Ibid.*, pp. 142–43; trans. pp. 54–55.
25. See Fārābī, *al-Madīna al-Fāḍila,* chap. 29.
26. *Ibid.*, pp. 132–34.

large measure of Aristotelian naturalism, al-Fārābī considered Rational Justice an ideal which he equated with the *jus divinum*. Like Plato, al-Fārābī maintained that such a form of justice can exist only in an ideal republic—Fārābī's Virtuous City—but as the *jus divinum*, the soul of man should comprehend its full meaning before it can eventually attain it in Heaven. Any other form of justice, whose standard is shorn of the qualities of excellence and perfection, is an injustice even though it is called justice in ignorant, erring and other cities.

Rational Justice as the Expression of a Social Contract

Fārābī's concept of Rational Justice, though closely related to Greek philosophy, strayed considerably from al-Kindī's notion of Rational Justice which emphasized Greek naturalism. Ibn Sīna, despite Fārābī's initial influence on him, seems to have shown greater interest in naturalism than his predecessors, which rendered his concept of Rational justice more identical with the *jus naturale*.[27] He expressed his concept of justice in terms of a social contract theory, on the basis of which his Just City is founded. Some have attributed the idea of a social contract to al-Fārābī,[28] which may be perhaps only indirectly implied in his theory of the Virtuous City; but it is more clearly stated in Ibn Sīna's design of the Just City. No Muslim philosopher before him did so explicitly state that a political order came into existence on the basis of an original contract ('iqd), formally agreed upon between the Ruler and his people. In the Just City, Ibn Sīna describes the form of the contract to consist of specific conditions laid down by the

27. Abū 'Alī al-Ḥusayn, generally known as Ibn Sīna, was born in 370/980 at Afshāna (a town near Bukhāra in Transoxiana) to a family of good standing in public service and scholarship. His father was a governor in the service of the Sāmānid dynasty, whose seat of government was in Bukhāra. From early life, he distinguished himself as a physician and philosopher, and he entered into public service first as a physician and then as a vizīr. Upon the fall of the Sāmānid dynasty, he served as vizīr under several princes in Isfahān and Hamadhān. He was a prolific writer whose influence extended beyond the region where he held official positions, and his works were translated into Latin. He died in Hamadhān in 428/1037. For his life, see Ibn Khallikān, *Wafayāt al-'Ayān*, I, 419–24; and for translation of his autobiography as repeated in Qifṭī and Ibn Uṣaybī'a, see W. E. Gohlman, *Life of Ibn Sīna* (Albany, N.Y., 1974).

28. See Jamīl Ṣlība, *Min Aflāṭūn Ila Ibn Sīna*, p. 64.

founders of the city in accordance with a scale of justice agreed upon by the parties concerned. Those who were born in the city or joined it afterward were bound to accept the political order on the basis of a *pactum tacitum.* In accordance with this order, each man was granted a rank and a function which would fit his natural aptitude and the degree of excellence he had acquired as a member of society. The function and rank of each man would be assigned in accordance with the aims of the political order of the city.[29]

How did Ibn Sīna arrive at such a theory of justice?

In the formulation of his theory, Ibn Sīna has drawn on both Greek philosophy and Islamic traditions.[30] Unlike al-Fārābī, who did not address himself to the question of how the Virtuous City was established, Ibn Sīna envisioned his Just City as a body of citizens who felt the need for getting together to establish a political community through consensus and tacit agreement. This line of reasoning seems to have led him to the conclusion that the men who founded the earliest form of an association (al-mushāraka) must have first negotiated the terms of the agreement ('iqd, contract), which became binding on all who subsequently accepted to become members of the city either by birth or by association. On the basis of the original contract upon which the city was founded, said Ibn Sīna, such a city must be called not merely a virtuous city but a just city.[31]

To achieve its ends, the city must have a Law and a Ruler entrusted with both executive and legislative powers. Such a Ruler must be a prophet, endowed with special qualities by virtue of his moral character and the divine authority embodied in the prophecy. As a prophet,

29. See Ibn Sīna, *Kitāb al-Shifā': al-Ilāhiyāt II* [Book of Healings: Metaphysics II], ed. Mūsa, Dunya, and Zāyid (Cairo, 1380/1960), p. 441. Portions of this work are translated by M. E. Marmura, "Avicenna, Healing: Metaphysics X" in Lerner and Mahdi, *Medieval Political Philosophy: A Sourcebook* (New York, 1963), pp. 99–110.

30. In his autobiography, he complained that he read Aristotle's *Metaphysics* forty times without understanding it until he chanced upon reading al-Fārābī's *On the Object of the Metaphysica,* when the object of that philosophy became clear to him. However, the idea that ancient society was founded on a tacit concept of social contract is not new in Arab tradition. According to al-Mas'ūdī, the first political community was founded when Kiumarth, a grandson of Adam, was proclaimed king by a few men who felt the need for rulership. An agreement was reached between them that Kiumarth should rule in accordance with their common good. This story is also reported by Ṭabarī. See al-Mas'ūdī, *Murūj al-Dhahab,* ed. Bell, I, 261–62; and Ṭabarī, *Ta'rīkh,* I, 171.

31. Ibn Sīna, *Kitāb al-Shifā',* p. 441.

he would be the Prophet-Ruler and the legislator who lays down the law to organize the human relationship in all its aspects. Since such a Ruler is a rarity and will not always be in evidence, his Law is destined to remain valid after him. The purpose of the Law is to establish a political order based on justice and to enable men to attain happiness in this world and in the hereafter. Although he pays lip service to the destiny of man (and he reiterates Fārābī's idea of the soul and the attainment of happiness in the hereafter), the achievement of happiness on Earth is the primary concern of Ibn Sīna's Just City. To achieve justice for all, its class-structure and its political and economic orders are worked out in as fairly detailed manner as possible.

The Just City is composed of three classes: the administrators, the artisans, and the guardians. For each class there must be a leader, under whom there are other leaders, down to the common run of men. Nobody remains idle, unless he is ill. Those who refuse to work would be reprimanded or sent into exile. The assignment of rank and function in accordance with the qualities and acquired capabilities of each citizen is the responsibility of the Ruler who acts with the utmost rigor, fairness, and prudence, with the welfare (al-khayr) of the city as a whole as his goal. Justice as the end of Ibn Sīna's city appears more clearly defined than in Fārābī's city by an emphasis on the aggregate interests of the citizens, their security, and in the maintenance of public order.

To maintain public order and insure continuity and harmony, a public fund is called for, drawn partly from duties on imports and the income from agricultural produce, and partly from the penalties for violations of the Law. The fund might also be used as a source of income for the guardians and for citizens who are either ill or handicapped.[32]

Nobody in the Just City should be permitted to engage in frivolous or unproductive crafts. Those who are engaged in such practices as usury and gambling must be outlawed. Stealing and other harmful acts beneficial only to the wrongdoers are prohibited. Nor are immoral professions—prostitution and others—permitted, because they are likely to compromise social institutions considered to be the

32. Ibn Sīna proposed that citizens who are permanently ill or crippled should also be assisted from the fund, although some suggested that they should be put to death. He held that such treatment would be cruel and unjust. At any rate, he said, their number is not so great in society to cause hardship to others. See *ibid.*, p. 447.

cornerstones of the public order. Indeed, the Law should be strictly enforced to maintain the unity of the family and to regulate divorce and inheritance on an equitable basis. Love, says Ibn Sīna, is the bond for the stability of the family and care for the children; divorce should be discouraged by denying women the right to make the separation.[33]

For the stability of the City, Ibn Sīna saw the need for a law prescribing the mode of succession to the Prophet-Ruler. He proposed that succession should be by designation, as the choice of rulers by the public breeds dissension and partisanship. However, if the Prophet-Ruler or the second Ruler dies without designating a successor, Ibn Sīna proposed to follow the precedent set by the Caliph 'Umar (d. 22/644), who appointed a committee to choose one in consultation with the people. But if another candidate proclaims himself a Ruler (Imām) by virtue of power or wealth, then it would be the duty of all citizens to oppose him and, if necessary, to put him to death. If the self-appointed Ruler claims that his rival were afflicted with an imperfection, and his claim proved to be valid, it would then be in the best interests of the citizens to accept him. In accordance with such a rule of succession, Ibn Sīna's concept of political justice seems to be based on perfection and excellence rather than on legitimacy, contrary to the prevailing Sunnī doctrine of political justice. As a philosopher, he preferred to follow the concepts of Plato's philosopher-king and al-Fārābī's Prophet-ruler even though they run contrary to the Sunnī concept of the Imamate.[34] Since perfection and excellence are relative concepts, they are likely to stir controversies among rival parties and therefore seem inconsistent with the goals of harmony and stability which Ibn Sīna considered to be the very basis of the Just City.

As for the enemies of the Just City who stand against the Law, they are considered rebels and must be brought under control by force. If they persist, they should be put to death. Were they to surrender, they would be entitled either to some useful crafts or treated as slaves. If a city other than the Just City possesses laws and justice considered

33. Ibn Sīna did not argue against divorce in principle, but he felt that since "women are quick to follow passion and not very rational," the act of separation should not be initiated by them (*ibid.*, p. 450).

34. Ibn Sīna's concept of legitimacy based on the principles of designation and perfection is in accord with the Shī'ī doctrine of the Imamate. Unlike al-Fārābī, who was brought up in a Shī'ī family, Ibn Sīna was the son of a Sunnī father. His stress on the principles of perfection and designation, however, is based on rational rather than on religious grounds.

praiseworthy, it should be left in peace unless there would be a call for the jihād (just war)—presumably proclaimed by the Imām—whereby they should be treated in accordance with the Revealed Law.[35]

The Ruler, in the enforcement of the Law, should treat all men equally and impose penalties on all who act in disobedience to the Law. The penalties must be in proportion to the degree of violation of Law and morality. In all his actions, the Ruler should maintain a standard of justice based on the principles of moderation and the middle (al-wasaṭ). The latter is the principle of the "golden mean," which Ibn Sīna envisaged should be the general rule governing the conduct of citizens in their personal as well as public affairs. The purpose of the principles of moderation and the mean is to enable the citizen to cultivate the highest virtues necessary to realize justice. This kind of justice, according to Ibn Sīna, is justice in the practical sense. Combined with theoretical justice, presumably the *jus divinum,* ultimate happiness would be attained—"he who is able to achieve these prophetic qualities would become virtually a Divine man worthy of worship after God and should be the one entrusted with the governance of the servants of God; he is the worldly Sovereign and God's appointed Caliph over the world."[36] In contrast with al-Fārābī, whose concept of justice is utopian, Ibn Sīna's concept of justice is practical, qualified by Islamic religious and moral principles. Such a concept of justice reveals elements of naturalism, which brings it in line with Kindī's Rational Justice.

In contrast with both al-Kindī and al-Fārābī, who sought in varying degree to achieve the harmony of Reason and Revelation, Ibn Sīna's more naturalistic concept of justice, could hardly be regarded as supporting such endeavors. Nor was his way of life an example of an effort to achieve the purification of the soul to which he often referred in his writings, since he rarely restrained his indulgence in sensual habits and material luxury. For this reason, al-Ghazzālī, who was not opposed to Reason in principle, denounced the lip service paid by the philosophers to religious morality as a means to disguise their indulgence in mundane affairs. His cryptic remarks were made specifically against Ibn Sīna's life-style. He claimed that they defended religious and moral principles not for being of divine nature but for being useful in maintaining union in the family and stability in the commu-

35. For the law and justice among nations, see chap 7.
36. Ibn Sīna, *Kitāb al-Shifā'*, p. 455.

nity.[37] In taking such a critical attitude, al-Ghazzālī rejected the findings of philosophy, but he accepted the combined methods of Revelation, Reason, and Mysticism as the pathways to the Truth. The synthesis of these methods was hailed as a great intellectual achievement which remained prevailing in Islamic lands until it was challenged by the empirical method of the modern age.

Rational Justice as Natural Justice

It was not only Ghazzālī's attack on the falāsifa that checked the spread of rational standards. Perhaps even more important was the failure of philosophy to provide a fully convincing rationale for the harmony of Reason and Revelation. Before a similar reaction against philosophy in Western Islamic lands took place, another attempted solution for the harmony of Reason and Revelation was advanced by three philosophers in Western Islamic lands—Ibn Bājja, Ibn Ṭufayl, and Ibn Rushd—who were able to keep philosophy held in high esteem for another half a century before Ghazzālī's method prevailed. Since our primary concern is with justice, the question of the harmony of Reason and Revelation will be dealt with from that perspective. But a few words on Ibn Rushd's background may be illuminating.[38]

Before he became committed to philosophy, Ibn Rushd was brought up in the tradition of the Ash'arī theology, and in law he was a follower of the Mālikī school. After he studied Greek philosophy, his discourses on Religion and Law became more original and often critical of the dogmatic method of Muslim theologians, which incurred their displeasure and prompted them to denounce his philosophy. In his commentaries on Plato and Aristotle, divorced of neo-Platonism, he appeared in the eyes of his contemporaries as the scholar whose primary fidelity was to philosophy and not to Islam even though he sought to demonstrate in earnest the possible harmony of Reason and

37. Ghazzālī, *al-Munqidh Min al-Ḍalāl* (Beirut, 1959), pp. 47–48.

38. Abū al-Walīd Ibn Rushd, known in the West by his Latin name, Averroes, was born in Qurṭuba (Cordova) to a family well-known for learning and public service in 520/1126. He served first as a judge (Cordova and Granada) and then as a physician to the Caliph Abū Ya'qūb Yūsuf (and later his son al-Manṣūr), who entrusted him with the task of writing a commentary on Aristotle's philosophy. He also wrote works on jurisprudence, medicine, and philosophy, but he was known in Europe as the commentator on Aristotle. He died in 595/1198 at the age of seventy-two. For his life, see Ibn Abī Uṣaybi'a, *'Uyūn al-Anbā' fī Ṭabaqāt al-Aṭibbā'* (Beirut, 1965), pp. 530–33.

Revelation. Only from the perspective of Ibn Rushd's theory of justice, however, will we be able to demonstrate whether he was able to provide a more convincing rationale than his predecessors.

Although Ibn Rushd wrote many works, only in three that have reached us did he discuss the concept of justice directly. Two are commentaries on Plato's *Republic* and Aristotle's *Ethics,* and the third is a treatise on the Islamic creed to which he applied the rational method.[39]

Before he addressed himself to the concept of justice, Ibn Rushd sought first to discuss the possible application of Reason to religious questions.[40] He pointed out that he entirely disagreed with Ash'arī, the leading advocate of Sunnīsm, who held that the measure for distinguishing just from unjust acts is set forth in the Law, under the rules of "permissions" and "prohibitions," denoting that all prohibited acts must be considered unjust and all others just. It follows, said Ibn Rushd, that there is really nothing inherent in the nature of things to guide man on questions of justice and injustice except the Law.

Justice, according to Ash'arī, is nothing but the manifestation of God's Will—if an act is commanded by God, it must be just and if it is prohibited, it must be unjust, even if it appeared to man as unjust, since He alone knows that which is just or unjust.[41] In other words,

39. The Arabic texts of Ibn Rushd's commentaries on Plato's *Republic* and Aristotle's *Nichomachean Ethics* were lost, but Hebrew and Latin translations are available. The former has been rendered into English in two critical editions: (1) by E.I.J. Rosenthal, entitled *Averroes' Commentary on Plato's Republic* (Cambridge, 1956); and (2) by Ralph Lerner, entitled *Averroes on Plato's Republic* (Ithaca, N.Y., 1974). I have used both translations, as each has certain merits, although each author rendered Ibn Rushd's work from a different perspective. Ibn Rushd's commentary on Aristotle's *Ethics,* called the Middle Commentary, is being prepared for translation by Lawrence Berman. Ibn Rushd's book on the Islamic creed, though long remaining unknown, has been published in two critical editions: (1) by Marcus J. Müller, entitled *Philosophie und Theologie von Averroes* (Munich, 1859); and (2) by M. Qāsim, entitled *Kitāb Manāhij al-Adilla fī 'Aqā'id al-Milla* [Treatise on the Methods of the Proofs in the Creed of the (Islamic) Religion] (Cairo, 1955). Ibn Rushd's treatise on the harmony of Revelation and Reason, which has indirect bearing on justice, entitled *Kitāb Faṣl al-Maqāl,* ed. Nādir (Beirut, 1961), is rendered into English by George Hourani, under the title *Averroes on the Harmony of Religion and Philosophy* (London, 1961).

40. In the *Manāhij al-Adilla,* Ibn Rushd discussed the rational method in relevance to specific questions, but in the *Faṣl al-Maqāl* he dealt with the subject in broad philosophic terms.

41. Ibn Rushd, *Manāhij,* p. 223.

there is no measure by virtue of which man may be able to know whether an act is just or unjust other than legal permission or prohibition.

Such a doctrine, said Ibn Rushd, is absurd. For, he went on to explain, it would be contrary to both Revelation and Reason were we to argue that justice cannot possibly be known by its inherent goodness. For, if this were the case, then the belief in more than One God would be something neither good nor evil by itself save that it is prohibited in the Law. Such a presumption, says Ibn Rushd, is contrary to the Revelation. For, as stated in the Qur'ān, not only God describes Himself as just, but He also made it clear that "whoever does an injustice does so to himself" (Q. III, 178; VIII, 53; XXII, 10), clearly indicating that it was taken for granted that man could by himself distinguish between justice and injustice.[42]

Perhaps someone, said Ibn Rushd, may ask: what then is the meaning of the Revelation, "He [God] leads astray whomever He will, and He guides whomever He will" (Q. XIV, 4)? In the strictly literal sense, said Ibn Rushd, one may conclude from this Revelation that only God decides on questions of Justice and injustice. But, he maintained, the deeper meaning of this text cannot possibly be taken to imply that God is unjust, because it is contrary to other texts which confirm that He is always just and cannot possibly be unjust.[43] The Revelation in question would be more intelligible if taken to mean that some may be led astray by conditions conducive to evil which He had already created and to which men of evil propensities might be drawn to do unjust acts.[44] What if some would ask why did God create evil propensities at all, since their creation may amount to injustice? The reply, said Ibn Rushd, is that their creation is a manifestation of Divine Wisdom. As part of His grand design, God provided that evil shall be inherent in the nature of some men, but most men were indeed endowed with goodness, since no good would be known unless a greater good (al-khayr al-akthar) existed side by side with a lesser evil

42. In his commentary on Plato's *Republic,* Ibn Rushd also reproached the theologians for their assertion that there is nothing in the nature of things which distinguishes good from evil or just from unjust acts other than that which is indicated in the Law (Sharī'a) on the grounds that man possesses no will of his own apart from God's Will, which created both man and his acts (see Rosenthal, *op. cit.*, pp. 185–86; and Lerner, *op. cit.*, pp. 80–82).

43. See Q. IV, 45: "God will not be unjust to anyone the weight of a note."

44. Ibn Rushd, *Manāhij,* p. 234.

(al-sharr al aqal). The significance of the Divine Wisdom is enshrined in a Revelation which runs as follows:

> God to the Angels:
>
> I am setting forth in the Earth a khalīfa (vicegerent).
> They [the Angels] said: What, wilt thou set therein one who will do corruption there, and shed blood, while we proclaim thy praise and call Thee Holy?
> He [God] said: Assuredly I know that you know not. (Q. II, 28)

The significance of this text, according to Ibn Rushd, is that it explains the possible existence of good and evil, provided that the former exists in greater quantity than the latter, and that the need for the existence of some evil rather than its complete absence is inherent in the nature of things.[45] But if one would question the wisdom of the existence of such texts, the reply is that it is necessary to explain by example that God is the creator of both good and evil on Earth and that there exists One God only and not two, as some have already believed that there existed two gods, one who created the good and another the evil.[46] Moreover, Ibn Rushd pointed out that God did not create good and evil for the sake of good and evil; He created the good for the sake of goodness in itself and created evil for the sake of goodness also, just as He created fire for a certain good, although fire may accidentally cause an evil. Needless to say, he added, the existence of fire is obviously justified despite its accidental evil.

But someone may ask, said Ibn Rushd, what is the meaning of the Revelation, "He [God] shall not be questioned as to what He does, but they [men] may be questioned" (Q. XXI, 23). Is this text consistent with justice? It is true, Ibn Rushd said in reply, that men do justice because they desire to obtain the benefit of goodness for themselves, but God assuredly does not need the good for Himself. He does justice because justice flows from His perfection and not because He realizes His perfection by doing justice. If God's Justice, said Ibn Rushd, is thus understood, it would be different from human justice. But one does not have to agree with the theologians that God's Will

45. *Ibid.*, pp. 235–36.

46. In accordance with the tradition of classical philosophy, Ibn Rushd said, it may be necessary to explain to the multitude by rhetorical expressions the harmony of Revelation and Reason, but the allegorical method of interpretation which some theologians (i.e. the Mu'tazila) have used is an entirely different matter (see *ibid.*, pp. 236–37).

should not be qualified with Justice. Such an argument would be contrary to Reason and Law. If God's Will should not be qualified with Justice, then one would have to conclude that there exists nothing which is inherently just or unjust. And if God is described as Just in the same way as man is just, then God becomes deficient in Essence, since God, unlike man, does justice for the sake of justice, while man does justice as a service to others for the sake of his survival.[47]

Having established the harmony of Reason and Revelation, Ibn Rushd proceeded to discuss his ideas of justice making a distinction between the Divine and Human justice (Rational Justice). He made it clear that despite differences in sources (Greek and Islamic), the notion of justice embodied in both is ultimately the same. In setting forth his theory of human justice, Ibn Rushd has drawn on both Plato and Aristotle, making a distinction between the theoretical and practical forms of justice with an emphasis on the latter.[48] Justice, like other virtues, does not exist in its perfect form in a vacuum, said Ibn Rushd; it attains its perfection only when men are citizens of the state. Just as virtues are faculties of the soul, he added, justice is the highest virtue of man as a citizen. But justice is not just one virtue; it is, as Plato said, the sum of all virtues.[49] "It consists," he said, "in no more than every citizen following the activity for which he is best qualified by nature."[50] He went on to explain that this is conceivable only when the state is functioning in accordance with the guidance provided by the speculative science (philosophy) and governed by its masters. These are the ruling classes of the state just as the intellect is the ruling part of the soul. So justice means that each man (or class) does what he (or the class) has to do in proper measure and time.

Ibn Rushd distinguishes between virtues like wisdom and courage which are closely connected with one class only, and virtues like justice and temperance ('iffa) which are manifestly connected with all classes of the state. In agreement with Aristotle, he says that the virtue of temperance is connected with all, although Plato insists that temper-

47. *Ibid.*, pp. 237–38.

48. Although Ibn Rushd made use of both Plato's *Republic* and Aristotle's *Ethics*, he seems to have shown greater attachment to Aristotle's ideas, not without modification, especially in characterizing Rational Justice as natural justice.

49. Ibn Rushd, *Commentary on Plato's Republic*, pp. 114–15.

50. *Ibid.*, p. 115.

ance is a virtue confined to craftsmen. Justice is the virtue necessary for all.

In the realization of justice—indeed, in the realization of all virtues—Ibn Rushd said, in agreement with Aristotle, that three conditions are required. First, it is not only knowledge of the nature of virtues that is necessary; action is even more important. Second, the souls of the young must be inculcated with these virtues and cultivated to the point of perfection; if evil is ever in possession of some, it must be removed. Third, the qualities and virtues, whenever they are combined and render other virtues perfect, must be specified.

Ibn Rushd then turned to the question of how to inculcate and cultivate these virtues into the souls of the citizens. There are obviously two methods: First, by persuasion, either rhetorical and poetical for the multitude or the rational (speculative) for the elect; and second, by force. The first method is for the citizens who had already been accustomed to it from youth, and the other is for the adversaries and all those who are not sensitive to the appeals of virtue. The latter is evidently not for the citizens of the Virtuous State; it is for states whose public order is not based on virtues. In dealing with these states, whose rulers resort to force to correct their citizens, there is no other way than to resort to war. The Law, says Ibn Rushd, indicates how the two methods can be applied. If persuasion is not heeded, war becomes just (jihād) against rebels as well as unbelievers.[51] Since preparation for war is impossible without the cultivation of the virtue of courage, the citizens should cultivate this virtue in preparedness for war when it becomes necessary. Just as wisdom is the virtue necessary for the realization of justice within the state, so courage is necessary for the realization of justice in the relationship between nations.

Ibn Rushd, in agreement with Plato, maintains that justice can be realized only in a state founded upon a set of virtues, namely, wisdom, courage, temperance, and justice. Whenever these virtues are fully cultivated, the state becomes an ideal state. A few words about each virtue may be called for.

Wisdom includes possession of theoretical and practical knowledge concerning governance and Law. Men who are endowed with this rare quality are very few; they may be found only among the philosophers and those who are capable of governing the State. The rulers of the

51. For jihād as just war, see chap. 7.

Ideal State, said Ibn Rushd in agreement with Plato, "are necessarily the Philosophers."[52]

Courage as a virtue is the quality of strength against such emotions as fear and desire, which can be attained by education, especially in music and gymnastics. This virtue is most needed by the guardians whose responsibility is to maintain order and protect the state from its enemies.

Temperance and justice are in a different category from wisdom and courage. Whereas the last two are ordinarily found among rulers and guardians, temperance and justice are virtues necessary for all men. Temperance may be defined as the middle or the mean in human behavior—in eating, drinking, sexual intercourse, and others—and the man who is temperate "is he who can, of his own accord, remain permanently in this middle position." He can control himself and restrain "the soul from pleasures and desire." "It is said," Ibn Rushd adds, "that the temperate man is the most courageous and master over himself."[53] Just as the man who is by his intellect the master over the inferior, so is the temperate state more courageous than others and a master over itself. In order to attain such a quality, temperance should exist not only in one class but in all—the rulers and the ruled alike.

Finally, justice as a virtue is the quality of fairness and self-control. It is the quality by which the state can survive and claims to continue as long as the rulers and the multitude are in agreement "to keep that which the laws demand," namely, that "everyone . . . does that business for which he is fitted by nature, and does not long for what he does not possess."[54] In other words, the ideal state is the Just State by reason of the quality of justness with which all its citizens are clothed, just as wrongdoings reduce other states to "states of injustice" or "erring states."

Justice is maintained in the state as long as each citizen pursues the virtue most fitting to his class. The Just State is characterized as wise, courageous, and temperate, provided that these virtues exist in the state in their true measure, so that the rational faculty (Reason) rules over the other faculties.

Justice, in order to endure, is dependent on the Ruler who presides

52. Ibn Rushd, *op. cit.*, p. 157.
53. *Ibid.*, p. 158.
54. *Ibid.*, p. 160.

over the destiny of the state. Such a Ruler must be a philosopher, because he is the only one who desires knowledge and investigates its nature (separated from matter) and is able to teach it. Knowledge may be taught to the few either by the rational or demonstrative argument; the multitude can be taught only by rhetorical and poetical methods. In order to succeed, the philosopher should master both the theoretical and the practical arts, just as the king, in order to perfect the art of governance, is in need for the qualities of wisdom and intellect. The lawgiver obviously needs the same qualities. Indeed, the qualities of the philosopher, the king, and the lawgiver are the same. The Imām, Ruler of the Islamic state, must possess all of these qualities.

Should the ruler be a prophet? Ibn Rushd's answer to this question in general is in the affirmative.[55] Apart from being a prophet or a philosopher, however, the Ruler must be endowed with a set of natural qualifications such as disposition to theoretical knowledge, love for the truth, high-mindedness, courage, fluency in speech, good memory, control over desires that are not proper for rulers (like sensual desires and love for money), and—last but not least—justice. Since the existence of the prophet is a rarity, as Fārābi and Ibn Sīna have already pointed out, Ibn Rushd stressed the personal qualities of the Ruler upon whom the survival of the state is dependent. Thus it would be tempting to conclude that were the state to be a just state it should be presided over by a Ruler possessing the theoretical and practical qualities without having first been ruled by a prophet. In such a state Rational Justice may be equated with the *jus naturale*.

The opposite of the Just State are the erring or wrongdoing states where injustice prevails. Like Plato, Ibn Rushd identifies four types of states apart from the Ideal State; in each a different scale of justice is maintained. The first is the state whose order is based on honor, which is called timocracy. In such a state, justice is subordinate to honor and to other qualities. As an end, honor may be combined with wealth and power and may tempt men to overpower each other and do evil and injustice. Men of honor are masters and their status corresponds generally to the degree of honor they attain. Rulers possess the ability to distribute honors in pursuit of the measures that preserve their control. This, says Ibn Rushd, is the kind of justice that exists in timocracy.[56]

55. *Ibid.*, p. 177.
56. *Ibid.*, p. 211.

The second type, called plutocracy, is ruled by a few whose power rests on wealth. So wealth, not virtue, is the measure of the quality of men. The Ruler, the most powerful and perhaps the richest, combines with wealth an ability to govern successfully and consequently he is the master of the state, provided he allows his men to acquire wealth and let them enjoy it indefinitely. Wealth and power are the privilege of the few, but the majority, possessing no claim to privilege, are poor and oppressed.

The third type is the democratic state in which everybody is free from restraints and each is entitled to do whatever his heart desires. The aims and qualities of men vary—some love honor, others wealth, and still others tyranny. But there may be some who possess a few virtues and are moved by them. All arts and dispositions come into being, and it is possible that an "ideal state" as well as other types of states may emerge out of these varied dispositions. The man who is truly just is the one who has the power of leadership. The majority, at the mercy of whoever becomes the master, are plundered and oppressed by the more powerful, but these are often tempted to commit excesses "just as it happens in our own time and in our own state."[57] When the conditions deteriorate and the rulers can no longer distribute wealth among supporters, they resort to imposing heavy taxes. Consequently the common run of men, encouraged by dissatisfied supporters, try to shake off the oppressors, but the masters seek control by force. The State, supported by a few (including religious leaders), becomes tyrannical. The end of such a state is reduced to nothing more than to serve the master and to fulfill his wishes. This state is obviously the opposite of the Just State. Only in the Just State can the citizen attain justice equal to his natural abilities.

Ibn Rushd chose to discuss his concept of justice in the form of commentaries on Plato's *Republic* and Aristotle's *Ethics,* but the theory of justice that emerged from his pen is not merely a reproduction of Greek notions. The purpose of his commentaries, whether intended to validate the concept of justice drawn from pagan Greek

57. Ibn Rushd makes the following remark about the state of injustice in his own community: "The association among many of the Muslim rulers today are communities exclusively based upon houses (dynasties). Of the law, only that which observes the first law (the sacred law) is left among them. It is clear that in his State all property appertains to the house. Therefore they are sometimes forced to bring out of the house acquired treasure and allot it to those who fight on their behalf. Herein tribute and imposts (gharāma) have their origin. Thus men will be of two categories: a category called the masses and another called the mighty." *Ibid.,* p. 214.

sources or to harmonize Greek (representing Reason) and Islamic (representing Revelation) sources, has been the subject of controversy from the time his commentaries made their appearance until the modern times. Among his contemporaries, Ibn Rushd was considered merely a follower of Aristotle (indeed, he was also a great admirer of Plato), and he was denounced as a philosopher who undermined Islam under the guise of harmonizing Reason and Revelation. His works were repudiated—at one time they were burned and kept out of circulation—and later superseded by Ghazzālī's teachings which were taken to stress Revelation, although Ghazzālī never repudiated Reason and he did indeed recognize it as consistent with Revelation. In the modern age, under the impact of Western secular thought, there has been a revival of interest in Ibn Rushd's philosophy and the use of Reason as a method to validate the adoption of Western concepts and institutions as consistent with Islamic traditions. Some Western scholars have maintained that Ibn Rushd and other Muslim philosophers (al-falāsifa) paid only lip service to Islam by advocating the harmony of Reason and Revelation because of the heavy-handed official policy in support of Revelation, but in reality they disguised their fidelity to Greek philosophy, which stressed naturalism, in order to escape compulsion and censorship.[58] Today Muslim scholars have tried to defend the falāsifa's fidelity to Islam and hailed their method of the harmony of Reason and Revelation as a great contribution to philosophy.[59] To modern scholars, Ibn Rushd is considered more relevant to resolve questions arising from the impact of Western culture on Islam than Ghazzālī, although Muslim scholars (Revelationists) still adhere to Ghazzālī's methods.[60]

58. For the emphasis of naturalism in al-Kindī's philosophy, see R. Walzer, *Greek to Arabic,* (Oxford, 1926), chap. 1. Leo Strauss has overstressed the fidelity of the falāsifa to Greek naturalism, arguing that they concealed between the lines their views on the grounds of compulsion and censorship. See Strauss, *Persecution and the Art of Writing* (Glencoe, Ill., 1952), chaps. 1–2 (cf. the writer's review of this book in *The Muslim World,* XLIII, (1953), 136–38). Ralph Lerner, accepting in principle Strauss's viewpoint of the falāsifa's primary loyalty to Greek philosophy, has taken the same position concerning Ibn Rushd, though considerably modified, without contesting Ibn Rushd's fidelity to Islam (see Lerner, *op. cit.,* pp. xv–xvii).

59. Muḥammad 'Abduh, in his debate with Faraḥ Antūn (d. 1922) on the conflict between religion and science, defended Ibn Rushd's fidelity to Islam in his attempted method of the harmony of Reason and Revelation (see M. 'Umāra, ed. *al-'Amāl al-Kāmila li al-Imām Muḥammad 'Abduh* [Beirut, 1972], III, 496–513). See also Abū Rīda, *op. cit.,* I, 52–58; and M. Qāsim, *Ibn Rushd* (Cairo, 3rd ed., 1969), pp. 53–61, 72–76.

60. See chap. 9.

Despite the opposition of theologians, Ibn Rushd seems to have stood firmly by his fidelity to both Islam and philosophy. Indeed, there is nothing in his extant works giving evidence that he was cynical or doubtful about religious beliefs. He took it for granted that Reason can answer all questions on matters of faith. In his attempted harmony of Reason and Revelation, though rejected by Muslim theologians, he found among the Latin thinkers in Europe followers (often called the Averroists) who accepted this harmony which gained ground over time. But other Latin thinkers considered it unsound in principle and labelled it the doctrine of the twofold truth. St. Thomas Aquinas, though disagreeing with some of Ibn Rushd's ideas, seems to have implicitly endorsed his doctrine of the twofold truth by making a distinction between the truth arrived at by philosophy and the truth arrived at by theology. He maintained that to handle philosophical questions one must be a philosopher, and to handle theological questions one must be a theologian.[61]

The distinction between the theological and philosophical aspects of a problem is made nowhere more clearly than in Ibn Rushd's theory of justice. In making a distinction between Divine and human justice, he made it clear that human justice, arrived at through Reason, is imperfect, whereas Divine Justice, known through the Revelation, is an expression of God's perfection. These two levels of justice are but the ideal and practical aspects of the concept of justice—the theologians laid down its ideal formulation and the philosophers sought to find its elements from the experiences of man. In his theory of justice, Kindī held that the ultimate truth is one, but Ibn Rushd said that human justice is imperfect and therefore necessarily different from Divine Justice. The ultimate truth is not one, since the scale of justice of each aspect is derived from an entirely different source. But a harmony of the two, as Ibn Rushd demonstrated, can be found, notwithstanding the possible existence of discrepancy between the two.

Ibn Rushd's philosophy of the harmony of Reason and Revelation was introduced into Europe by his Jewish disciples, who formed the link between Muslim and Christian thinkers. Just as Christian scholars who spoke the Arab tongue had translated the works of Greek philos-

61. For a discussion of Ibn Rushd's twofold doctrine and its impact on European thinkers, see Etienne Gilson, *Reason and Revelation in the Middle Ages* (New York, 1938), chaps. 2–3; H. A. Wolfson, "The Twice Revealed Averroes" *Speculum,* XXVI (1961), 373–93.

ophers into Arabic in the early 'Abbāsid period, so did the Jewish scholars who lived in Spain under Arab rule transmit the works of Muslim philosophers and their commentaries on Plato and Aristotle into Latin.[62] Among those who had perhaps the greatest influence in this process was Mūsa B. Maymūn (Maimonides). He was born in Spain (530/1135) and educated in the Jewish and Islamic traditions, and lived in Morocco for a short time before he finally settled in Egypt. He died in 601/1204.[63] Although a contemporary and follower of Ibn Rushd, he studied first more thoroughly the works of al-Fārābī and did not become a follower and commentator on Ibn Rushd until after he went to Egypt. He was a philosopher in his own right, and wrote a treatise on Jewish law, titled *Dalalat al-Hā'irīn* (Guide of the Perplexed), in which he set forth his philosophy of law based on the harmony of Reason and Revelation. He described the Divine Law as a rational system and therefore as the perfect law; all other laws, called *nomos*, are the product of human experience and therefore imperfect. Like Ibn Rushd, he dealt with justice on two levels—the Rational and Divine—the latter being the embodiment of perfection and the former the product of human Reason and therefore imperfect. Divine Justice can be realized on Earth only through man's respect for and obedience to the Law. In consummation of his obedience to the Law, man achieves the perfection of the soul and ultimately his happiness and justice.[64]

Perhaps no less significant are Ibn Maymūn's commentaries on Muslim philosophers, especially on Ibn Rushd's philosophy and the transmission of their works into Europe leading to the establishment of the school of Averroism. Its central theme is the harmony of Reason and Revelation, and justice is dealt with as an essentially moral concept. Despite his popularity among European thinkers, Ibn Rushd's philosophy was rejected by Muslim thinkers and his concepts—justice and others—were almost entirely disregarded until the modern age

62. See DeLacy O'Leary, *Arabic Thought and Its Place in History* (London, 1922), chaps. 10–11.

63. For the life of Ibn Maymūn (Maimonides), see Ibn Abī Uṣaybi'a, *op. cit.*, pp. 582–83; Ibn al-Qifṭī, *op. cit.*, pp. 317–19.

64. Maimonides, *Guide of the Perplexed,* trans. R. Lerner and M. Mahdi, *Medieval Political Philosophy* (New York, 1963), pp. 91–225; Ralph Lerner, "Moses Maimonides," in Strauss and Cropsey (eds.), *op. cit.*, pp. 81–99; Lenn E. Goodman, "Maimonides' Philosophy of Law," *Jewish Law Annual,* I, 72–107.

when, under the impact of new streams of thought, his rational concepts have become relevant to contemporary Islamic society.[65]

Closely connected with philosophical justice is ethical justice. Indeed, the two overlap, as some of the writers on ethical justice were philosophers in their own right.

65. See chap. 9.

5

Ethical Justice

The supreme end for which we were created and towards which we have been led is not the gratification of physical pleasures but the acquisition of knowledge and the practice of justice: these two occupations are our sole deliverance out of the present world into the world wherein is neither death nor pain.

—Abū Bakr al-Rāzī

Ethical justice is justice in accordance with the highest virtues which establish a standard of human conduct. In accordance with legal justice, man is commanded to observe a minimum standard of duties; but in accordance with ethical justice, man is commended to conform to the highest possible standard of good. Justice, in the words of Aristotle, is "the greatest of virtues . . . and in it every virtue is comprehended."[1] The highest virtues are taken to be implied in the Relevation, but Muslim writers have drawn their ethical standard not only from Islamic but also from foreign (Greek, Persian and others) ethical sources. In their theories of ethical justice, however, they consciously sought to harmonize Islamic with foreign notions and values. Like philosophical justice, ethical justice was discussed on two levels—Divine and human—and most writers tried to correlate the two, though some dealt with one or the other independently, making no effort to relate the one with the other.

Ethical Justice and the Doctrines of Voluntarism and Involuntarism

To posit what justice ought to be, the writer on ethical justice must presuppose that man is endowed with a voluntary faculty which deter-

1. Aristotle, *Nichomachean Ethics* [1129^{b}13].

mines his conduct towards other men. In Islam, however, the doctrine of voluntarism was by no means acceptable to all believers, as the evidence in the authoritative sources is not clear as to whether it is in favor of voluntarism or involuntarism. This vagueness, concerning not only justice but also other matters, gave rise to the opposing schools of Qadar and Jabr.

The Khārijites were perhaps the earliest thinkers in Islam to initiate the debate on justice, and they discussed not only its political aspect but also its ethical implications. Although they advocated the doctrine of qadar (voluntarism) and held that man is responsible for his actions on the political plane, they were not all in agreement that he is completely free to determine his actions on the ethical plane. Ethical measures are too closely connected with religious duties and therefore must be determined within the framework of the Revelation.

Differences on the relationship between religious and moral obligations came to the surface on the occasion of a dispute between Shu'ayb and Maymūn about a debt which the former owed to the latter. Upon Maymūn's demanding the payment of the debt, Shu'ayb replied, "I shall give it to you, if God will." "God has willed that you should give it to me now," replied Maymūn. "If God had willed it, I could not have done otherwise than give it to you," said Shu'ayb. Thereupon Maymūn said, "Verily, God has willed what he commanded; what he did not command, he did not will; and what he did not will, he did not command." Failing to settle the issue, they agreed to refer the matter to 'Abd al-Karīm B. 'Ajarrad, the Khārijī leader, then in prison during the governorship of Khālid B. 'Abd-Allāh in 'Iraq (105/724–120/738), for an opinion. In reply, 'Abd al-Karīm said:

> Our doctrine is that what God willed came about, and what he did not will, did not come about; and we do not fix sū'an (evil) upon God.[2]

'Abd al-Karīm's reply, which arrived shortly after his death in prison, gave rise to differences of opinion on the interpretation of the text. Maymūn, invoking the statement "we do not fix evil (immoral purpose) upon God," declared that 'Abd al-Karīm approved of his opinion that God does not predicate evil, whereas Shu'ayb, on the

2. See Ash'arī, *Maqālāt al-Islāmiyyīn,* I, 165–66; passage translated in W. M. Watt, *Free Will and Predestination in Early Islam* (London, 1948), pp. 32–34.

strength of the statement "What God willed came about, and what He did not will did not come about," insisted that 'Abd al-Karīm confirmed his opinion. The disagreement may be said to have centered on the ethical question: Can God do injustice? Shu'ayb maintained that He can, because it is an expression of His Will; Maymūn argued that it would be impossible to ascribe evil to God, and injustice is evil. Thereupon, the disagreement between Maymūn and Shu'ayb led to a split into two schools of thought. The followers of Maymūn—the Qadarites—asserted the principle of voluntarism by virtue of which man possesses the capacity to choose between good and evil and is held responsible for all his acts. The followers of Shu'ayb were Jabarites, who held that man's acts, predicated by God, must be considered valid as an expression of His Will, and therefore the question of good and evil is irrelevant. To the Jabarites, God's justice must be subordinate to His Will, and moral issues should therefore be settled in accordance with the Law. To the Qadarites, however, justice is closely connected with morality and determined by Reason (in accordance with the doctrine of qadar, voluntarism); therefore, man would be blamed for his disregard of the ethical standard of justice. It was taken for granted that Reason would guide man to do good rather than evil.

Ḥsan al-Baṣrī, whom we met before, though considered to be a Qadarite, rejected the views advanced by the followers of Shu'ayb that the scale of ethical justice was predestined, although he equated justice with piety and righteousness (moral good). He made a distinction between ethical and political justice, holding man responsible for the former but not the latter. He maintained that the Revelation is clear on questions of political justice, as prescribed in the Qur'ān in no uncertain terms: "Obey God and the Apostle and those in authority among you" (Q. IV, 62). On the strength of this Revelation, he preached obedience and loyalty to the authorities and repudiated all the political agitation which the leaders of heterodox sects had aroused against Sunnī rulers. Since political justice is an expression of the Will of the Sovereign, final decisions on all questions of political justice must be made by the Caliph himself, presumably as God's representative on Earth.

But ethical justice falls into an entirely different category. In accordance with the doctrine of al-Ḥasan, God commands mankind as a whole to follow an ethical standard of justice, but does not predicate the individual's moral acts; each man is responsible for his own wrongdoing. "Guidance flows from God," said al-Ḥasan, "but wrongdoing comes from man."[3] In accordance with this doctrine, whoever holds that his acts are commanded by God is considered a hypocrite (munāfiq) and should be blamed for his wrongdoing, but should not be punished since he would be judged by God in the hereafter. As a man who equated justice with righteousness, al-Ḥasan maintained that the measure of justice is ethical, determined by religious morality; no legal or theological sanctions need be invoked.

An entirely different scale of ethical justice was laid down by the Ṣūfīs or the Muslim mystics. Owing to their deep contemplation and solitude, they stressed a set of values which might have the effect of bringing about an injustice against one's own self. Aristotle said that there can be no injustice toward one's self, as no one chooses to hurt himself; if he ever did, he would do injustice towards the state.[4] But the Ṣūfīs, believing in humility, poverty, and complete surrender of voluntarism, have consciously renounced their personal claims; therefore, their acts of voluntarism may be considered a form of self-inflicted injustice. In the subjective sense, the man who accepts deprivation and surrenders his free will may derive an inward satisfaction or happiness (moral good); but in the objective sense, there is an injustice which may affect more than the person concerned. Whereas the Ṣūfī concept of Divine Justice is expressed in terms of love and beauty, its measure of justice is forgiveness and mercy. In the words of Abū Sa'īd B. 'Alī al-Khayr (d. 441/1049), the Ṣūfī scale of ethical justice is defined as follows:

> Whoever has seen me and has done good work for my family and disciples will be under the shadow of my intercession hereafter.
>
> I have prayed God to forgive my neighbors on the left, on the right, in front, and behind, and He has forgiven them for my sake. . . .
>
> I need not say a word on behalf of those around me. If anyone has mounted an ass and passed by the end of this street, or has passed my house or will pass it, or if the light of my candle falls on him, the least thing that God will do with him is that he will have mercy upon him.[5]

3. See chap. 2, section on Political Justice as Righteousness.
4. See *Nichomachean Ethics* [1134^{a}32 and 1137^{b}34].
5. R. A. Nicholson, *Studies in Islamic Mysticism*, pp. 217–18.

Since most Ṣūfīs have preferred to lead a life of quietude and detachment, their attitude towards wrong-doers was expressed in terms of forgiveness and mercy, free of condemnation or blame. Their notion of "ethical justice" might well be called theistic love and beauty which, like the Sun shining on all mankind, makes no distinction between those who do good and evil.

Ethical Justice as the Expression of Divine Virtues

Most writers on ethical justice were concerned with the practical aspects of justice and sought, by composing mirrors for princes and manuals for laymen, to delineate what might be called moral blueprints for human conduct. A few thinkers like Miskawayh and Rāzī showed an interest in ethical theory and tried to formulate a standard of justice in which Islamic values were embodied. They made it clear that ethical justice was not merely a set of religious and legal duties, but also moral obligations or dispositions toward good and evil, which man ought to undertake were he to pursue justice in accordance with an ethical standard.

Like the falāsifa (philosophers), writers on ethical justice dealt with the subject on two levels—Divine and human. In this section, it is proposed to discuss ethical justice as an expression of Divine virtues; in the following section, ethical justice will be dealt with as an expression of human virtues. Three thinkers—Miskawayh (421/1030), al-Ghazzālī (505/1111) and al-Ṭūsī (570/1174), who distinguished themselves as leading writers on ethical theory—are chosen, because each has stressed a somewhat different aspect of justice. The ethical notions of the three may be taken to provide a general theoretical framework for ethical justice.

The first, Aḥmad B. Muḥammad Miskawayh, may be regarded as perhaps the most important thinker to discuss ethical theory, as he dealt more directly with the ethical aspect of justice. In his treatise entitled *Tahdhīb al-Akhlāq* [The Refinement of Character] he devoted an important portion of the work to justice;[6] and in a shorter

6. Aḥmad B. Muḥammad Miskawayh, *Kitāb Tahdhīb al-Akhlāq wa Taṭ-hīr al-'Araq* [Book of the Refinement of Character and the Purification of Veins] (Cairo, 1322/1905), trans. Constantine Zurayk, *The Refinement of Character* (Beirut, 1968), chap. 4.

study, dealing specifically with the theory of justice, he posited a set of abstract postulates on the nature and components of ethical justice.[7] In both works, Miskawayh has drawn on Greek ethical theory—Plato and Aristotle in particular—and on some of the later Greek writers who lived in the later period of the Roman Empire. He was also an ethical philosopher in his own right, as he refined some of the Greek concepts and reformulated them within the context of Islamic morality. It is, however, not our purpose to trace the Greek origin of his ethical concepts, since this has already been done by other scholars, but rather to focus our discussion on his ethical ideas expressed in terms of the Islamic concepts of justice.[8]

Miskawayh divided justice into three categories: natural, conventional, and Divine Justice. He followed the categories set by Aristotle, but added a fourth, called "voluntary." He said, however, that this kind is included in the other three categories. Aristotle made a distinction between natural justice, which exists in nature, and conventional justice, the product of human acts, and he contended that justice concerning the relationship among the gods falls into the category of natural justice.[9] In an effort to achieve harmony of Greek philosophy and religion, Miskawayh sought to reconstruct Aristotle's categories within an Islamic context. Divine Justice is thus defined not as governing the moral relationship among gods but as the relationship between God and man; natural justice as governing the relationship among physical or natural bodies, expressed in abstract or numerical terms; conventional justice as governing the moral relationship among men and expressed in Aristotelian and Neo-Platonic concepts; and voluntary justice, though presumably included in all the three, must fall in the category of human or conventional justice, as it has no direct bearing on Divine or natural justice.

"As to Divine Justice," says Miskawayh, "it exists in metaphysical and eternally existing things. The difference between Divine Justice and natural justice, even though the latter is eternal, is that Divine

7. Miskawayh, *Risāla fī Māhiyyat al-'Adl* [Treatise on the Nature of Justice], edited and rendered into English by M. S. Khan, entitled *An Unpublished Treatise of Miskawayh on Justice or Risāla Fī Mahiyyat al-'Adl li Miskawayh* (Leiden, 1964). This treatise, written in answer to a question put forth to Miskawayh by Abū Ḥayyān al-Tawḥīdī (d. 413/1023), is highly abstract in nature.

8. For a discussion of the Greek sources on which Miskawayh has drawn, see Richard Walzer, *From Greek to Arabic* (Oxford, 1962), p. 220ff.

9. *Nichomachean Ethics* [1134^{b}18].

Justice exists in something other than matter, whereas the other [natural justice] has no other existence except in matter."[10] It is, in other words, a spiritual relationship between man and God which transcends the physical relationship between man and nature or between man and man. Expressed in Islamic terms, it is the fulfillment of man's legal and religious duties toward God.[11] But to these, Miskawayh adds a moral obligation—the repayment of God's favors which man ought not fail to observe. "For," he went on to explain, "whoever is given a certain good, no matter how small it may be, and does not see the necessity of repaying it in some way, is an unjust man. . . . Although God is beyond the need of our assistance and efforts, it is disgracefully absurd and abominably unjust not to observe any obligation towards Him nor to offer Him, in return for His benefits and favors, what would remove from us the mark of injustice and of failure to fulfill the stipulation of justice."[12]

What are man's obligations to God? Miskawayh, accepting Aristotle's notions of Divine obligations as filtered to him in a translation of the *Nichomachean Ethics,* expressed them in Islamic moral and religious values. He pointed out that people hold different views about man's obligations towards God. Some, he said, hold that the performance of prayers, fasting, and the offering of sacrifices are absolutely necessary, whereas others are satisfied with the acknowledgement of His existence, His beneficence, and the glorification of His name. Still others desire to gain His favor by commendable acts, and there are those (like the Ṣūfīs) who maintain that man's obligations can only be fulfilled by means of a mystical unity with God. Moreover, there are those who contend that man's obligations do not have to be fulfilled in just one single way—indeed, each one may, in accordance with his class or rank, follow his own way. Apart from that, Miskawayh said that the philosophers and other men of learning held that the worship of God may be carried out in one of the following ways:

> The worship of God consists of three things: true belief, right speech, and good action. Action is divided into the bodily such as fasting and prayers, and the non-bodily, such as transactions and the

10. Miskawayh, *Risāla fī Māhiyyat al-'Adl,* p. 20, trans. Khan, p. 31.
11. Miskawayh, *Kitāb Tahdhīb al-Akhlāq,* p. 39, trans. Zurayk, p. 106.
12. *Ibid.*, pp. 39–40, trans. 106–8.

jihād. Further, transactions are divided into exchanges, marriages, and methods of mutual assistance.[13]

Finally, in the classification of the fulfillment of moral obligations, Miskawayh was not unaware that some men may act like just men in appearance but in reality may not be just. In other words, they often pretend to be just. Therefore, he suggested that not only the outward but also the inward performance of the obligation must be examined. To be truly just, he went on to explain, men must fulfill all the purposes of justice and act in accordance with them as well as with other purposes. For they may pretend, as hypocrites often do, to act as just men but, in reality, they are not just at all. "The truly just man," he said, "is he who harmonizes all his faculties, activities, and states in such a way that none exceeds the others . . . desiring in all of this the virtue of justice itself and not any other object. . . . He can achieve this only if he possesses a certain moral disposition of the soul out of which, and in accordance with which, all his activities come forth."[14] As Aristotle said, justice is not a portion of virtue but the whole of virtue; and injustice—the opposite of justice—is not a portion of vice but the whole of vice.[15] Justice as the whole of virtue is ethical justice, which Miskawayh maintained is quite consistent with Islamic teachings, as moral principles, enshrined in the Law and Traditions, are the ultimate goals of the Islamic religion.

Like Miskawayh, Abū Ḥāmid al-Ghazzālī did not only draw on Greek ethical philosophy, but also made use of the writings of Muslim philosophers who attempted to harmonize Greek ethics with Islamic traditions. In his *magnum opus,*[16] he dealt with the practical aspects of ethical justice and laid down an elaborate code of morality designed to serve as a guide for human conduct.[17] In his attempt to indicate the right path of justice, Ghazzālī first examined the scope of the theological and philosophical notions of justice which he found wanting. Having taught for a short while in Baghdad, where he was a popular lecturer at the newly established Nizāmīya University, he began his

13. *Ibid.*, p. 40, trans. 109.

14. *Ibid.*, p. 100.

15. Aristotle, *Nichomachean Ethics* [1129^{b}13; 1130^{a}6].

16. Ghazzālī, *Iḥyā' 'Ulūm al-Dīn* [Cairo; Bulaq, 1289/1872), 4 vols.

17. Perhaps one of the best summaries of this code of morality may be found in Ghazzālī's *Kitāb al-Adab fī al-Dīn* (on the margin of Miskawayh's *Kitāb Tahdhīb al-Akhalāq* [Cairo, 1322]).

journey (483/1091) to Damascus and then went to Jerusalem and Makka, where he lived in seclusion as a mystic and practiced the Ṣūfī way of life. His journey, as he described it, was "the search for the truth."[18] Later he returned to his native town of Ṭūs (where he was born in 450/1059) and led a life of piety and righteousness. After these varied experiences, he wrote his major works in which he combined the methods of Reason, Revelation, and Mysticism. In this synthesis, he incorporated Greek, Persian, and other foreign notions, and tried to keep a balance which he called the "mean" (alwasaṭ)[19] in his concept of justice. In the pursuit of this method, he was influenced by his teacher Abū al-Ma'ālī al-Jūwaynī (d. 478/1085), who taught at Ṭūs.[20]

Ghazzālī was a prolific writer and his works deal with almost all conceivable questions of theology, philosophy, and mysticism. The debate on justice naturally did not escape his searching mind, but he formulated no new theory of justice, nor was justice as a concept central in his writings. He was deeply interested in ethics and dealt with justice from an essentially ethical view point. Like the Mu'tazila and the philosophers, he dealt with justice on two levels—Divine and human. Man's conduct, he maintained, is guided by Divine Justice, as an expression of God's Will, and by Rational Justice, as an expression of man's free will (qudra) granted to him by God.[21] The Law, the embodiment of Revelation, governs man's external actions, and Reason governs man's actions from within. The two provide guidance to pursue justice and good. Whereas the Law, consisting of God's commands and prohibitions, indicates what is good and just, Reason explains why some of the rules are just and why others are unjust, as the Law sets forth only the category of obligations, some are legally binding and others are commendable (morally binding).[22]

Ghazzālī's concept of justice may appear as a combination of Rational and Revelational notions; he seems to have shown an interest

18. For these experiences, see Ghazzālī's intellectual autobiography, entitled *al-Munqidh Min al-Ḍalāl* [Deliverance from Error]; trans. W. M. Watt, *The Faith and Practice of al-Ghazali* (London, 1953).

19. He also used the term "al-mizān" (balance).

20. For the life of Juwaynī, see Tāj al-Dīn-al-Subkī, *Ṭabaqāt al-Shāfi'īya al-Kubra* (Cairo, 1323/1905), III, 249–85; F. H. Maḥmūd, *al-Juwaynī: Imām al-Ḥaramayn* (Cairo, 1964). For the life of Ghazzālī, see Subkī, *op. cit.*, IV, 101–45.

21. Ghazzālī, *al-Iqtiṣād fī al-'Itiqād* (Cairo, n.d.), pp. 43–44.

22. See Ghazzālī, *al-Mustaṣfa Min 'Ilm al-Uṣūl* (Cairo, 1937), I, 2–3, 7–35.

only in its ethical aspect.[23] It consists of moderation (i'tidāl) and the mean (al-wasaṭ), which he began to develop in Baghdad before he turned to mysticism. In a work entitled *Mishkāt al-Anwār,* he describes the role of intuition (iḥā'), a mystical method in the determination of justice. He redefined Reason (considered earlier as a power [qudra] implanted in man by God) as "light" (nūr), a word often used in the Qur'ān as the equivalent of Divine Wisdom, inspired by God to guide man along the path of the truth and justice. Justice, as understood by Māturīdī and Bāqillānī, is an expression of God's Will and embodied in the Law; on all other matters, concerning which there is nothing in the Law to indicate what is morally just or unjust, Reason guides man to distinguish between the two. Reason, according to Ghazzālī's doctrine of the light (nūr), is the channel by virtue of which Divine Wisdom is inspired. This Wisdom is enshrined in the virtues (al-faḍā'il) and manifested in man's conduct to do the good. Ethical justice is thus an expression of human virtues (which Ghazzālī dealt with in detail in his earlier works), but it is ultimately derived from Divine Justice.[24]

In his later years Ghazzālī seems to have considered the mystical method as overriding, while Reason—the instrument which enables man to distinguish between justice and injustice—was relegated to the level of a medium for Divine intuition. While the intuitive method may be said to have raised man to a higher spiritual level by virtue of direct communication with Divine Wisdom, in practice it meant that man would be completely dependent on Revelation.

Ethical Justice as the Expression of the Highest Human Virtues

No Muslim thinker who wrote on ethics had been so deeply committed to Reason as the only method to acquire knowledge as al-Rāzī.[25] It

23. For Ghazzālī's exposition of this aspect of Justice, see pp. 120–21.

24. Ghazzālī, *Mishkāt al-Anwār* [Niche of Light], ed. 'Affīfī (Cairo, 1383/1964).

25. Abū Bakr Muḥammad B. Zakarīya al-Rāzī was born at Rayy (near Tihrān) in 251/865. He began to study medicine when he had already reached the age of thirty, having spent his earlier years in music. He went to Baghdad which had become the center of learning in Islamic lands, where he studied under the masters of medicine and began to practice his new profession with competence. Returning to take charge of the public hospital in Rayy for a short time, he later went to Baghdad to occupy the

is true that the philosophers (al-falāsifa) had also depended heavily on Reason, but most of them sought the harmony of Reason and Revelation and dealt with justice on two levels—Divine and human. Rāzī, however, though he believed in God and in the doctrine that He is "the God of Justice," maintained that Divine virtues can be attained only through Reason. He made no acknowledgment of the need for Revelation. Indeed, he seems to have written a book on prophecy (which, needless to say, has not survived), in which he stated that Reason is superior to prophetic inspiration.[26] For this reason, Rāzī's views on ethics have been condemned, and only his writings on science and medicine were highly valued.[27] Rāzī aspired to be acknowledged as a philosopher, and he wrote an intellectual autobiography and a treatise on human virtues in which the concept of ethical justice is discussed.[28]

According to Rāzī, the acquisition of knowledge and the pursuit of justice are the ultimate ends of human existence. In the tradition of Greek philosophy, he asserted that the aim of life is not the gratification of physical pleasure, but the acquisition of knowledge and the realization of justice.[29] Pleasure, he goes on to explain, is prompted by passion; but Reason "urges us to eschew present pleasure for the sake of other objects which it prefers." For God, who "loves us to have knowledge and to be just," does not desire that man should suffer pain—He "will punish those of us who inflict pain, and those who deserve to be pained, each according to his deserts." Pleasure and pain on Earth will come to an end, Rāzī held, while the pleasures of the next world, where no death exists, are everlasting. No man, needless to say, should be prepared to purchase a pleasure that perishes at

---

same position until he retired to his native town where he spent the rest of his life. Despite blindness in the latter part of his life, Rāzī continued to show interest in science and medicine. He dedicated his famous book on medicine, entitled *Kitāb al-Mansūrī* (known in Europe as *Liber Almansoris*), to his friend al-Manṣūr, Governor of Rayy. He died in 313/924. For his life and thought, see Ibn Khallikān, *Wafayāt al-A'yān*, IV, 244–47.

26. P. Kraus and S. Pines, "al-Rāzī," *Encyclopaedia of Islam*, 1st ed., III, 1136.

27. Meyerhof hailed him as "the greatest physician of the Islamic world and one of the great physicians of all time." M. Meyerhof, "Science and Medicine," *Legacy of Islam* (London, 1st ed., 1931), p. 323.

28. Rāzī, "Kitāb al-Sīra al-Falsafīya," in *Rasā'il Falsafīya*, ed. Kraus (Cairo, 1939; Beirut, 1973), pp. 99–111; trans. A. J. Arberry, "Rhazes on the Philosophic Life," *Asiatic Review*, 45 (1949), 703–13.

29. *Ibid.*, p. 101, trans. p. 705.

the price of an infinite pleasure that endures. "This being so," he warns, "it likewise necessarily follows that we ought not to seek any pleasure, the attainment of which would inevitably involve us in the commission of an act barring our deliverance into the World of Spirit, or that would oblige us in this present world to suffer pain exceeding both quantitatively and qualitatively the pleasure we have chosen."[30] It is evident that Rāzī, who takes it for granted that man is in possession of free will and guided by Reason, would prefer to make a choice in favor of the deferred pleasure in the hereafter than the immediate pleasure on Earth. The "philosopher" (the man of Reason), he said, "may sometimes eschew many of these lawful pleasures (mubāḥāt) in order thus to train and habituate his soul, so that it may be easier for him to give them up when the occasion requires."[31]

While the enjoyment of physical pleasures is permitted under the Law, Reason, according to Rāzī, urges man to forego such an enjoyment in lieu of the more everlasting spiritual pleasure in the second life. Rāzī admits that the Revelation urges man to pursue the pathway of justice, but it does not provide the measure to distinguish between just and unjust acts. Such a measure is provided by Reason which enables man to choose the pathway which he ought to pursue. By the same token, Reason may guide man to comprehend the highest virtues, the attainment of which can bring about a realization of justice. But how does Reason, one may ask, provide the guidance necessary to comprehend the highest virtues and what are those virtues?

In the *Spiritual Physick,* Rāzī said that he had examined the life of great philosophers who set an example of what the standard of justice ought to be. Such a standard, embodying the highest virtues, consists of the following: (1) continence ('iffa), (2) compassion (raḥma), (3) universal benevolence (al-nusḥ li al-kull), and (4) the endeavor to secure advantages to all men (al-ijtihād fī naf' al-kull). By contrast, the men who pursue the path of injustice and oppression are those who seek to overthrow the regime and do all the kinds of acts which are prohibited—disorder (al-harj), mischief (al-'ayth) and corruption (al-fasād).[32] Some men, Rāzī held, may pursue a life of wrongdoing because they follow doctrines which are in themselves bad and inherently evil, like followers of certain heresies which allow deceit and

30. *Ibid.*, pp. 101–102, trans. pp. 705–6.
31. *Ibid.*, p. 102, trans. p. 706.
32. Rāzī, "Kitāb al-Ṭibb al-Rūḥānī," *Rasā'il Falsafīya,* p. 91.

treachery toward their opponents.[33] Not only were their acts considered to be harmful to the community, but also to themselves. Such men, Rāzī warned, cannot be persuaded to change their evil way of life, except by serious discourse to bring them back to Reason and justice. The impact of classical theory is clearly evident in Rāzī's concept of ethical justice; he sought to discuss its components in familiar Islamic terms.

In his discussion of injustice, Rāzī broaches the problem of pain. Although he is opposed in principle to the inflicting of pain on any sentient being, he permits pain either in the form of Retributive justice or in the form of hardship to avert still greater pain, such as taking bitter and disagreeable medicine and the pain accompanying surgical operations. Beasts may also be put to hard labor, provided they are not treated too harshly, or unless exceptional circumstances arise and it is necessary to rescue someone from danger or to escape from the enemy.

As for the killing and slaughtering of animals, Rāzī held that this should only be done with carnivorous and not with domestic animals. Lions, tigers and wolves, which cause great mischief, might be hunted; snakes and scorpions and the like, which are harmful and not needed for any use, might be killed and exterminated. He held that there are two reasons for killing these animals: first, if they are not destroyed, they will destroy many other animals; second, the souls of animals, unlike the souls of man, cannot escape from their bodies, whereby the killing of animals may liberate their souls from their bodies and lead to their release.[34] But domestic animals should be handled gently. Since there is no hope for the soul to escape their bodies, he said, Reason would not have permitted their slaughter at all. However, he admitted that the philosophers have held different opinions on the matter and that Socrates was against the slaughtering of animals. The notion that animals are in possession of souls which cannot be released, except by killing them, was not shared by other Muslim thinkers. Most thinkers held that animals do not have souls, and some, such as the Mu'tazila, who admitted that their slaughter was an act of injustice, maintained that they would be compensated in the hereafter.

33. Razi cited the examples of the followers of Dayṣan and the Red Khurramīs who held it lawful to mislead their enemies, and the Manicheans who refused to give water, food, or medical care to those who did not share their opinion. See *Ibid.*, pp. 91–92, trans. p. 101.

34. Rāzī, *Kitāb al-Sīra al-Falsafīya*, pp. 104–5, trans. pp. 707–8.

While Rāzī discussed ethical justice as an expression only of Reason, equating it with God's Wisdom, Miskawayh and Ghazzālī dealt with justice on two levels—Divine and human—and tried to relate the one with the other. Since the theories of Miskawayh and Ghazzālī about Divine Justice have already been dealt with, we will discuss now their ideas about ethical justice on the human level.

According to Miskawayh, ethical justice as an expression of virtues falls into the category of conventional justice. Human virtues are divided into two kinds: One may be called particular and the other general. The general is the kind upon which all men are agreed, such as the transactions in gold which men have used as the standard for fixing the values of labor and services.[35] Conventional justice, the product of human experience, is either "established by consent and convention," or determined by inquiry and long deliberation but not by whims or accidental events. Particular justice is a kind of justice that develops in one country or city (or even between two persons), consisting of measures essentially of equal rights binding on the parties concerned. This kind of justice, in the words of Aristotle, is called contractual justice, a form of legal justice based either on the law or custom of the land.[36] Finally, voluntary justice, the product of human experience (which may well be a form of conventional justice),[37] is an expression of the soul and the peaceful cooperation of its faculties. This cooperation of the faculties, says Miskawayh, stands in relation to the body and is maintained by the activities of the soul.[38]

Like Aristotle, Miskawayh maintained that conventional justice is the mean, or the middle, between two extremes, while injustice is one of the two extremes. Indeed, every virtue, he explained, is a form of an equilibrium, and justice is but a name which embraces all virtues.[39] Four virtues, considered to be the highest human qualities, are as follows: Wisdom (al-ḥikma), temperance (al-'iffa), courage (al-

35. Like Aristotle, Miskawayh dwells on the use of money and indicates how gold and silver came into use as measures of value (see the *Risāla fī Nihāyat al-'Adl,* pp. 18–18, trans. pp. 29–30).

36. *Ibid.*, p. 19, trans. p. 30.

37. Miskawayh, *Risāla,* p. 12, trans. p. 21.

38. *Ibid.*, p. 19, trans. p. 31. In the *Tahdhīb al-Akhlāq,* Miskawayh (quoting Plato) said, "When man acquires justice, every part of his soul illuminates every other part, for all the soul's virtues are achieved in it. Then the soul rises and performs its particular activity in the best possible way. This is the happy man's nearest approach to God." Miskawayh, *Tahdhīb al-Akhlāq,* p. 41, trans. pp. 110–11.

39. Aristotle's *Ethics* [1133^{b}33–35]; however, Miskawayh attributed this concept to Plato. See *Tahdhīb al-Akhlāq,* p. 41, trans. p. 111.

shajā'a), and justice (al-'adl). Each is made up of a set of overlapping dispositions, the highest of which is enshrined in justice.[40]

The foregoing virtues became the familiar theme of ethical justice in Muslim writings. Although originally drawn from Greek sources (especially the works of Plato and Aristotle), they were gradually Islamized and expressed in religious and moral values, as set forth in the writings of Rāzī and Miskawayh. Abū Ḥāmid al-Ghazzālī and Naṣīr al-Dīn Ṭūsī, drawing in particular on Miskawayh's writings, contributed to this process in which Greek and Persian ethical values were assimilated. In his discussion of which ethical principles man ought to pursue, Ghazzālī provided believers with a justification under the category of commendable (mandūb) acts of the Law.[41] As set forth by Ghazzālī, the standard of ethical justice which provides guidance consists of four virtues, which may be summed up as follows:

1. Wisdom (al-ḥikma), the quality of mind by which man makes choices: he distinguishes between good and evil and restrains himself from extreme acts under such pressures as rage and anger, and maintains a balance between foolhardiness and swindling. Such a balance, considered by the Prophet one of the "goals of believers," is implied in the principle of the "mean" and hailed as the very essence of justice.[42] "Whoever is given Wisdom," in the words of the Revelation, "has been given much good" (Q. II, 272).

2. Courage (al-shajā'a), the quality of fury and indignation (al-quwwa al-ghaḍabīya) which may be described as a form of moral courage, neither rashness and hastiness (tahawwur) nor cowardice (jubn), but a state in the middle of the two. Guided by Law and Reason, courage urges man to conduct himself properly, pursue the right or straightforward path (al-sirāṭ al-mustaqīm)[43] and avoid the wrong. It also prompts him to be resolute on some occasions and compassionate on others.

40. Miskawayh held that, above all, ethical justice should include the following: friendship, concord, family fellowship, recompense, fair play, honest dealing, amiability and piety (some of the original manuscripts of Miskawayh's *Tahdhīb* add a few other dispositions which Constantine Zurayk considers as interpolations by a later writer. See Miskawayh's *Refinement of Character,* trans. Zurayk, pp. 20–21 (notes).

41. For the meaning of commendable acts, see p. 143.

42. Ghazzālī, *Ma'ārij al-Qudus,* pp. 67–74; *Mizān al-'Amal,* p. 264ff.

43. "Al-Ṣirāṭ al-mustaqīm" (the straightforward path) is the path of the Law (Sharī'a).

3. Temperance (al-'iffa), the quality of moderation by virtue of which man follows the middle course between two extremes of greed and antipathy, tries to be fair to others and moderate in his way of life. It is, in other words, an expression of "the golden mean."

4. Justice (al-'adl), which is not just one virtue but the "whole of the virtues." It is the perfection of all virtues, consisting of the "state of balance" (equilibrium) and of moderation in the conduct of personal and public affairs. Above all, it is an attitude of fairness (inṣāf) which urges man to pursue that which might be described as the "path of justice."[44]

But what is the "path of justice"? The path of justice, Ghazzālī said, is "al-ṣirāṭ al-mustaqīm" (the straightforward or the right path), by virtue of which man attains happiness in this world and in the hereafter.[45] By happiness Ghazzālī did not mean physical possessions but spiritual satisfaction which can only be attained in the acquisition of knowledge (Divine and human) which enables man to reach the state of near perfection on Earth, in preparation for the attainment of the ultimate state of perfection in Heaven.[46] This kind of knowledge, he said, may be obtained either by Reason or Revelation. The latter provides guidance for the achievement of Divine Justice (in the hereafter) and the former governs man's actions in his personal and public affairs in this world. But the real happiness, said Ghazzālī, is not worldly happiness (happiness on Earth is only metaphorically so-called), because the real and eternal happiness can be realized only in Heaven, where man will find himself in the presence of God, seen seated on His Throne.[47]

The opposite of justice is jawr. It may be described as a form of vice.[48] While justice is a state of moderation, no such state can possibly exist in evil, just as there is no moderation or a state of middle between order and disorder. Heaven and Earth, said Ghazzālī, are founded on two pillars—order and justice—without which man cannot possibly survive.

Naṣīr al-Dīn Ṭūsī (d. 672/1274), the last of the scholars in the

44. For a discussion of Ghazzālī's four virtues and the impact of Greek philosophy on his ethical ideas, see M. A. Sharīf, *Ghazzālī's Theory of Virtue* (Albany, N.Y., 1965), chap. 2.

45. Ghazzālī, *Mizān al-'Amal*, p. 294.

46. Ghazzālī, *Ma'ārij al-Qudus*, p. 133; *Mizān al-'Amal*, p. 295.

47. Ghazzālī, *Mizān al-'Amal*, p. 304.

48. See note 15.

tradition of Miskawayh and Ghazzālī, lived in a crucial time when the capital of Islam was captured by Hulago in 656/1258 and 'Abbāsid rule came to an end.[49] He wrote a treatise on ethics (akhlāq-i Nāṣirī) called the *Nasirean Ethics,* after his name, which has been described by one scholar as "the best known ethical digest to be composed in medieval Persia, if not in all medieval Islam."[50] Like Miskawayh his theory of justice is based essentially on Greek theory to which he made no mean contribution, whereby his concept of ethical justice appeared in harmony with Islamic teachings.

Ṭūsī's theory of ethical justice is based on two fundamental concepts of "equivalence" (musāwāt) and "oneness" (waḥda), with an emphasis on the latter as having the highest rank in superiority and perfection embodied in the concept of the One (the nearer is the person to One, the nobler is his existence). "Among the virtues," he said, "none is more perfect than the virtue of justice, as is obvious in the discipline of ethics (ṣinā'at-i akhlāq), for the true mid-point is justice, all else being peripheral to it and taking its reference therefrom." The mid-point is the equilibrium, the umbra of oneness, devoid of any deficiencies and excesses. "Were it not for equilibrium," he went on to explain, "the circle of existence would not be complete for the generation of the three generables (the animals, vegetables and mineral kingdoms) from the four elements is dependent on equable mixings."[51]

Since justice is essentially a notion of equivalence, it follows that the just man would be he who is in favor of "proportion" and "equivalence," and whoever is in favor of disproportion and inequivalence would be an unjust man. Moreover, the just man is

49. Ṭūsī was born in 597/1201 in Ṭūs (a town in northeast Persia). He studied science and philosophy and was a prolific writer. Before he defected to become a counselor to Hulago, the Mongol conqueror, in 645/1247, he was in the service of the Ismā'īlī governor of Quhistān, to whom he dedicated his treatise on ethics. For the rest of his life he was fully involved in public affairs and scholarship. In public life, his personal conduct often deviated from the rules he set forth in his works, for which he was reproached. For his life, see Kutubī, *Fawāt al-Wafayāt* (ed.), 'Abd al-Ḥamīd, II, 306–12; and the introduction of G. W. Wickens to his translation of Ṭūsī's ethics, *The Nāsirean Ethics* (London, 1964), pp. 9–13. The latter work has been set forth in a popular treatise entitled *Akhlāq-ī Jalālī* [The Jalālian Ethics] by Muḥammad B. As'ad Jalāl al-Dīn al-Dawwānī (d. 900/1501), trans. W. F. Thompson, *Practical Philosophy of the Muḥammadan People* (London, 1839).

50. See Wickens's introduction to *The Nāsirean Ethics,* p. 9.

51. Tūsī, *Nāsirean Ethics,* p. 95.

expected to practice justice first with regard to himself, and then towards others.[52] The just ruler is an arbitrator in equality and in stopping mischief. He is also expected not to award himself more goods and advantages than others. Were he to depart from this rule, he would be practicing tyranny (the opposite of justice). For justice, as Aristotle said, is not part of virtue, but all virtue in its entirety, and injustice is not part of vice, but vice in its entirety.[53] The man in authority would be held in high respect if he were just, according to Ṭūsī, although the common people would be likely to respect him if he were wealthy or of noble descent. Similarly, Aristotle pointed out that people generally respect the man in authority in accordance with his reputation of nobility, descent and wealth, but men of reason realize that only wisdom and justice can provide the necessary qualities for good government.[54]

In discussing the various aspects of ethical justice, Ṭūsī begins with an account of man's due to God, who is the bestower of all good leading to justice. Since his discussion of this aspect of justice follows the same line of reasoning as Miskawayh, who has drawn on neo-Platonic sources, it is perhaps unnecessary to provide a summary essentially the same as that of Miskawayh.[55]

Second to man's due to God, Ṭūsī discusses other aspects of justice in man's conduct towards other men, such as the relationship between justice and liberality (generosity), favors, affection, and others. Justice, he said, is manifested in the acquisition of wealth and is closer to effect, whereas liberality is manifested in the disposition of wealth and therefore is closer to the act. "It is for this reason," he went on to explain, "that people love the liberal man more than the just, notwithstanding the fact that the order of the universe depends more on justice than on liberality."[56] Since the liberal man acquires wealth, not for wealth's sake but to expend it, the love of man is for his lavishness and not for his acquisitiveness, although he is on guard against waste and prodigality. So justice is embodied in liberality according to Ṭūsī. "Every liberal man is just," he states, "but not every just man is liberal."

52. Aristotle said: "the best man is not he who exercises his virtue towards himself but he who exercises it towards another" (*Nichomachean Ethics*, 1130^{a}6).

53. Ṭūsī, *Nāsirean Ethics*, pp. 98–99.

54. *Ibid.*, p. 99.

55. *Ibid.*, pp. 100–105.

56. *Ibid.*, p. 105.

But a difficulty arises which calls for an explanation. "Since justice is a matter of free will (amrī-yī ikhtiyārī)," he said, "acquired in order to win virtue and merit praise, then injustice (jawr)—which is its opposite—must also be a matter of free will, acquired in order to win vice and merit blame; thus, the existence of injustice is impossible of realization." According to Ṭūsī, in such a situation man often prefers to listen to his will rather than to reason, and in becoming a tyrant he chooses evil. But Ṭūsī admits that there is a better answer which is attributed to Master Abū 'Alī (presumably Miskawayh), whom he quotes as follows:

> Since man has diverse faculties, it is possible that the one may motivate an act contrary to what is required by another faculty; thus, an angry man, or one excessively given to appetite or one who is quarrelsome in drink, freely chooses acts, without the counselling of reason, which—once indulged in—he subsequently regrets. The reason why this is so is that where the upper hand is held by the faculty demanding the act in question, that act seems fair; moreover, since that faculty has striven to subjugate the reason and to make use of it, the reason has no scope to criticize; but once the assault of that faculty dies down, the (real) abomination and corruption become apparent. As for those people characterized by the felicity of virtue, their reason is never overcome, and the procession of a fair act becomes habitual to them.[57]

What about the relationship of favor to justice? "Favor (tafaddụl)," says Ṭūsī, "is praiseworthy, but it has no part in justice, for justice is equivalence, while favor is augmentation." It follows that favor must be blameworthy, if justice is the equivalence and the mid-point, and favor is deficiency from the mid-point. Ṭūsī considers such a reasoning absurd and provides another answer which puts favor in the category of just acts. He describes favor as "circumspection (ihtiyāṭ) in justice"; therefore, it no longer becomes a deficiency in relationship to the centrality of justice, just as generosity is a mid-point between prodigality and augmentation and temperance is a mid-point between greed and sluggishness. He added that

> favor cannot be realized without prior observance of the conditions for justice, which first fulfills the obligation of merit (istiḥqāq) and then, out of circumspection, adjoins an augmentation thereto. But if, for example, one gives all one's wealth to an undeserving man, leaving the

57. *Ibid.*, pp. 105–6.

> deserving at a loss, one is not showing favor, but behaving as a spendthrift (mutabadhdhir), for justice has been neglected.[58]

So favor is considered as "justice in augmentation," and he who shows favor is a just man rather than blameworthy. Indeed, Ṭūsī seems to consider favor even superior to justice, were justice to be taken to extreme lengths, but not in the sense that it lies outside justice.

Injustice (jawr), as has often been reiterated, is the opposite of justice ('adl). As a scholar committed to Reason, Ṭūsī maintains that man is inclined to do justice, yet he often inflicts an injustice among other men. What causes injustice, one may ask? Injustice, according to Ṭūsī, is the product of harm done by one man to another. There are four causes which lead to harm: (1) appetite, the consequence of which is depravity, (2) malice, the consequence of which is jawr (opposite of justice), (3) error, the consequence of which is grief (ḥuzn), and (4) anguish, the consequence of which is anxiety and regret (ḥayra and ḥasra). Appetite may cause injustice without intention of doing harm, but a malicious man may cause it for the sake of the pleasure of inflicting harm on others. As for error, the harm may occur but is not necessarily caused by malice. As for anguish, its cause is external to the object to which no harm was intended, as in the case of someone injured or killed by colliding with an animal ridden by a person who holds him in affection. Such a person, suffering anguish, perhaps ought to be pitied and helped rather than blamed. But, if a person, either out of drunkenness or outrage, commits the act, he ought to be punished for the act and not merely blamed.[59] But injustice is not only caused by harm, for, as Ṭūsī himself pointed out earlier, it might be the result of imbalance and excess caused by irrational acts. Reason might be immobilized by outrage; consequently, against his best judgement, man is led to inflict an injustice, an act which he later regrets. Ṭūsī held that not all people are slaves of their outrages, for there are some in whom "by felicity of virtue, their reason is never overcome, and the procession of a fair act becomes habitual to them."[60] Such men, whose Reason is habitually on guard against intemperance and excess, are always just.

58. *Ibid.*, p. 106.
59. *Ibid.*, pp. 99–100.
60. *Ibid.*, p. 106.

Ethical Justice as the Moralization of Justice

Ethical justice is often expressed in terms of certain values to justify human acts that are outwardly in accord with conventional ethics, but in reality are not necessarily the expression of the highest virtues. Strictly speaking, such kind of justice is not ethical justice but "ethical justification" for ulterior motives. It may also be called the moralization of justice and not moral justice.

Two sets of writers may be distinguished who dealt with this form of ethical justice from different perspectives: first, the writers who sought to justify their own behavior patterns on ethical grounds; second, the authors of counsels for kings, often called "mirrors" of princes, who wrote elaborate manuals providing ethical rationale for the conduct of royalty and men in high offices. The first type consists of ethical literature based on the writer's own experiences as well as the experiences of others whose careers had been the subject of social censure and who tried to defend their conduct by setting forth their own standard of ethical justice. Ibn Ḥazm, a man who had varied experiences as a statesman and a scholar, may be cited as an example in this category, as he laid down an elaborate code of ethics which may be regarded as an apologia for his disagreement with statesmen and scholars who repudiated his views and attacked him, not on ethical but on credal or political grounds. The other category, the so-called mirrors of princes, consists essentially of anecdotes and sayings of ancient wisemen, which Muslim writers have compiled to provide guidelines for their rulers on how they should conduct themselves in the governance of their people. Muslim writers have summarized ancient wisdom and the careers of old rulers to provide ethical blueprints for their rulers. The literature on the subject abounds in quantity, but in quality it varies considerably from manuals to highly sophisticated treatises, including literary works telling allegorical tales which warn kings and men in high authority against ill-advised and unjustified acts. It is exceedingly difficult to provide even a summary of works in such a rich field, but perhaps two or three examples might be illuminating.

For moral self-justification, the example of Ibn Ḥazm is perhaps the best in his time. Born in 384/944, Ibn Ḥazm was influenced partly by the surroundings of his father's household, but mainly by the vicissitudes of the events following the fall of the Umayyad dynasty under which he and his father had served. He suffered a moral crisis following imprisonment and exile, and he lost most of his property which was confiscated by the state. Withdrawing from politics, he found solace in learning. But even in solitude, he was not granted the peace of mind. His literary works were attacked by most scholars of his time, mainly because he changed his adherence from one school of law to another, first from the Mālikī to the Shāfi'ī and then from the Shāfi'ī to the Ẓāhirī, despite his significant contributions to law, theology and literature. Since the Mālikī school was then prevailing in Spain, most of the Mālikī scholars turned against him. In his contest with opponents, he proved to be an able debater and defended himself with sharp tongue and impressive arguments. Apart from that, he was recognized by both foes and admirers as a great scholar, and his commitment to learning was never in doubt. To his admirers, he became founder of the Ẓāhirī school of law.[61]

Ibn Ḥazm died in 456/1064, having spent most of his later years in contemplation and writing. He tried to understand the nature of human character and the underlying norms governing human behavior. His findings, based partly on his experiences and partly on the ethical writings of Muslim philosophers, are set forth in his book on ethics. In this book he described in terse words the patterns of human behavior and laid down a code of ethics that he hoped might improve the ethical standard of his age, which he found unworthy of human dignity.[62] The central theme of his moral code is the existence of two types of men: the man who desires pleasure—drinking, sex, material gains, and other things—and the man who desires wisdom, knowledge, and piety. The pleasures of the latter, he said, are superior to the pleasures of the former, as demonstrated by the men of wisdom, knowledge, and piety who have always abandoned worldly pleasures

61. For the life of Ibn Ḥazm, see his autobiographical work entitled *Ṭawq al-Ḥamāma* [Code of the Dove], ed. Petrof (Leiden, 1914), trans. Nykl (Paris, 1981) and Arberry (London, 1953); Ibn Kallikān, *Wafayāt al-A'yān*, III, 13–17; Abū Zahra, *Ibn Ḥazm* (Cairo, 1954).

62. His book on ethics is entitled *Kitāb al-Akhlāq wa al-Siyar* [Treatise on Ethics and Conduct], edited with a French translation by Nada Tomiche (Beirut, 1961); see also his *Risāla fī Mudāwāt al-Nafs wa Tahdhīb al-Akhlāq wa al-Zuhd fī al-Radhā'il* [Treatise on the Cure of the Soul and the Refinement of Character and the Renunciation of Vices], in *Rasā'il Ibn Hazm* [Ibn Ḥazm's Treatises], ed. Iḥsān 'Abbās (Cairo, n.d.), pp. 115–73.

in favor of the highest virtues (al-faḍā'il). It is hardly necessary to say that one might agree with Ibn Ḥazm that no man is in a better position to know which of the two kinds of pleasure is superior than the man who has experienced both. On the strength of his own experience, Ibn Ḥazm had no hesitation to say that he belonged to the second category.[63]

From a scrutiny of the two types of men, Ibn Ḥazm turned to the search for the underlying cause which prompted men to choose between pleasure and knowledge. He found the answer, he said, in just one reason: to overcome anxiety (al-hamm). He used this term, however, not in the strict sense of anxiety, but in the broad sense of human concern, which includes grief and distress as well as worries about all sorts of things—material as well as non-material—which men often seek to overcome. From his own experience, he found that nobody could possibly bear the burden of concern for too long. All men—believers as well as unbelievers—endeavor to overcome their worries, although the method used by each varies from one to another. As far as he was concerned, Ibn Ḥazm found that nothing in life proved more gratifying than to turn to God and work for the next life. It is the surest and most direct way to achieve solace and inward satisfaction. Everything else seemed to Ibn Ḥazm to be misleading and futile.[64]

Since he was constantly the target of attack by scholars and political opponents, Ibn Ḥazm counseled to pay no attention to them, and he said, "It is folly to think of any one who can possibly escape slanders and abuse."[65] He found in the pursuit of justice and virtue an escape from vice and injustice. All wise men, he said, have come to the same conclusion through Reason; but were some to find it difficult to tolerate slander, they would find peace of mind in religion.[66]

Ibn Ḥazm's notion of justice may be regarded as a rationalization of his behavior pattern and an ethical justification for his failure in politics. He tried to find an escape in scholarship, but the world of learning, though acknowledging his scholarship, was not prepared to tolerate his doctrines or the method he employed to defend them. He keenly felt that he was ignored by a society that appeared unjust to

63. *Ibid.*, p. 13.
64. *Ibid.*, pp. 14–15.
65. *Ibid.*, p. 17.
66. *Ibid.*, pp. 77–79.

him. He responded by laying down a moral code which would vindicate his conduct and "cure" (to borrow his own word) the vices of his age.

As the founder of a new school of law, Ibn Ḥazm failed in his efforts because the austere Ẓāhirī doctrines proved inadequate for the needs of believers and very soon vanished from Spain. But his writings on ethics and jurisprudence aroused greater interest and continued to influence scholars in succeeding generations.

The second category of works on ethical justice are the so-called mirrors of princes. Mirrors scarcely deal with the conceptual aspect of justice, as they essentially consist of guidelines and general rules intended to enhance the position of royalty and assert its claim to loyalty and legitimacy. Since a number of these works can be found in translation, to which the reader may be referred,[67] only two writers have been singled out, each representing an aspect of ethical justice from a different perspective. The two writers are Abū al-Qāsim al-Ḥusayn al-Maghribī (d. 418/1026), Vizīr and Court Counselor; and Abū al-Ḥasan al-Māwardī (d. 450/1058), Judge, Counselor and emissary of the Caliph.

Maghribī was the son of a vizīr who subsequently held the same office as his father and became a counsel for kings.[68] In the composition of his mirror, he has drawn on his personal experiences in public life as well as on the experiences of other courtiers and vizīrs.[69] His work is divided into three parts: the first is devoted to the private life of the king; the second, the king's dealings with the upper class; and the third, the king's attitude towards the general public. For each aspect of the king's conduct, Maghribī proposes a different set of rules and general guidelines. In the first part, he counsels the prince to pay attention to his physical condition, for negligence in his physique might affect his ability to govern, and consequently his rule might

67. See Niẓām al-Mulk, *Siyāsat-Nāma,* or *Siyar al-Mulūk* [The Book of Government, or The Rules for Kings], trans. Hubert Darke (London, 1960).

68. Abū al-Qāsim al-Maghribī served under several rulers in Egypt, Syria, and 'Iraq, but in the latter part of his life he was involved in palace intrigue and fell from grace. Even before he gave up public service, he composed poetry and showed an interest in literature, but after retirement he became fully dedicated to literary pursuits until his death in 418/1026. For his life, see Ibn Khallikān, *Wafayāt al-A'yān,* I, 428–33.

69. Abū al-Qāsim al-Maghribī, *Kitāb al-Siyāsa* [Treatise on Conventional Ethics], ed. Sāmī al-Dahhān (Damascus, 1948).

become unjust. For this reason, the prince is well advised to take regular meals and undergo exercises for the upkeep of his physical condition. Nor should the prince indulge in drinking, for the habit of drinking might adversely affect the discharge of his duties as a sovereign. If he ever wanted to drink, he should drink in private and with moderation so that he could enjoy himself without compromising his dignity. Moreover, he should not indulge in any kind of pleasure which might distract him from work, although some kind of entertainment which does not adversely affect his regular work is absolutely necessary.

The prince must keep himself well-informed about the world as well as about the affairs of his own country. He must also be prompt in his dealings, fulfill all promises, and compliment as well as admonish—even punish—those who fail in their duties. Loyalty of all public servants should be solicited by inspiring confidence in them rather than by arousing suspicion and fear. Above all, the prince must be just in all his acts. He should do so, not only as a duty to his people, but as an act of piety—in gratitude of God's favor (ni'ma) for entrusting to him the task to rule with justice. The prince must always bear in mind that justice is an ethical obligation required by convention and sanctioned by religion.[70]

The second and third parts of the treatise consist of counsel on how the prince should deal first with the men to whom he has entrusted public service—courtiers and others—and then with the people as a whole. In dealing with each group, his immediate objective is not necessarily the same; he needs the former to assist him in governing, whereas his demand from the latter is loyalty and support. In order to achieve his aim, the prince should pay particular attention to cultivate the qualities and character of public servants.

Public servants should be well-trained, each in his profession, and carefully watched to encourage them to do their work properly. Moreover, they should be corrected when they err. Their conduct, based on respect and confidence, should be cultivated by various means. First, the prince should be kind to them, in accordance with the Prophet's saying that "the hearts of men are attracted to those who have been kind to them,"[71] and take an interest in their own personal affairs.

70. *Ibid.*, p. 62 (see Q. 38, 25).

71. *Ibid.*, p. 69. The Prophet's saying may be found in Siyūṭī, *al-Jāmi' al-Ṣaghīr,* I, 488; and *al-Fatḥ al-Kabīr,* II, p. 62.

Second, he should forgive them for unintentional faults in order to keep their morale high. Third, he should not restrict them from pursuing their own interest and pleasures so that they would not be overburdened with work. Fourth, he should be prepared to listen to them and heed some of their entreaties.

These are the general rules of guidance. There are some specific matters to which the prince should pay particular attention. He is well-advised to choose the Chief Secretary (Kātib al-Rasā'il) from among men who are highly cultivated, eloquent in speech, and capable of keeping secrets and pursuing all matters entrusted to them. The Chamberlain (al-Ḥājib) should be chosen from among men who are agreeable, well-mannered, and able to handle all kinds of men who call on the prince. The tax-collector (jābī al-amwāl) should be a man well-known for his good conduct, fairness, and justness (munṣif and muntaṣif); he should also be attentive and tolerant. The Army Commander (Qā'id al-Jaysh) should be a courageous and good soldier, knowledgeable in weaponry and conditions of the army, as well as prudent so that he can command respect and fear in the courts of foreign countries and among foreign emissaries and spies. The Chief of Police (Ṣāḥib al-Shurṭa) should be a stern and earnest person who can be firm with men who are prone to disturb the public order, and capable of finding them wherever they may hide. In the meantime, he should be honest, reliable, temperate, and prepared to give good advice. The Judge (al-ḥākim) should be a wise man and knowledgeable in the Law. He must also be a man of integrity and of just character (qāḍī 'adl).[72] The Inspector (al-Muḥtasib) should be honest, knowledgeable in the affairs of his profession (well-acquainted with the fluctuation of prices and ways of cheating), and able to protect public interests. Complaints about violations of the Law are of two kinds: some, criminal in nature, should be dealt with by the police, and others, underground, by the Inspector. Finally, the Messenger (al-Mutawajjih fī al-Rasā'il) should be an agreeable person, fluent in tongue, and reliable in his ability to deliver oral messages accurately from memory. It is taken for granted that each of these men, whether the head of a department or a Courtier, should be prepared to deal with his subordinates in a manner agreeable to the Prince in order to

72. See chap. 6, section on Procedural Justice.

obtain their cooperation in achieving order, stability and justice in the kingdom.

With regard to the people as a whole, the Prince is obviously unable to cope with all of their affairs, since their number is always increasing and their personal affairs are complicated; he should, therefore, limit his interference in their personal affairs and concentrate on the requirements for the maintenance of public order and the pursuit of justice.[73] His immediate objective should be to hold the community together and obtain its loyalty, not always by force, but by firm and tolerant policy. The Prince should also try to keep fairly close to his people—to know their dignitaries, scholars, and other prominent men, and to look after their public interest. Dignitaries and scholars should be required to frequent the Court and keep in touch with him. Others—the rank and file—should not be completely ignored; those who are well-behaved should be recognized. Those who commit injustices and indecencies should not be left unpunished, and each should receive punishment in accordance with the seriousness of his crime. Measures of justice should be applied to all, without distinction, for if discrimination and corruption were ever allowed, injustice (jawr) and corruption (fasād) might lead to the downfall of the kingdom.[74] In order to hold the country firmly under control, the Prince should order that all public roads within each city be inspected and that the identity of all who enter or leave be known to the authorities; nobody should be allowed to enter or leave the city without permits. Even postal correspondence and the mail should be subject to inspection in order to prevent fraud and irregularities. Finally, the Prince should keep himself well-informed about all events and happenings outside his kingdom in order to protect it from foreign intrigues or sudden attack by the enemy.

The other writer, Abū al-Ḥasan al-Māwardī, was a jurist and Chief Justice (Qāḍī al-Quḍāt) under Caliph al-Qādir bi-Allāh. He is well-known to Western scholars as the author of a treatise on the principles of government,[75] but his two treatises on ethics are not as widely

73. *Ibid.*, pp. 67, 73.
74. *Ibid.*, p. 76.
75. Abū al-Ḥasan 'Ali al-Māwardī, *Kitāb al-Aḥkām al-Sulṭānīya* [Treatise on the Principles of Government], ed. Engeri (Bonn, 1853). For life of al-Māwardī, see al-Khaṭīb al-Baghdādī, *Ta'rīkh Baghdād* (Cairo, 1349/1931), XII, 102–3; Subkī, *Ṭabaqāt*, III, 304–14; Ibn Khallikān, *Wafayāt*, II, 444–45.

known. One of them is a counsel for Vizīrs, and the other a manual for the public.[76] In the first work, the counsel is addressed to the Minister of State whose duty is to serve the Prince and assist him in the conduct of public affairs; in the second, a code of ethics is laid down for the public. In both it is made clear that unless ethical principles were taken seriously into account, the regime might be undermined and the legitimacy of the Prince questioned. Māwardī's ethical code is based partly on Religion and Law and partly on that which he called the truth (al-ḥaqq). The term truth is used in the sense of ethical justice.[77] Although Māwardī was essentially a jurist who served the Caliph on the bench and on diplomatic missions, he was also known as a writer on ethics who sought to assert the legitimacy of the Caliphate on the basis of law and justice. Above all, he was a great defender of Sunnīsm, which was then challenged by Shī'ī heterodox creeds—the Buwayhīs in 'Iraq and Persia and the Fāṭimids in Egypt. He tried by his works on law and ethics to confirm the legitimacy of Sunnī rule. For this reason, he counseled the Buwayhī Vizīr that his service to the Caliph should be in accordance with the principles of law and justice, presumably in conformity with Sunnīsm, the official creed of the 'Abbāsid Caliphate. In order to augment the authority of the Caliph, Māwardī pointed out that law and justice should be enforced not only in words but in deeds. He counseled toleration and warned that arbitrary rule would create resentment between rulers and their subjects, and aggravate sectarian conflicts, such as those that have already been wrecking the Sunnī and Shī'ī communities in Baghdad and elsewhere. He advocated peace and order and went on to plead that even if force were used by one party against another, the Vizīr would be well-advised to refrain from using it. Force, he warned, should be used only as a last resort.[78]

As jurist and writer on ethics, Māwardī developed the concept of ethical justice as a mixture of ethical and legal norms. He was genuinely concerned about the dwindling authority of the central government. By emphasizing the overriding authority of the Caliph, he

76. Māwardī, *Qawānīn al-Wazāra wa Siyāsat al-Mulk* [Rules for the Vizirate and the Conduct of Authority], ed. Riḍwān al-Sayyid (Beirut, 1979); *Adab al-Dunya wa al-Dīn* [Temporal and Religious Ethics], ed. Muṣṭafa al-Saqqa (Cairo, 1973).

77. Māwardī, *Qawānīn al-Wazāra,* pp. 122–23; for the meaning of the truth to imply ethical justice, see al-Muṭarrazī, *al-Mughrib,* I, 132.

78. *Ibid.,* pp. 145–46; cf. p. 123.

sought to maintain the unity of the State at a time when the house of Islam was menaced by foreign invaders at its gates and was torn by dissident sectarian conflicts. He admonished the Caliph to recognize self-appointed provincial governors, provided they acknowledged his supreme authority and supported him against the forces of dissension and foreign pressures. He considered order and justice as absolutely essential, for without them neither the integrity nor the stability of the state could be maintained.[79]

The three aforenamed—Ibn Ḥazm, Maghribī and Māwardī—are scrutinized as examples of writers who dealt with ethical justice either as rationalization of personal behavior patterns or moralization of the conduct of a public figure. Thus the highest virtues were not used for the refinement of character, but for the justification of ulterior motives. Neither the ethical scholars nor the authorities were able to repair the scales of justice when its fundamental principles and ideals were called into question. The new circumstances in Islam—the threats of Mongols from the East and the Crusades from Europe—had so radically altered the internal conditions of Islam that the debate on justice was bound to adopt new concepts and variables. Scholars like Ibn Taymīya, al-Ṭawfī, Ibn Khaldūn, and others called for a thorough reconsideration of prevailing doctrines. New concepts, such as "maṣlaḥa" (public interests), "siyāsa shar'īya" (political law) and "'aṣabīya" (a form of social solidarity), came into vogue. These were not entirely abstract notions, but practical steps to meet the demands of new conditions and social habits. The debate on justice gradually turned to the social aspect, and its components called for a redefinition of justice. Before dealing with the social aspects of justice, however, we should discuss legal justice at this stage on which the scholars were in agreement that it represents the minimum standard laid down in accordance with the Revelation to be enforced by the state.

79. Māwardī, *al-Aḥkām al-Sulṭānīya,* pp. 53–57.

6

Legal Justice

Justice means acting in obedience to God [i.e., to His Law].
—Shāfi'ī

Legal justice is justice in accordance with the law. Etymologically, justice is a legal term and the literal meaning of *jus* and *justum* necessarily overlap; however, the meaning of justice has considerably been extended to imply not only legal but also other aspects. So law and justice may coincide, as some elements of justice may be embodied in the substance of the law; but law may or may not have justice as an objective, depending on whether the law was laid down to achieve justice or some other goals. In Islam, Law (Sharī'a) is closely intertwined with Religion, and both are considered the expressions of God's Will and Justice, but whereas the aim of Religion is to define and determine goals—justice and others—the function of Law is to indicate the path (the term Sharī'a indeed bears this meaning) by virtue of which God's Justice and other goals are realized.

The Law provides no specific measure to distinguish between just and unjust acts. It devolved therefore upon the scholars to indicate the underlying principles of justice which would serve as guidelines to distinguish between just and unjust acts. Although these principles have not been brought together and correlated into a coherent theory of legal justice, they may be grouped into two categories, each embracing a distinct aspect of justice. These aspects may be called the substantive and the procedural, and the meaning of justice in each necessarily varies from one to the other.

The first category consists of those elements of justice which may be contained in the substance of the Law. But it is not the law, which is only a set of regulatory rules that determines how much of the elements of justice its substance must contain; the lawmakers decide how much (in quality and quantity) it must contain. The Sharī'a, consisting of the laws drawn from Revelation and Wisdom (Qur'ān and Traditions) as well as from derivative sources (consensus and analogy), is considered to contain the justice laid down by the Divine Legislator. The scholars, in the great debate about justice, indicated the elements of justice which the Law contains.

The second aspect of justice is procedural. It is conceivable that a certain system of law may be completely devoid of elements of substantive justice, and yet it possesses rules of procedure which are observed with a certain measure of coherence, regularity, and impartiality, constituting that which is called formal justice. Due process of law, a well-known procedure to Western jurists, is an aspect of formal justice. Procedural rules of justice, however, vary from one system of law to another; but each system, if ever to be acceptable to a given society, must develop its own procedural rules, including their impartial application, in accordance with the mores and social habits of that society. The more advanced these procedural rules, the higher is the quality of formal justice revealed in that particular system of law. Whenever these rules are ignored or inappropriately applied, procedural injustice arises. Legal injustice might also result from a decision considered contrary to the letter or the spirit of the law. But this kind of injustice falls, strictly speaking, in the category of substantive justice.

Substantive Justice

Substantive justice is the internal aspect of the law, and the elements of justice contained in the law constitute a declaration of "rights and wrongs." In the Islamic vocabulary the "rights and wrongs" are called the "permissions and prohibitions" (al-ḥalāl wa al-ḥarām) and form the general and particular rules of the Islamic *corpus juris* (Sharī'a). The Law does not specify under the categories of permissions (ḥalāl) and prohibitions (ḥarām) what is the measure which distinguishes just from unjust acts; it merely states that believers must fulfill their duties (farā'iḍ) under the first category and abstain from others under prohibitions. It was taken for granted that all obligatory acts must be just, since they are the expressions of God's Will and Justice, and that all prohibited acts are unjust, on the grounds that the Revelation cannot possibly inflict an injustice on believers (Q. VIII, 53). In their inquiry into the nature and scope of legal obligations, the scholars were able to discern the underlying principles governing the distinction between just and unjust acts. Taken together, these principles determine what the ultimate goals or purposes of the Law (maqāṣid al-Sharī'a) ought to be.

What are these purposes? The first and foremost is the principle of "general good" (al-khayr al-'ām), which is indeed implied in the Revelation and intended to promote the public welfare of believers (Q. XLVIII, 18–19); the Law is the path to guide men to do the good and to avoid evil. More specifically, the Law is designed to protect the public interest (maṣlaḥa), since man is not always aware of what is good for him and his people (Q. II, 216), only God knows that which is in the best interest of all.[1] Although there is no specific reference to maṣlaḥa in the Qur'ān, there are several references as to how to do the good and how to avert the harm (mafsada) and other evils (Q. II, 200–205). Moreover, the Prophet is reported to have said in a Tradition that "no injury should be imposed nor an injury be inflicted as a penalty for another injury" (lā ḍarar wa lā ḍirār), presuming that the general good and public interest must be protected.[2]

From the early Islamic period, the Caliphs often made decisions on the basis of the general good and the precedents established by them were followed by their successors. Mālik (d. 179/795), founder of the Ḥijāzī school of law, is reputed to have been the first to use maṣlaḥa as a basis for legal decisions, and later jurists followed the precedent set by him.[3] Ghazzālī stated in no uncertain terms that maṣlaḥa, defined as the furthering of "manfa'a" (benefit) and the averting of "mafsada," is an ultimate purpose of the Law.[4] It was, however, Najm al-Dīn al-Ṭawfī (d. 716/1316), a Ḥanbalī jurist, who not only considered maṣlaḥa a legal concept, but went so far as to argue that if maṣlaḥa were to be in conflict with a textual source, it should override on the grounds that it is the ultimate purpose of the Legislator.[5] In the

1. For the meaning of the term "maṣlaḥa," see my article "Maṣlaḥa," in *Encyclopaedia of Islam,* 2nd ed.; Musṭafa Zayd, *al-Maṣlaḥa fī al-Tashrī' al-Islāmī* (Cairo, 1954); Malcolm Kerr, *Islamic Reform* (Berkeley, 1966), pp. 80–86.

2. For text of the Tradition, see Zayd, *op. cit.*, pp. 14–15 (Appendix).

3. See Shāṭibī, *I'tiṣām* (Cairo, 1356/1937), II, 281–316.

4. Ghazzālī, *al-Mustasfa* (Cairo, 1356/1937), I, 139–40; Shāṭibī, *al-Muwāfaqāt* (Cairo, n.d.), I, 25–37.

5. For text of Ṭawfī's treatise on "maṣlaḥa," see Zayd, *al-Maṣlaḥa* pp. 14–48 (Appendix).

modern age, under the impact of Western law, jurists take it almost for granted that maṣlaḥa is a source of legal decisions and the grounds on which reform has been justified. Muḥammad Bin 'Āshūr, former rector of the Zaytūna Mosque in Tunis, insisted that maṣlaḥa is the primary purpose of legislation and should therefore be the basis for all legal decisions.[6]

Does the Sharī'a seek to protect the collective interests of the community as the primary object or the interest of the individual believer? An examination of the public and private "rights and duties" indicates that the purpose of the Law is to protect the interests of believers as a whole; the interests of the individual are protected only in so far as they do not come into conflict with the general interest. A case in point is the Law governing ownership of property. Does the Law first protect private or public ownership? If private ownership came into conflict with public ownership, which one should prevail?

In legal theory, all property belongs ultimately to God on the grounds that He had created everything in Heaven and Earth. But for the survival of mankind, God granted man the right to enjoy property. So we may conclude that God is the "owner" of property in principle, and that He has granted man only the right of "possession." It is not clear, however, whether God has granted possession collectively or left the mode of distribution to man. As a result, two schools of thought have developed; the first maintained that property must be possessed collectively, the other is in favor of distribution and the individual's right to acquire and transfer property from hand to hand. The latter school, which argued in favor of private ownership, prevailed, and the Law tended on the whole to affirm the principle of individual ownership. But in practice, the Law provided restrictions which qualified private ownership consisting of measures such as the zakāt (legal alms), a tax for the poor;[7] the waqf, the right of the owner to immobilize part or the whole of his estate but not its income to his successors[8]; the shuf'a, the right of the co-owner of an estate to acquire

6. See Muḥammad al-Ṭāhir B. 'Āshūr, *Maqāṣid al-Sharī'a al-Islāmīya* [Purposes of Islamic Law] (Tunis, 1366/1946), p. 63ff.

7. The zakāt is a tax which obligates the well-to-do to contribute to the welfare of the poor—indeed, to all who cannot work, whether because of old age or illness, without discrimination on the grounds of race or religion. This tax is a concession of private to public ownership.

8. For an exposition of the classical theory, see Hilāl B. Muslim al-Ra'y, *Kitāb Aḥkām al-Waqf* (Hyderabad, 1355/1935). M. Abū Zahra, *al-Waqf* (Cairo, 1959).

the entire property by paying the price for which the vendor has offered it for sale;[9] confiscation of private estate by the state;[10] and certain restrictions which inhibit the exercise of private property rights.[11] These and other qualifications and restrictions demonstrate that Islam is primarily concerned with public welfare, and that in a conflict between public and private interests the latter must be subordinate to the former.[12]

Closely connected with the general good as an ultimate purpose of the Law is the principle of happiness. Happiness has been the theme of inquiry by many philosophers and utopian writers, and Muslim scholars shared the views and aspirations of their peers in other countries on the subject, but not unnaturally they discussed it within the framework of Islamic traditions and experiences. However, little or nothing may be found on the subject in early Islamic literature and most writers seem to have urged the pursuit of piety and righteousness and made only vague references to happiness in Paradise. Some, like al-Ḥasan al-Baṣrī, held very pessimistic views about life on Earth, and went so far as to say that men were not brought into the world in order to be happy.[13]

Under the impact of Greek philosophy, especially the writings of Plato and Aristotle, the falāsifa were perhaps the earliest Muslim thinkers to state clearly and emphatically that the ultimate purpose of life is happiness.[14] Since the textual sources are not quite clear on

9. Mālik, *al-Muwaṭṭa'*, ed. 'Abd al-Bāqī (Cairo, 1370/1951), II, 713–18; Abdur Rahim, *Muhammadan Jurisprudence* (Madras, 1911), pp. 272–73; Faraḥ Abū Rāshid, *al-Shuf'a* (Beirut, 1956).

10. For example, if a new street were to be constructed which requires the demolition of a few houses or if the construction of a canal requires the use of a private estate, the confiscation of the houses and the estate by the state is legal, but compensation must be adequately provided. Moreover, the individual owns only the surface of the land, the sub-surface and minerals are considered public property.

11. The person is inhibited in the disposal of his property were he to be insane, drunkard, or under duress. He is also inhibited if he apostatized or if he were in death-illness. If a person is no longer solvent, he loses legal capacity until he regains solvency. Since the drinking of wine and eating of pork are prohibited, the believer is not expected to own such property, though he may sell them to unbelievers.

12. The writer has drawn freely from his article, "Property: Its Relation to Equality and Freedom in Accordance with Islamic Law," in *Equality and Freedom: Past, Present and Future,* published by the International Association for the Philosophy of Law and Social Philosophy (Wiesbaden, 1976), pp. 177–85.

13. Ibn al-Jawzī, *al-Ḥasan al-Baṣrī,* ed. Sandubī (Cairo, 1350/1931), pp. 38–40.

14. Fārābī was perhaps the first Muslim philosopher to discuss happiness as the ultimate end of life in all its aspects. Like Aristotle, he considered the highest form of

whether happiness will be found only in Paradise and not necessarily on Earth, the scholars advanced different answers to the question. Some, like Ibn Ḥazm and Ghazzālī, maintained that life on Earth is not for happiness and pleasure, but for hard work and perhaps even endurance and suffering, as it is but a short span in which the believer should lead a strict and puritanical life in preparation for the eternal life and happiness in Paradise.[15] Others, like al-Āmidī and other jurists, held that the purpose of the Law is to achieve happiness both in this life and the next world.[16] While the falāsifa were in agreement with other scholars concerning the premise that the real and everlasting happiness is in Paradise, they held that happiness on Earth is not for pleasure, fame, or wealth, but for contemplation and the acquisition of learning. Summing up the divergent views of the scholars, the followers of the eclectic Brethren of Purity (Ikhwān al-Ṣafā'), who flourished in the fourth/tenth century, set forth their position on the matter as follows: happiness may be achieved on Earth and in Heaven through the paths of Revelation and Reason, but not all believers would be able to attain it in both: some may attain it through the path of Reason in this life, but not in the hereafter; others hope to attain it in the hereafter through the path of Revelation, but may not be able to attain it on Earth; still others may attain it neither on Earth nor in Heaven, if their way of life proved contrary to Reason and Revelation.[17] It may be argued, however, that believers who hope to attain ultimate happiness in Heaven, whether through Reason or Revelation, derive an inner satisfaction by equating the path of life they chose with justice, even though at the expense of hardships in life on Earth.

---

happiness to be achieved not through pleasure, but through contemplation—the experience of rational power peculiar to human beings—and the cultivation of the highest virtues (al-fadā'il). Justice, said Fārābī, is the highest virtue which man tries to cultivate in the fulfillment of happiness (see Abū Naṣr al-Fārābī, *Kitāb Taḥṣīl al-Sa'āda* [Treatise on the Acquisition of Happiness] (Hyderabad, 1345/1926); and *Kitāb al-Tanbīh 'ala Sabīl al-Sa'āda* [Treatise on the Pursuit of Happiness] (Hyderabad, 1346/1927).

15. Ibn Ḥazm, *Kitāb al-Akhlāq wa al-Siyar* [Treatise on Ethics and Conduct], ed. Tomiche (Beirut, 1961), p. 13; Ghazzālī, *Kitāb al-Iqtiṣād fī al-'Itiqād* [Treatise on the Abridgement of the Creed], ed. al-Awwa, (Beirut, 1969), pp. 72–73; and *al-Mustaṣfa* (Cairo, 1356/1937), I, 2–3.

16. Abū al-Ḥasan al-Āmidī, *al-Iḥkam fī Uṣūl al-Aḥkām* (Cairo, 1347/1928), I, 5.

17. See Khayr al-Din al-Ziriklī, ed., *Rasā'il Ikhwān al-Ṣafā'* [Epistles of the Brethren of Purity] (Cairo, 1347/1928), I, 257–58.

Finally, the general principles of good character (makārim al-akhlāq) are universally agreed upon as one of the fundamental purposes of the Law, and the believers are commanded by God to observe them with good faith (Q. XXXI, 16; XLIX, 13). Although the rules of conduct before Islam, often described as harsh and rugged, continued to be honored after the rise of Islam (especially such customs as personal honor, hospitality, and courage), the Prophet stressed such values as kindness, mercy and justice, which gradually modified and eventually superseded earlier customs and practices. The Prophet's moral teachings are summed up in a Tradition ascribed to him, in which he declared that he was "sent to further the principles of good character."[18] Moral and religious values became in time important elements of the law and were often used as a basis for legal decisions.[19]

In addition to ultimate goals, a set of general principles might be regarded as corollary maxims of justice. Perhaps the very basic is the principle of "intent" (nīya), which presupposes that the Law must be observed in good faith. A religious sanction to this principle was invoked by a Tradition from the Prophet, which stated that human acts must be judged "by that for which they are intended."[20] The nīya implies the *animus*, which produces legal effects, and it is expressed in a declaration of intention.[21] In legal theory, the nīya, not the form or the written word of the Law, must first be taken into consideration; only if the implicit meaning is not clear, the literal or the explicit meaning of the text must be considered.

Closely related to good faith, indeed based on it, is the obligation to fulfill the terms entered into a contractual arrangement. Even in

18. This Tradition is to be found neither in the standard compilations of Traditions nor in other early texts, but it was reported by writers on ethics as early as the third/ninth century and often quoted subsequently to endorse the principle of "good conduct" (makārim al-akhlāq). For a discussion on the origin and meaning of this Tradition, see Bishr Fāris, *Mabāḥith 'Arabiya* [Arabic Studies] (Cairo, 1939), p. 38ff.; J. A. Bellamy, "The Makārim al-Akhlāq by Ibn Abī L-Dunya," *Muslim World*, LIII (1963), 100–119; Cf. Walzer and Gibb, "Akhlāk," *Encyclopaedia of Islam*, new ed., I, 326.

19. For a discussion of early Arab moral values, see Fāris, *op. cit.*, p. 93ff.

20. See Bukhārī, *Ṣaḥīḥ*, ed. Krehl, II, 119; III, 35 and 413.

21. The principle of the nīya is based on a Tradition in which the Prophet said: "acts shall be [judged] in accordance with the nīyas" (Bukhārī, *Ṣaḥīḥ* I, 22–23). The jurists tended to equate nīya with the principles of *bona fide* and *animus* in law. See Shāṭibī, *Muwāfaqāt*, I, 149–50; Jalāl al-Dīn al-Suyūṭī, *al-Ashbāh wa al-Nazā'ir* (Cairo, 1356/1938), pp. 7–50. See also *al-Majalla* (Articles 2–3 and 68).

the case of an oral promise, the believer is admonished to live up to it. The contract, once made between the parties by mutual consent, is binding in accordance with the principle *pacta sunt servanda,* embodied in the Revelation "not to break pledges after making them" (Q. XVI, 93). Not only believers are legally bound to fulfill their obligations, but also morally urged to abide by them. Only under threat or duress (and perhaps in grave deception, in the form of ghabn faḥish) can a contract or a pledge be cancelled.

Finally, the ideas of freedom, equality, brotherhood, and toleration are often stated as goals in the authoritative sources, and they find literary expression in the works of philosophers and ethical writers. Although these ideas have close bearing on justice, jurists and theologians have not strictly speaking considered them as fundamental purposes of Law. However, brotherhood and toleration have been considered as important moral and religious obligations. The nature and scope of each of these concepts might call for a definition.

Freedom has been used in two different though not unrelated meanings: one is essentially theological to denote free-will (ikhtiyār), concerning which there was sharp disagreement between Rationalists and Revelationists; the other is strictly legal, to define the relationship between slavery and freedom.[22] The Law sets forth the rights and obligations of owners and slaves; but no special "bill of rights," in the modern sense of the term, is provided to protect individual rights.[23] In the chapter of the Law on devotional duties ('ibādāt), defining the relationships between man and God, man can claim no specific right against God; he has only duties towards Him, which he must fulfill in order to be rewarded with Paradise. Above all, man is under obligation to worship God (Q. LI, 56), and to associate no other god with Him (Q. IV, 51 and 116). But in his relationship with other men, man's rights and duties are defined and determined in accordance with a scale of justice consisting of a set of principles in which freedom, equality, toleration, and brotherhood are included. With regard to his status as a member of the community, the basic principles are

22. As an "ethical term" denoting "noble character," Rosenthal says it was in vogue in ancient Hebrew and Arab societies and continued to have some social significance under Islam in the relationship between free men and slaves. See F. Rosenthal, "ḥurriyya," *Encyclopaedia of Islam,* new ed., III, 589; and *Concept of Freedom in Islam* (Leiden, 1960).

23. For the legal relationships between freemen and slaves, see R. Brunschvig, "'Abd," *Encyclopaedia of Islam,* new ed., I, pp. 26–40.

freedom (ibāḥa) and innocence (barā'a)—man is free to act unless forbidden by the Law, and he is considered not a wrongdoer unless he broke the law: *nulla crimen sine lege*.[24] Moreover, the Law has made a clear distinction *(a)* between permitted acts (halāl) and forbidden acts (ḥarām); *(b)* between the recommended (mandūb) and objectionable acts (makrūh) which fall between these two extremes, or ḥalāl and ḥarām, and in regard to which the believer has a choice, but neither is forbidden or obligatory; and *(c)* the category of Jā'iz, between the recommended and objectionable acts, to which the Law is indifferent, and the believer has freedom of action. However, beyond the scale of legal justice, individual freedom is scarcely defined in terms of political and theological justice.[25]

The principles of brotherhood and equality, forming the very foundation of the community of believers (umma), are given far more literary expression than freedom. All men who believe in the One God and in the message of His Apostle are considered brothers in religion and equal members of the community, without distinction on ethnic or social grounds. "The most honorable of you in the sight of God," man has often been reminded, "is the most pious and God-fearing of you" (Q. XLIX, 13). In declaring Islam open to all men, the Prophet stated in a treaty with the people of Madīna (1–2/622) "the protection of God is one (and is equally) extended to the humblest of believers."[26] Such brotherhood and equality were the privileges only of believers, but no barrier was set before anyone who wished to join the community of believers. The umma, as the Prophet stated in another provision of the treaty, is held together, in distinction from other peoples, by the invisible threads of brotherhood and equality. But since non-Muslims were accorded citizenship in the Islamic state, the concept of the state necessarily became broader in meaning than the umma, and the internal relationships among the various communities as well as their relationships with the outside

24. For the basic principles of freedom (Ibāḥa) and innocence (barā'a), see Ghazzālī, *op. cit.*, Vol. 1, 40; Shāṭibī, *Muwāfaqāt*, I, pp. 109–30; and Ṣaliḥ Bin Sa'd al-Laḥidān, "al-Muttaham wa Ḥuququh fī al-Sharī'a al Islāmīya," *al-Nadwa al-'Ilmīya al-Thālitha* (Riyād, 1402/1982).

25. See chaps. 2 and 3.

26. See text of the Prophet's treaty with the people of Madīna in Ibn Hishām, *Sīra*, I, 341ff. (English translation in my *War and Peace in the Law of Islam*, pp. 206–29).

world were defined and regulated in accordance with a standard of justice determined by the Law.[27]

Finally, moderation and toleration are not only principles of legal justice; they are also moral and religious obligations. The first reveals the flexibility of the Law and the conditions under which the believers can discharge their duties; the other defines the attitude of Islam towards non-Muslim communities whether within or outside Islamic lands. Designed to protect the believer's interest and promote the general good, the Law is not intended to impose obligations beyond the capacity of believers to fulfill them. A certain relaxation of the Law is deemed necessary. This relaxation is permitted in accordance with the principle of moderation, consisting of equity and justice, by virtue of which the individual would be able to maintain a balance between an obligation and his capacity of fulfillment (Q. II, 185; XXII, 78).[28] The principle of toleration requires the State to grant protection to other communities that share belief in the One God were they to live in the Islamic State, and to refrain from the use of force whenever negotiations and peace were entered into between Muslims and non-Muslims.[29]

Procedural Justice

Procedural justice is the external aspect of the Law by virtue of which substantive justice is realized. This aspect of justice, often called formal justice, is manifested in the degree of regularity, meticulousness, and impartiality in the application of the Law. As a procedural form of justice it may not seem as significant as substantive justice, but in reality it is no less important and its processes are intricate and highly complicated. Without it, the elements of justice would become of academic value, just as a hidden treasure loses its value unless it is put into use. Even if little or no elements of justice were to be found in the law, the individual could derive satisfaction if the law were applied with regularity and impartiality. Indeed, no legal system, whether ancient or modern, could claim endurance were it to be found want-

27. For the concept of the "umma" as a community of believers, see Sir Hamilton A. R. Gibb, "The Community in Islamic History," *Proceedings of the American Philosophical Society* 107 (1963), 173–76.

28. See Shāṭibī, *al-Muwāfaqāt,* II, 346ff.

29. See chap. 7.

ing in procedural justice, notwithstanding that the modes of its manifestation vary from one system to another.

The experience of Islam in procedural justice demonstrates again the truth that man in earlier societies was more habitually inclined to trust the judge who enjoys a good reputation than to trust the judicial system.[30] This truth is perhaps nowhere more clearly revealed than in the emphasis paid to the status and the qualifications of judges and witnesses in the Islamic judicial system. Although the structure of the court was relatively primordial, the qualities of the judge were defined with particular care. The judge was the central figure in the judicial process. He was, in the words of Qāḍī ʿAbd al-Jabbār, the Chief Judge whom we met before, the "qāḍī ʿadl" (just judge);[31] and likewise the witness is called "shāhid ʿadl" (just witness), because "ʿadl" (justice), second only to the faith, is the highest quality a man should possess were he to be chosen a judge or a witness. Before the qualities and qualifications of the "just judge" and "just witness" are examined, the special meaning of the concept of justice (ʿadl) relative to the judicial process calls for clarification.

The early jurists used the term "ʿadl" as a quality of the judge in a relatively broad sense, stressing religious and moral values. In his work on jurisprudence, Shāfiʿī, founder of the school of law bearing his name, stated in defining the term "ʿadl," that it "means acting in obedience to God," and went on to explain that by "obedience to God" he meant "obedience to the Law" in the pursuit of justice.[32] Since the statements "obedience to God" and "obedience to the Law" are too broad for a definition of "ʿadl," Shāfiʿī provided us with a more specific definition in describing the "Shāhid ʿadl" (just witness), in which he stressed in particular two qualities: "truthfulness" and "good behavior."[33] Later jurists, in citing a number of specific qualifications, set forth a higher level of religious and moral perfection, revealing the increasing demand for strictness in order to protect the judge from pressures. Thus in describing the just person, al-

30. As a reaction to this ancient tradition, man in the modern age seems to be inclined to trust "government by law" rather than "government by men" on the grounds that highly developed legal and judicial systems provide a more objective standard of justice than the quality of justness in the man (or men) who presides over its processes.

31. Qāḍī ʿAbd al-Jabbār, *al-Mughnī*, VI, 48–49.

32. Shāfiʿī, *al-Risāla*, p. 25 (trans. Khadduri, *Islamic Jurisprudence*, pp. 70–71).

33. *Ibid.*, pp. 492–93 (trans. pp. 298–99).

Māwardī (d. 450/1059), Chief Judge under the Caliph al-Qā'im, stated that he must be "truthful, trustworthy, sinless, and beyond suspicion of bias in all religious and temporal actions."[34] To these moral qualities, which most jurists considered absolutely necessary, the judge must be: (1) an adult, free, and a male believer; (2) sound in the senses, especially in sight and hearing, though some jurists (Mālikī in particular) make reservations about sight, as he might be assisted by someone who acts as an aide; (3) sane and sound in all faculties in order to be able to exercise good and discriminating judgement and cope with subtle and complex problems; and (4) in the possession of an adequate knowledge of the Law, both in its fundamental principles and rules as well as an ability to exercise legal reasoning through analogy (qiyās) and make the right and just decisions in accordance with the recognized sources of the Law.[35]

The qāḍī (judge), belonging to the community of religious scholars ('ulamā'), was highly respected and revered, owing to his knowledge of Religion and Law and his concern about morality. In spite of this, in the Umayyad and early 'Abbāsid periods jurists often refused the office of judge because of political pressures.[36] Later jurists displayed greater eagerness to serve as judges and often rendered legal advice to the Imām. The judges, indeed the whole community of scholars ('ulamā'), were considered the light of the world and custodians of Religion and Law after the Prophet.[37] The judge, the nā'ib (delegate-representative) of the Imām, was appointed either directly by the Imām or by the provincial governor on his behalf. Once appointed, the qāḍī could act independently. Contrary to modern practice, no appeal was entertained, although the qāḍī could reverse his judgement if a procedural error were detected.[38] Recourse from the qāḍī's

34. Māwardī, *al-Aḥkām al-Sulṭānīya,* ed. Engeri (Bonn, 1853), p. 109.

35. See Māwardī, *op. cit.,* pp. 107–11; *Adab al-Qāḍī,* ed. Sirḥān (Baghdad, 1972), I, 618–48; Ibn Farḥūn, *Tabṣirat al-Hukkām,* I, 17–25.

36. For the reluctance of Mālik and Abū Ḥanīfa, founders of the Mālikī and Ḥanafī schools of law, to serve as judges, see Ibn 'Abd al-Barr, *al-Intiqā',* pp. 43–44, 170–171.

37. See Shāṭibī, *al-Muwāfaqāt,* I, 69–77.

38. See Shāfi'ī, *al-Risāla,* p. 450 (trans. Khadduri, p. 274). That the judge may reverse his judgment seems to have been an early practice and was confirmed in a letter from the Caliph 'Umar (d. 22/634) to Abū Mūsa al-Ash'arī, Qāḍī of Baṣra. The letter, probably the product of a later date, gave an official expression of the practice. See Ibn Qutayba, *'Uyūn al-Akhbār,* I, 66; Ibn al-Azrak, *Badā' i' al-Sulūk,* I, 255–56; for translation, see H. J. Liebesny, *Law of the Near and Middle East* (Albany, N.Y., 1975), pp. 240–41.

judgement to the Imām, which was not necessarily part of judicial procedure, obviously bears no resemblance to the appellate system. The Qāḍī al-Quḍāt (Chief Judge), the supreme judicial office created by the Caliph Hārūn al-Rashīd (d. 193/809), did not constitute a higher degree of jurisdiction, since he was entrusted with essentially administrative functions and not with an appellate power. As nā'ib of the Imām, or lieutenant of the governor, the qāḍī was the only judge in the court, since the bench of several judges was unknown and the judicial system adhered to the principle of a single judge. However, in practice the judge often had a *concilium,* consisting of a group of jurists who could advise him but had no deliberate function. This is a measure to avoid error. Before discussing court hearing, perhaps the question of determining the qualifications of witnesses must be taken up to this point, as it is of particular importance in the judicial process.

Like the judge, the witness (Shāhid), whose testimony is considered the objective evidence (al-bayyina) on the strength of which the judge makes a decision, must also be a person of just character (Shāhid 'adl).[39] The minimum requirement is that he must display justness at the time when his testimony is provided. In his scrutiny of the qualifications necessary for the witness if his testimony were to be accepted, Shāfi'ī stated:

> The testimony of witnesses should be carefully considered: if we detect a certain bias or an excessive interest in the person on whose behalf they are testifying, we do not accept their testimony. If they testify regarding a difficult matter beyond their ability to comprehend, we do not accept their testimony, for we do not believe that they understand the meaning of that to which they have testified. We do not accept the testimony of . . . witnesses who make many errors in their testimony.[40]

Later jurists laid down further requirements and specified the conditions under which they apply. The philosopher Ibn Rushd, a Mālikī judge in his own right, stated that the witness must be a free and adult believer and above all he must be "just" in accordance with the Revelation that the "two witnesses of just character" (Q. LXV, 2), specifying the minimum requirements for the acceptance of testimony. Moreover, some jurists argued that a sinful person (fāsiq)

39. Māwardī, *Adab al-Qāḍī,* II, 3-58; Ibn Farḥūn, *op. cit.*, I, 169ff.
40. Shāfi'ī, *Risāla,* pp. 381–82 (trans. Khadduri, p. 245).

should not qualify even if he repented, but most jurists were inclined to accept his testimony if he repented.[41] Only in a testimony for adultery, four witnesses of just character are required (Q. IV, 19–20; XXIV, 4), but in all other cases a minimum of two men or one man and two women are considered satisfactory (Q. II, 282).[42] The testimony of each witness of just character must be supported by another witness of just character called the muzakkī, and the justness of character of each other witness must be confirmed by another person of just character. The qualifications of witnesses are considered of utmost importance to insure impartiality and justice in the judicial process. Once the preliminary steps are taken, the judge would be ready for the hearing and for the final decision. In the letter of instructions to Abū Mūsa al-Ash'arī, the guidelines for decision-making have been set forth, but these, as noted earlier, seem to have been the product of a later date. Perhaps one of the earliest authoritative statements on the subject may be found in Shāfi'ī's answer to a question on the subject, in which he said:

> I should make a decision against a person either on the basis of my knowledge that the accusation made against him was right, or on his [own] admission. If neither had the knowledge or if he did not confess, I should decide against him on the basis of [the testimony of] two witnesses [of just character]. Since witnesses may make errors or be confused my knowledge and the [defendant's] admission would be stronger [evidence] against him than the [testimony of] two witnesses. I should [also] decide against him on the strength of [the testimony of] one witness and the [plaintiff's] oath; but [such evidence] is weaker than the [testimony of] two witnesses. I should also decide against him if he refused to take an oath whereas the plaintiff did take an oath; but [such evidence] is weaker than the [testimony of] one witness and the oath, since the accused's refusal might have been the result of his fear for his reputation or his feeling that the matter was too insignificant for an oath, whereas he who did swear an oath on his own behalf might be a covetous or debauched person.[43]

This process, described by Shāfi'ī as it existed in the third/ninth century, continued in its essentials to the modern age, though not without refinements, as a model of judicial procedure. The essential

41. Ibn Rushd, *Bidāyat al-Mujtahid,* II, 386; Ibn Farḥūn, *op. cit.*, I, 170.

42. Shāfi'ī, *Risāla,* pp. 147–48 (trans. Khadduri, pp. 146–47); Ibn Farḥūn, *op. cit.*, I, 205ff.

43. Shāfi'ī, *Risāla,* p. 600; (trans. Khadduri, pp. 351–52). For a more detailed account of hearing, see Māwardī, *Adab al-Qāḍī,* II, 240ff.

elements are as follows: (1) admission by the accused as the primary evidence, (2) the testimony of two just witnesses, and (3) the oath of either party and the testimony of one witness. In the modern age, testimony is regarded as the objective evidence whereas admission is an essentially subjective evidence. In the past, Religion was a sanction to Law, and the believer was not expected to tell the untruth against himself. Nor would he take an oath in the name of God unless he considered his testimony to be true. Only an impious (fāsiq), known to disregard Religion, may feel that he is under no compulsion to tell the truth by taking an oath. For this reason, a fāsiq is considered an unjust witness, and impiety (fisq) is an antonym of justice. But in the modern age other precautions are under consideration, to which we shall have an opportunity to return.

Were these judicial processes adequate to insure legal justice? There were, indeed, certain discrepancies between substantive and procedural justice, which rendered the judicial process inadequate to insure substantive justice. These discrepancies, as well as irregularities in the administration of justice, have adversely affected the standard of legal justice.

Disparity between Substantive and Procedural Justice

In legal theory, substantive and procedural justice are two aspects of justice defined and determined by the public order of a given society; therefore, there should be no disparity or conflict between them. But in practice no public order is so hierarchical and cohesive as to be immune to the possible existence of some kind of disparity between the two.

In Islam, the standard of substantive justice, consisting of a set of religious and moral values highly esteemed in the public eye, is far from being realized by the judicial process, despite the stress laid on the qualifications for the office of judge and the meticulousness of the law of evidence. Moreover, the development of the judicial structure is confined to the establishment of subsidiary judicial organs operating independently from the court system. Above all, no uniformity or consistency in procedural justice exists, partly because the judges were not required by such rules as the rule of *stare decisive,* which would make their decisions consistent with the decisions of a higher court as well as consistent with one another.

As a consequence, procedural justice was maintained not by a unitary judicial process but by a complex system, partly judicial and partly administrative in character. Nor was the Law codified (in the modern sense of the word) and applied uniformly as a coherent system throughout the land. Differences in judicial procedure existed not only between the two major divisions in Islam—the Sunnī and Shī'ī—but also between the schools of law. Differences on credal and legal grounds necessarily led to differences in the administration of justice from one locality to another.

Because of differences among early rival parties and groups on questions of political justice, as noted before,[44] the jurists preferred to grapple with the problems of law-making outside the state, and some of them refused to serve as judges. As a result the Law tended to develop as a jurist law, notwithstanding the fact that the decrees issued by the state were incorporated into the body of the Law whenever they were found in conformity with textual sources.

After the establishment of the 'Abbāsid dynasty in the second/eighth century, the jurists were gradually drawn to serve in the state, and the need for establishing some form of harmony and coordination in the legal system was discussed in high political circles. Ibn al-Muqaffa' (d. 139/756), a functionary in the provincial administration of Baṣra, submitted a memorandum to the Caliph Abū Ja'far al-Manṣūr, in which he suggested a set of proposals touching on all aspects of the administration of justice—military, civil, fiscal, and judicial—designed to improve the system by codifying all the laws into a coherent legal system.[45] More specifically, he called the attention of the Caliph to the discrepancies in judicial decisions from province to province and from court to court in dealing with similar cases, concerning which there should have been one coherent standard of justice applied with impartiality. Some judges, Ibn al-Muqaffa' went on to explain, claimed that they made their decisions on the basis of the Prophet's Sunna (Traditions), but in reality the Sunna they applied was "no Sunna at all" (in Ibn al-Muqaffa's words), and they followed their own predilections in the name of Sunna. Others, claiming to make their decisions on the basis of analogy (qiyās), inflicted an

44. See chap. 2.

45. For text, see 'Abd-Allāh B. al-Muqaffa', "Risāla fī al-Ṣaḥāba," *Rasā'il al-Bulaghā*, ed. Kurd 'Alī (Cairo, 3rd ed., 1946), pp. 117–34.

injustice on one or the other party, although the purpose of analogy was to seek equity and fairness whenever there was no specific rule applicable to a particular situation. To reform the judicial process, Ibn al-Muqaffa' proposed that a unified code derived from the recognized sources of the Law should be issued by the Caliph and applied to all the lands.[46]

Ibn al-Muqaffa', needless to say, was not the only one who called the attention of the Caliph to discrepancies and irregularities in procedural justice; indeed, the Caliph al-Manṣūr himself seems to have realized that the judicial system was in need of reform. It is said that on the occasion of his pilgrimage to Makka, he urged Mālik (d. 179/795), head of the Ḥijāzī school of law, to compose a digest of law based on the Sunna of the Prophet, for possible adoption as the standard *corpus juris;* but Mālik, perhaps expressing the prevailing opinion among his peers, did not think that his digest should be the only text to be followed in the lands.[47] Indeed, the jurists were opposed to the idea that the authorities should impose a single code of law, as each leading jurist had his following and was inclined to develop his own school of law, resulting in the existence of diverse legal doctrines, rather than to accept a unified code of Law (although eventually only four schools of law were recognized under Sunnī Islam). It is true that diversity in doctrines may enrich the legal system as a whole, and the jurists, invoking a Tradition in which the Prophet is reported to have said that "disagreement among the scholars is a mercy for my people," sought to justify the trend toward diversity rather than uniformity in the legal system.[48] But despite agreement on fundamentals, differences among the schools were accepted at the expense of uniformity in the legal system.

Perhaps no less significant was the reassertion of an old legal device called al-ḥiyal al-shar'īya, a form of casuistry by virtue of which an act may seemingly be lawful in accordance with the literal (external) meaning of the Law, but could hardly be in conformity with the spirit or the general purposes of the Law.[49] Cases in point may be found in almost all branches of the Law, but one or two may suffice to make the

46. *Ibid.*, pp. 126–127.

47. See Ibn 'Abd al-Barr, *al-Intiqā'*, pp. 40–41; Abū Zahra, *Mālik,* pp. 188–89.

48. The jurist al-Sha'rānī composed a digest of law discussing differences among the jurists based on the Tradition that the differences among scholars is a blessing. See Sha'rānī, *Kitāb al-Mizān al-Kubra,* (Cairo, 1351/1932) I, 36–40.

49. The word "ḥiyal" is the plural of "ḥīla" which literally means a trick or stratagem; in law it is technically used as a legal channel or a medium for an extra-legal

point clear. A woman seeking divorce but unable to obtain it without her husband's initiating the divorce was told to apostatize on the grounds that the wedlock between husband and wife would be cancelled if she changed her religion (presumably with the intent of returning to Islam after the divorce). Likewise, a man may wish to bequeath an estate to one of his children in greater quantity than his share, although he cannot do so under the law of inheritance. But if he declared before his death that he was indebted to a certain man with a specific sum of money, the debt must be paid before distribution of the inheritance (presumably the man to whom the fictional debt was paid will transfer the sum to the child designated by the father).[50] These and other cases, especially those relating to business transactions, were recorded and taken to court for litigation, and the judge often found himself bound to decide on the evidence presented to him. Thus the ḥiyal, a legal concept consciously used as a means to achieve an otherwise illegal end, became an expediency—a legal fiction—which virtually meant the subordination of substantive to procedural justice.

The concept of ḥiyal was not unknown before Islam, and ancient law dealt with it. The Prophet, who admonished against its use, made an allowance only in situations of extreme hardship which did not compromise justice. A case in point is the Biblical story of Jacob who had taken upon himself to strike his wife with a hundred lashes, but he was relieved of the severity of his oath by Divine Revelation to strike her gently with a "bundle of rushes" (Q. XXXVIII, 43). On the strength of this Biblical precedent, the Prophet made an allowance, only in situations of extreme hardship which would not compromise justice, but he warned against possible abuses.

From early Islam, controversy raged among jurists on the validity of the ḥiyal and its relevance to legal justice. At the outset, it centered around critical situations and business transactions concerning which ambiguous statements were either made by persons not anticipating the adverse legal effect or made without the intent to fulfill them, such as "if I do such and such a thing (or if such and such a thing is

---

purpose (see Jurjānī, *Kitāb al-Ta'rīfāt*, p. 100). The nearest equivalent to al-ḥiyal al-Shar'īya in Western legal tradition is legal fiction, a term coined by Sir Henry S. Maine to imply an extra-legal act. See Maine's *Ancient Law*, chap. 2.

50. For other forms of ḥiyal, see Ibn Qayyim al-Jawzīya, *Kitāb I'lām al-Muwaqqi'īn 'an Rabb al-'Alamīn* (Cairo, n.d.), III, 264.

not carried out), my wife is divorced." In accordance with procedural justice, such an oath is binding, especially to jurists who recognized the literal meaning of the declaration. Because the intent is difficult to determine in human relationships, the Ḥanafī jurists argued, the Law should be applied in accordance with its literal meaning.

On the basis of this legal doctrine, the Ḥanafī jurists used the ḥiyal as a means to justify acts which otherwise would be illegal in accordance with the intent of the Law. To justify their doctrine, the Ḥanafī jurists maintained that in circumstances in which a person has taken an oath in an ambiguous expression, the oath is not binding on the strength of a Tradition from the Prophet, reported on the authority of the Caliph 'Umar, who said: "In ambiguous expressions, lying is inevitable."[51] In circumstances in which a person's oath leads to an unjust situation (mazlūm), the Ḥanafī jurists held, the oath is not binding. Even the Prophet, they asserted, made an exception in three instances—if one lies to make peace between two men, if one lies to his wife by making her promises, and if one lies in war.[52] Although Abū Ḥanafī was not unaware of possible abuses (as his disputations with a contemporary jurist demonstrate), his followers seemed inclined to follow more strictly the literal meaning of the Law and paid little or no attention to violations of the spirit of the Law.[53] A few examples might illustrate the point. A man, desiring a woman, would marry her not to live with her but with the intent of divorcing her immediately after the marriage, in order to avoid the penalty of adultery. Likewise, a co-owner of an estate wishing not to abide by the preemption right in accordance with the shuf'a sale, disposes of his part of the estate by giving it as a gift to another person (presumably on the assumption that the person will pay back the price agreed upon by an equivalent gift). Also, a man who desires to drink wine, which is prohibited by the Law, claims that under depression or other hardships he is justified to drink.[54]

These and other situations were rejected by jurists opposed to ḥiyal because they were contrary to the spirit of textual sources and to the

51. "Inna fī ma'āriḍ al-kalām la mandūḥa 'an al-kadhib" (Bukhārī, *Ṣaḥīḥ*, IV, bk. 90; and Ibn Qayyim, *I'lām*, III, 204–7).

52. Mubarrad, *al-Kāmil*, p. 632; Ibn Qayyim, *op. cit.*, III, 169–70.

53. See Abū Yūsuf, *Ikhtilāf Abī Ḥanīfa wa Ibn Abī Layla*, ed. Afghānī (Cairo, 1358/1938); and Ibn Qayyim, *I'lām*, III, 166ff.

54. For further cases, see Shaybānī, *Kitāb al-Makhārīj fī al-Ḥiyal*, ed. Schacht (Leipzig, 1930); Ibn Qayyim, *op. cit.*, III, 153–58, 213ff.

purposes of the Law. From the time of Abū Ḥanafī, many a jurist rejected the ḥiyal, and Ibn al-Mubārak (d. 181/797), a contemporary Traditionalist, denounced Abū Ḥanīfa as an apostate on the grounds that his doctrine of ḥiyal was a violation of the Law and contrary to Religion.[55] Mālik and Shāfi'ī, founders of two leading schools of law, were also opposed to the ḥiyal, although some of their followers made a distinction between one kind of ḥiyal they considered legal and others illegal. The Ḥanbalī jurists, especially Ibn Taymīya (d. 728/1328) and his disciple Ibn Qayyim al-Jawzīya (d. 751/1350), denounced the ḥiyal as contrary to textual sources on the grounds of deception (khud'a) and deceit (mukr).[56] Iby Qayyim insisted that it is inconceivable that an act prohibited by one law could possibly be permitted by another law under the same legal system.[57] But Ibn Qayyim made an exception in the case of a lease for rent, in which the owner of a house can register it in the name of his wife in order to avoid the possibility that the lessee might consider the absence of the owner as an excuse to delay payment of the rent. Such a device, he held, is not contrary to the Law.[58] Some Shāfi'ī jurists, like Shāṭibī (d. 790/1388) and others, were prepared to recognize other exceptions on the grounds of hardship or other extenuating conditions, like temporary marriage and the drinking of wine in non-Islamic lands, as their laws did not prohibit these practices.[59] But most jurists insisted that the believer must abide by his laws, especially those governing personal status, even though he may be in a country other than his own.[60]

It is possible to argue in favor of casuistry in cases of extreme hardship or in the inevitable choice between two wrongs, but it must be done only in exceptional circumstances. Moreover, an act contrary to the Law might be undertaken to protect public interest, in accordance with the doctrine of istiṣḥāb.[61] In such circumstances, the per-

55. For critics of Abū Ḥanīfa, see Abū Bakr al-Khaṭib al-Baghdādī, *Ta'rīkh Baghdād,* XIII, 403–24; cf. Abū al-Muzaffar 'Isa, *Kitāb al-Radd 'Ala al-Khaṭīb al-Baghdādī,* pp. 93–95.

56. Ibn Taymiya, *Iqāmat al-Dalīl 'Ala Ipṭāl al-Taqlīd,* 63ff.

57. Ibn Qayyim, *op. cit.,* III, 140ff.

58. For cases of ḥiyal considered lawful, see *Ibid.,* III, 210–13.

59. Shāṭibī, *Muwāfaqāt,* II, 378–80, 387–91.

60. For a summary of the views for or against ḥiyal, see A. A. Sharaf al-Dīn, *Ibn al-Qayyim al-Jawzīya* (Cairo, 1956), pp. 108–12.

61. For the doctrine of "istiṣḥāb," see R. Paret, "Istiḥsān and Istiṣlāḥ," *Encyclopaedia of Islam* (supplement), 1st ed., I, 255–59.

son may by necessity (*jus necessarium)* act in order to save his life or the life of others from death.[62] Apart from that, the practice of ḥiyal would be a travesty to legal justice. Only in the modern age, under the impact of Western judicial procedure, did the Muslim authorities make an effort to put an end to it, and some steps to improve the judicial process as a whole have been undertaken. Before the modern age, a modest attempt to limit the practice of ḥiyal had been made by invoking the doctrine of closure of expediency (sadd al-dharā'i') to counteract its harmful effects on legal justice.

Literally, the term dharī'a means a medium or a pretext.[63] As a doctrine it was invoked specifically against the practice of ḥiyal. The jurists who advocated this doctrine made it crystal clear that an act in conformity with the letter of one rule made with the intent of ignoring the purpose of another one is contrary not only to the purposes of the Law but also to textual sources.[64] In accordance with this doctrine, such practices as the shuf'a and marriage consciously not intended to endure were declared illegal. Moreover, temporary marriage and the drinking of wine in foreign lands, though the former is permitted under Shī'ī law and the latter prohibited under both Sunnī and Shī'ī laws, were declared illegal. In accordance with legal fiction, the latter is justified on the grounds of depression or hardship, and the former because the believer resided outside Islamic lands and not necessarily because foreign countries did not prohibit temporary marriage.[65] But in accordance with the doctrine of the closure of expediency, the believer is not permitted to seek casuistic justification for personal convenience. Such acts were indeed a travesty to procedural justice.

Equity and Judicial Procedure

In Islam as in other major legal systems—Roman law, the common law, and others—some form of equity came into existence when the judicial process was in need of reform by the adoption of a higher form of legal justice. It may seem strange indeed to speak of equity as a higher form of justice, especially in a system of law claiming to be

62. Ghazzālī, *Mustaṣfa,* I, 140–41.

63. For the meaning of dharī'a, see Ibn Qayyim, *op. cit.*, III, 119–20; Shāṭibī, *Muwāfaqāt,* II, 390–91.

64. For the doctrine of necessity, see Ibn Qayyim, *op. cit.*, p. 121ff.

65. Shāṭibī, *op. cit.*, pp. 388–90.

the embodiment of Divine Justice. But in reality, the standard of justice embodied in all law is not always applicable to all situations. For this reason, Aristotle speaks of the need for equity as the "corrective of legal justice," presuming that legal justice may be realized on two levels. "While both are good," he added, "the equitable is superior."[66]

In the experience of Islam, the equity that came into existence took the form of councils of Complaints (Mazālim) and sundry special courts designed to improve procedural justice as well as to provide a set of positive laws to deal with questions for which there existed no applicable rules in the Sharī'a. Like Roman and English equity, where the Praetor and Chancery court were to improve procedural justice, the Muslim authorities sought to establish Councils of Complaints (Mazālim) to deal with questions of procedural justice and litigation that did not come under regular court jurisdiction. But were the Mazālim and other related courts intended to fulfill the functions of equity courts?

It is not our purpose to discuss the composition and working of the Mazālim Councils, as this will take us far afield; only their relevance to legal justice will be dealt with.[67] The Mazālim Councils came into existence in the third/ninth century, although some form of procedural justice was achieved by occasional councils presided over by the Imām or his immediate subordinates much earlier. Like regular courts, they were to deal with private litigations, whether originated by an individual or a group of individuals or an administrative body, resulting in a wrong done to an individual, but they were not designed to pursue an appellate procedure. They were separate courts and applied essentially a set of political (almost secular) laws and not necessarily the Sharī'a. Moreover, the litigations that were considered outside the jurisdiction of regular courts, where the Sharī'a was applied, were taken directly to the Mazālim Councils. Those Councils, deriving their power of jurisdiction from the Imām and entrusted to men in high authority—vizīrs, governors and others—proved more efficient and their decisions were carried out more promptly than in

66. Aristotle, *Ethics* [1137ᵃ20].

67. For the composition and functions of the Mazālim Councils, see Māwardī, *op. cit.*, pp. 128–64; Emile Tyan "Judicial Organizations," in Khadduri and Liebesny, eds., *Law in the Middle East* (Washington, D.C., 1955), pp. 263–78.

regular courts. In this narrow sense, the Mazālim Councils may be said to have fulfilled the functions of equity courts.

However, since no rules or precedents were established to guide the Mazālim magistrates, their procedure often proved arbitrary and the litigation varied considerably from case to case. Some litigations were conducted by the Imām or his immediate subordinates, but in most cases by lesser functionaries to whom power of jurisdiction was delegated. Nor were these councils allowed to develop into a separate judicial system as equity courts, since they acted on the whole to serve the purposes of high authority and most jurists did not recognize them as courts at all, arguing that they had little or nothing to do with the Law.[68] For this reason, the Mazālim courts could hardly be regarded as truly equity courts and therefore could neither correct procedural justice nor improve on the judicial process.

Apart from the Mazālim Councils, there were other special courts established to deal with limited jurisdiction, defined by the purpose for which they were established or by the nature of the dispute. Such courts, applying the Law like regular courts, were set up for the army in the provinces. Others, to deal with specific civil litigations, were presided over by the Ḥājib (Chamberlain) deriving his power of jurisdiction from the Imām or the Vizīr.[69] Still others, dealing with criminal justice, were entrusted to the police, called the Shurṭa magistrate. But these courts, though separate from the regular courts, observed the same law enforced by the regular courts and could hardly be considered to function as equity courts.

Closely connected with the judicial process is the institution of the futya (iftā')—equivalent to the Roman institution of the *jus respondendi*—which represents a practical expression of the principle of consultation. The jurist who exercises iftā' is called the Muftī and his function consists mainly in answering questions relating to Law. Since the Sharī'a took the form of a jurist law, the need for interpretation was essential for its development. Moreover, the Muftī's opinion (fatwa) provided flexibility for the Law, as a reason for the fatwa was not required. So justice might be the basis for the Muftī's legal opinion, provided it was consistent with the general legal and moral prin-

68. Māwardī, *op. cit.*, pp. 140–41.

69. The Ḥājib may be the Court Chamberlain or a subordinate functionary appointed by the Court or the Wazīr (see Ibn al-Azraq, *op. cit.*, I, 269–74).

ciples of the Law. But the fatwas could lay no claim to changing principles or rules of law, as they were *responsa* to practical situations. In its early development, the futya was exercised by private jurists, but it gradually passed under State control and served as an instrument to effect a change in the scale of justice from perspective of the individual, guided by conscience and public morality, to the State, whose functionaries were not always sensitive to public opinion. Compilations of fatwas proved useful for the development of the Law and provided guidance for other Muftīs.[70]

As an institution supplementary to the judicial system, the bar is considered absolutely necessary to insure procedural justice. In Islam, the person to whom the interests of the party were entrusted was an agent (wakīl), and the arrangement between the client and the agent was a contract of agency. Although the role of the agent was closely connected with procedural justice, the agency was not considered as integral to procedure. In time, however, the agent's role became so important that the practice was acknowledged under the Ottoman legal system and instituted in the *Majalla*.[71]

Procedural justice, needless to say, proved inadequate for the requirements of justice under the Islamic legal system. Neither in structure, nor in working, were the courts fulfilling the purposes of procedural justice. In structure it was not unitary, since the judicial system was not correlated and the qāḍī was handicapped by the fact that he was not the sole authority to which all litigations were submitted and jurisdictional conflicts necessarily ensued. In its working, the judicial process was subject to political pressures, though in principle the qāḍī was immune and the Imām was charged with the duty to insure the achievement of justice in accordance with judicial processes. Men in high authority often tried to interfere in judicial procedure, and the appointment and dismissal of the qāḍī compromised the independence of the judicial system. The qāḍī was often subjected to increasing political pressures when local governors became either fully or semi-independent from the central authority. Only in the modern age, when Muslim states became fully sovereign, did the judicial system begin to change. In most Muslim states, the rulers have accepted the principle of separation of powers, although the courts have not yet become immune to political pressures.

70. For fatwas and the position of Muftī, see Shāṭibī, *al-Muwāfaqāt*, IV, 244–62.
71. See the *Majalla*, Article 1516; Tyan, *op. cit.*, pp. 248–51, 257–59.

But it was not only rulers and men in high authority who were responsible for procedural deficiencies. The scholars—qāḍīs, muftīs and others—were perhaps no less guilty for that sorry situation, since they considered themselves the custodians of legal justice. At first, the scholars were in favor of ijtihād (independent legal reasoning) which helped to maintain the flexibility of the Law and the official decrees were gradually absorbed into the Law. Their position against injustice and political pressure was defensible, as they were united in their efforts to uphold the rule of Law, despite differences on legal doctrines which were considered necessary for legal decisions in accordance with the Truth (the path of right and justice). But after the fourth/tenth century, when the ijtihād was gradually abandoned in favor of taqlīd (conformance to the canons of one of the recognized schools of law), their position became indefensible in the face of the rising power of local rulers and their differences on the degree of conformity to the law aggravated their subservience to political pressures. When Muslim states have finally accepted the principle of the separation of powers, the judiciary began to reassert procedural justice and challenge political pressures. Though they have not yet become fully independent, the courts, however, have made it clear that unless the judicial process acts freely legal justice cannot be achieved.

Retrospect

Just as law, which may be characterized as the control of all social controls, so legal justice may be taken as the measure which determines the aspect of justice that becomes binding on all men in society. Whereas other aspects of justice describe the elements of justice that ought to be pursued, legal justice indicates the pathway by which the other elements of justice can be translated into reality. For this reason legal justice has a greater practical significance than other aspects of justice and ranked higher in the eyes of many a believer than the creed. Indeed, legal justice provides perhaps the safest guidance for anyone who is in doubt about the validity of other aspects of justice, as it is essentially the product of wisdom and experience and not an abstract formulation of logic and idealism. The theologian Abū al-Hudhayl al-ʿAllāf, who hailed Reason as the highest human faculty to guide man in the pursuit of justice, admitted that when man is in doubt about justice on matters of detail, he should follow the standard of legal justice rather than the dictates of Reason, for although Reason may not be faulted on matters of general principles, it cannot be always the right guide on matters of detail. What Abū al-Hudhayl really meant is that the Law, tested by experience, is a more convenient rule of human conduct than an untested principle dictated by Reason.

Legal justice is the sum total of other aspects of justice, as it is the scale in which human acts are weighed. Other aspects of justice—theological, ethical, and others—will remain the subject of public debate until they become constituent elements in the scale of legal justice. In accordance with legal justice, each man is entitled to his legal rights, and he is obligated to pay the penalty for the injustices that he may commit. No other aspect of justice can advance a similar claim unless it is integrated or correlated with legal justice. It is perhaps not far from the truth to say that legal justice consists only of those elements that society has accepted as binding; those elements which society has not yet considered as binding may be regarded either as ethical or philosophical aspects of justice. Legal justice is thus the criterion of the immediate needs of society, whereas ethical, philosophical, or other aspects of justice are an expression of expectations. Legal justice is the channel through which the elements of other aspects of justice are gradually absorbed before they become binding.

7

Justice among Nations

We made you a nation in the middle[1]

— Q. II, 138

Justice among nations is essentially legal justice. Its standard is not necessarily the product of an agreement among all nations, but is determined by the hegemony of one or more nations playing the central role among them. From antiquity until the early modern age, no single public order proved capable of governing the entire world and, therefore, no single standard of justice was expected to prevail throughout the world. Instead, there existed, or co-existed, several public orders; each governed the relationship of a group of nations in such regions as the Near East, the Indian sub-continent, the Far East, and others. Under each order, one or two contesting empires dominated the relationship among the nations of that region and sought, in accordance with a scale of justice determined by the public order of that region, to play the central role in its enforcement.

Peace and justice seem to have been the two fundamental objectives of nations which sought to provide mankind with a public order regulating the relationship among nations, whether on the regional or global plane. Since no public order can endure indefinitely unless relative peace is established, peace may be said to have been the

Some of the material in this chapter has been freely drawn from my *War and Peace in the Law of Islam* (1955) and *The Islamic Law of Nations* (1965); but the relationship between the jihād as a doctrine of just war, and peace and justice as the objects of the Islamic public order have been considerably revised and reformulated as the central theme of this chapter.

1. According to most commentators, the meaning of the word "middle" in the foregoing Quranic Revelation is moderation and justice, denoting that in their relationship with other nations God has decreed that Muslims should pursue the principles of moderation and justice (see Tabarī, *Tafsīr*, ed. Shākir, III, 141–55).

overriding objective. But any public order devoid of justice tends to breed tensions and conflicts, and therefore would undermine and ultimately destroy the foundation on which peace is established. It is thus tempting to argue that justice is the key to a lasting peace and that peace and justice cannot be completely separated. Yet in human experience justice proved so compelling a goal in some societies that its pursuit often prompted men to break the peace. In the relationship among nations, peace proved to be the proximate, but justice is the ultimate objective, if public order were ever to endure.

The rise of Islam, with its universal appeal to mankind, necessarily raised the problem of how to establish its priority in the relationship between peace and justice. Islam, as we have already noted, is a political community endowed with a public order designed to govern its internal affairs as well as to conduct its relationship with other communities in accordance with a scale of justice determined by the Will and Justice of God. According to the Islamic public order, the Islamic community is the subject of God's Justice, whereas all other communities are the object of that justice. But if God's Justice is to reign supreme over the world, the validity of its public order must be acknowledged by all mankind. It follows that no other standard of justice would have been acceptable to Islam save the standard of God's Justice, which had to prevail, if necessary, by the sword.

Justice and the Islamic Public Order

The Islamic state, composed of a community of believers endowed with a message to all men, was a universal state. Its public order, derived from and exercised on behalf of God, was potentially capable of governing the whole of mankind. The state thus was the instrument with which Islam sought to achieve its ultimate objective—the establishment of God's Will and Justice over the world.

But the Islamic universal state, not unlike other universal states, could not establish peace and order in the world solely in accordance with its scale of justice. Outside it, there remained other communities with which it had to deal permanently. The world was split into two divisions: the territory of Islam (dār al-Islam), which may be called *Pax Islamica,* consisting of the territory over which Islamic justice ruled supreme, and the rest of the world, called dār al-Ḥarb, or the territory of war, over which other public orders prevailed. The first included the community of believers and other communities of the tolerated religions, collectively called Dhimmīs (People of the Book), consisting of Christians, Jews, and others known to have possessed scriptures, who preferred to hold fast to their own laws and creeds at the price of paying a poll tax (jizya) to Islamic authority. Relations between Muslim and non-Muslim communities under the *Pax Islamica* were regulated in accordance with special agreements recognizing the canon law and the scale of justice of each tolerated religious community on all matters relating to personal status. But any member of those communities could join the Islamic community and enjoy all its advantages at any moment by merely pronouncing the formula of the profession of the faith. Even without becoming a Muslim, one was not denied access to Islamic authority if he wished to avail himself of Islamic justice.[2]

The world surrounding the dār al-Islam is the dār al-Ḥarb, or "the territory of war." The territory of war was the object, not the subject, of Islam, and it was the duty of the Imām, head of the Islamic state, to extend the validity of its Law and Justice to the unbelievers at the earliest possible moment. The communities of the dār al-Ḥarb were regarded as being in a "state of nature," because they lacked the standard of justice granted to believers under the Islamic public order. But if an unbeliever (or the whole community of unbelievers) wished to adopt Islam without joining the Islamic community, he (or his community) could do so at any moment, just as any member of the tolerated religious communities under Islamic rule could do so, provided he observed the Law and Justice of Islam; but the convert from the dār al-Ḥarb would be under the moral obligation to migrate (hijra) to an Islamic land sooner or later, if the majority of his own people continued to uphold their public order.

The dār al-Islam was in theory neither at peace nor necessarily in permanent hostility with the dār al-Ḥarb, but in a condition which might be described as a "state of war," to use a modern terminology, because the ultimate objective of Islam was to establish peace and justice with communities which acknowledged the Islamic public order. But the dār al-Ḥarb, though viewed as in a state of nature, was not treated as a no-man's land without regard to justice. Islam pro-

2. For the legal status of these communities, see my *War and Peace in the Law of Islam* (Baltimore, 1955), chap. 17.

posed to regulate its relationship with the dār al-Ḥarb in accordance with a branch of its Law called the Siyar. Just as the Romans observed the rules of *jus gentium* in their relationships with other communities, so did the Muslims regulate their relationships with non-Muslims in accordance with the Siyar, or the law governing the conduct of the Islamic State with other communities.

The Siyar, a set of rules derived from the same textual sources as Islamic law (Sharī'a), possesses its own scale of justice based on Islamic principles as well as on Islam's experience with other peoples. Strictly speaking, the Siyar is not a separate system of law from the Sharī'a, but a chapter of its *corpus juris,* binding on all believers as well as on those who seek to protect their interests in accordance with Islamic justice. The scale of justice applied by the Islamic state in its relations with other states was based not necessarily on reciprocity or mutual consent, but was a self-imposed scale defined and determined in accordance with the Islamic public order.[3]

The Jihād as Just War

The instrument with which Islam sought to achieve its objectives was the jihād. Islam prohibited all kinds of warfare except in the form of jihād. But the jihād, though often described as a holy war, did not necessarily call for fighting, even though a state of war existed between the two dārs—dār al-Islam and dār al-Ḥarb—since Islam's ultimate goals might be achieved by peaceful as well as by violent means.

Strictly speaking, the word "jihād" does not mean "war" in the material sense of the word. Literally, it means "exertion," "effort" and "attempt," denoting that the individual is urged to use his utmost endeavors to fulfill a certain function or carry out a specific task.[4] Its technical meaning is the exertion of the believer's strength to fulfill a duty prescribed by the Law in "The path of God" (Q. LXI, 10–13), the path of right and justice. Thus the jihād may be defined as a religious and legal duty which must be fulfilled by each believer either by the heart and tongue in combatting evil and spreading the

3. For the nature and sources of the Siyar, see my *War and Peace,* chap. 3; and my *Islamic Law of Nations,* pp. 4–9.

4. See Zabīdī, *Tāj al-'Arūs,* ed. Hārūn, VII, 534–39.

word of God, or by the hand and sword in the sense of participation in fighting. Only in the latter sense did Islam consider the jihād a collective duty (farḍ al-kifāya) which every believer was bound to fulfill, provided he was able to take the field. Believers who could not take to the field nor had the means to do so were expected to contribute in weapons or supplies in lieu of fighting with the sword. Participation in the jihād in one form or another was a highly-prized duty and the believer's recompense, if he actually took to the field, would be the achievement of salvation and reward of Paradise (Q. LXC, 10–13) in addition to material rewards.[5] Such war, called in Western legal tradition "just war" *(bellum justum)*, is the only valid kind of war. All other wars are prohibited.

The jihād was the just war of Islam. God commanded the believers to spread His word and establish His Law and Justice over the world (Q. IX, 5). The dār al-Islam was the house of the believers where Law and Justice were given practical expression, and the dār al-Ḥarb was the house of the unbelievers and an object of the jihād. Religion, however, was and still is to be carried out by peaceful means, as there should be no compulsion in the spread of the word of God (Q. II, 257). The expansion of the state, carried out by the jihād, was an entirely different matter. Thus the jihād, a duty prescribed by Religion and Law, was surely as pious and just as *pium* and *justum* in the way described by St. Augustine and St. Thomas and later by Hugo Grotius.

In early Islam, the scholars like Abū Ḥanīfa (d. 150/768) and Shaybānī (d. 189/804) made no explicit declarations that the jihād was a war to be waged against non-Muslims solely on the grounds of disbelief. On the contrary, they stressed that tolerance should be shown unbelievers, especially the scripturaries (though not idolators and polytheists), and advised the Imām to wage war only when the inhabitants of the dār al-Ḥarb came into conflict with Islam. It was Shāfi'ī (d. 204/820), founder of the school of law bearing his name, who laid down a framework for Islam's relationship with non-Muslims and formulated the doctrine that the jihād had for its intent the

5. The promise of eternal life in Heaven, where believers attain Divine happiness and justice, is granted to all who fulfill the basic duties, but none would enable the believer to gain Paradise as surely as martyrdom in the jihād. See Sarakhsī, *Sharḥ Kitāb al-Siyar al-Kabīr li . . . al-Shaybānī,* ed. Munajjid (Cairo, 1957), I, 24–25. The material reward for the jihād is a share in the spoils.

waging of war on unbelievers for their disbelief and not only when they entered into conflict with the Islamic state.[6] The object of the jihād, which was not necessarily an offensive war, was thereby transformed into a collective obligation enjoined on the Muslim community to fight unbelievers "wherever you may find them" (Q. IX, 5), and the distinction between offensive and defensive war became no longer relevant.

The reformulation of the jihād as a doctrine of just war without regard to its defensive or offensive character provoked a debate among Shāfi'ī's contemporaries and led to a division of opinion among Ḥanafī jurists. Some, like Ṭaḥāwī (d. 321/933), adhered more closely to the early Ḥanafī doctrine that fighting was obligatory only in a war with unbelievers;[7] but Sarakhsī (d. 483/1101), the great commentator on Shaybānī, accepted Shāfi'ī's doctrine of the jihād that fighting the unbelievers was a "duty enjoined permanently until the end of time."[8] Scholars who came afterwards, until the fall of Baghdad at the hands of the Mongols in the thirteenth century, accepted the jihād as just war without regard to its offensive or defensive character.

Should the Caliph, head of the State, be obeyed if he invoked the jihād in a situation considered contrary to justice, it may be asked? According to the Orthodox doctrine of the Imamate, not to speak of Shī'ī doctrines, the Imām had to be obeyed even if he were in error. But on matters of foreign conduct of the state, the Caliph's powers were often questioned. In a war with the Byzantines, the Caliph Harūn al-Rashīd (d. 193/809) seems to have decided to use violence against the Banū Taghlib, a Christian community near the Byzantine borders, and to revoke their treaty with Islam on the grounds of their alleged sympathy with the Byzantines. Shaybānī, who was consulted on the matter, said in no uncertain terms that the Banū Taghlib did not violate the treaty and that an attack on them was unjustified, although he did not necessarily imply that if the Caliph issued an order, his order should not be obeyed.[9] Later when Islamic power was threatened, the scholars were dubious about the Imām's conduct if he violated his undertakings with the unbelievers, but Ibn Taymīya

6. Shāfi'ī, *Kitāb al-Umm*, IV, 84–85.

7. Abū Ja'far al-Ṭaḥāwī, *Kitāb al-Mukhtaṣar*, ed. Abū al-Wafā al-Afghānī (Cairo, 1320/1950), p. 281.

8. Sarakhsī, *Kitāb al-Mabsūṭ* (Cairo, 1324/1906), X, 2–3.

9. Khadduri, *Islamic Law of Nations*, pp. 34–35.

(d. 728/1328) spoke openly his mind in defense of Christian claims to protection when they were discriminated against even at the most critical time of danger to Islam.

Peace and Just War under the Islamic Public Order

In legal theory, the state of war existing between the dār al-Islam and the dār al-Ḥarb would come to end when the public order of the latter is superseded by the former. At such a stage the Law and Justice of Islam would reign supreme in the world. In practice, however, the dār al-Islam and the dār al-Ḥarb proved more permanent than the scholars had envisaged, and the believers gradually became more accustomed to a state of dormant jihād than to a state of hostility. In the meantime, Muslim justice was not denied to non-Muslims. If conditions of peace could not be completely established, contacts between Muslims and non-Muslims, on the personal and official levels, were nevertheless conducted by peaceful methods, although a state of war continued to exist in theory between Islam and other communities.

In accordance with the Law, the Ḥarbī—a person from the dār al-Ḥarb—was entitled to Islamic justice during the brief span of peace, whether by a peace treaty concluded between Muslim and non-Muslim authorities or by an amān (safe-conduct), granted either by an official or by private persons. A treaty, not exceeding ten years in principle, established peace between believers and unbelievers and granted the latter all rights of residents in accordance with Muslim justice (including the right of practicing their own religion) for the duration of the treaty.[10] In the absence of a treaty, the Ḥarbī (including his family and property) could enter the territory of Islam by virtue of an amām, obtained beforehand from any Muslim. Such an amām, ordinarily granted without difficulty, transformed the status of the Ḥarbī and his family from a state of war to one of temporary peace, with respect to his own private relations with the inhabitants of the territory of Islam. He would be granted security during his stay in Islamic lands and would be considered a permanent resident, subject only to the jizya (poll tax), if he and those who accompanied him

10. The treaty could be renewed for another ten-year term or more if the arrangement were agreeable to both parties.

stayed beyond one year. It is to this device that we should attribute the ease with which Muslims and non-Muslims crossed frontiers from one land to another for trade and for cultural and other purposes, whereby the justice granted under an amām virtually superseded the theoretical state of hostility under the jihād.[11]

Justice under neutrality had no place in accordance with the Islamic public order, if neutrality were taken to mean the attitude of a political community which voluntarily decided to refrain from hostile relations with belligerent parties. Since all communities of the dār al-Ḥarb, short of entering into treaty relations with Muslim authorities, were in theory in a state of war with Islam, none would be immune from the legal effects of the jihād. Only Ethiopia, declared immune from the jihād by virtue of doctrinal and historical consideration, attained a special status in its relationship with Islam. In early Islam Ethiopia had taken a sympathetic attitude toward Islam and protected its followers when they took refuge in its lands. Consequently, the Prophet decreed that all Ethiopian people would be in perpetual peace with Muslims, provided they refrained from taking hostile actions against them.[12]

In theory, all other lands that were spared the legal effect of the jihād or enjoyed peace and justice under the Islamic public order could do so only by virtue of peace treaties. But all treaties, regardless of the number of renewals, were regarded as temporary in theory, and the state of war was the normal relationship between the dār al-Islam and the dār al-Ḥarb.

The Jihād as Defensive War

The classical doctrine of the jihād made no distinction between defensive and offensive war, for in the pursuance of the establishment of God's Sovereignty and Justice on Earth the difference between defensive and offensive acts was irrelevant. However, although the duty of the jihād was commanded by God (Q. LXI, 10–13), it was considered to be binding only when the strength of the believers was theirs (Q. II, 233). When Islamic power began to decline, the state obvi-

11. For further details on the Law of amām, see my *War and Peace in the Law of* Islam, chap. 15.

12. Ibid., pp. 253–58.

ously could no longer assume a preponderant attitude without impairing its internal unity. Commentators on the jihād as a doctrine of permanent war without constraints began to reinterpret its meaning in a manner which underwent a significant adjustment to realities when conditions in the dār al-Islam changed radically. Some scholars, though still adhering to the principle that the jihād was a permanent state of war, argued that the mere preparation for the jihād would be a fulfillment of its obligation.[13] Not only did Islam become preoccupied with problems of internal security, but also its territorial integrity was exposed to dangers when foreign forces (the Crusaders and Mongols) from the dār al-Ḥarb challenged its power and threatened its very existence.

In those altered circumstances, scholars began to change their position on the question of whether the jihād, used against believers on the grounds of their hostility to Islam, was just. The doctrine of the jihād as a duty permanently imposed upon the community to fight the unbelievers wherever they might be found retained little of its substance. Ibn Taymīya, a jurist-theologian who was gravely concerned with internal disorder, understood the futility of the classical doctrine of jihād at a time when foreign enemies (Crusaders and Mongols) were menacing at the gates of dār al-Islam. He made concessions to reality by reinterpreting the jihād to mean waging a defensive war against unbelievers whenever they threatened Islam. Unbelievers who made no attempt to encroach upon the dār al-Islam, he asserted, were not the objective of Islam nor should Law and Religion be imposed upon them by force. "If the unbeliever were to be killed unless he becomes a Muslim," he went on to explain, "such an action would constitute the greatest compulsion," a notion which ran contrary to the Revelation which states that "no compulsion is prescribed by Religion" (Q. II, 257). But unbelievers who consciously took the offensive and encroached upon the dār al-Islam would be in an entirely different position.[14]

No longer construed as a war against the dār al-Ḥarb on the grounds of disbelief, the doctrine of the jihād as a religious duty

13. See Ibn Hudhayl, *Kitāb Tuḥfat al-Anfus Wa Sukkān al-Andalus*, ed. Merçais (Paris, 1936), p. 15.

14. Ibn Taymīya, "Qā'ida fī Qitāl al-Kuffār," *Majmū'at Rasā'il*, ed. Ḥamīd al-Fiqqī (Cairo, 1368/1949), pp. 115–46; and *al-Siyāsa al-Shar'īya*, ed. Nashshār and 'Atīya (Cairo, 1951), pp. 125–53.

became binding on believers only in the defense of Islam. It entered into a period of tranquility and assumed a dormant position, to be revived by the Imām whenever he believed Islam was in danger. It is true that the Ottoman sultans in their conquest of European territory often invoked the jihād, but in their actions they were neither in a position to exercise the rights of the Imām nor were their wars always religious in character.[15] Moreover, at the height of their power, the sultans came to terms with the unbelievers and were prepared to make peace on the basis of equality and mutuality with Christian princes, contrary to precedents. Elated by their victories against the unbelievers in Europe, they turned to eastern Islamic lands and brought them under their control when the Shī'a seized power in Persia at the opening of the sixteenth century, thus threatening internal unity. The Ottoman Sultan, though unable to subjugate Persia, provided leadership to Islamic lands under his control until World War I.

Just War and Secular War

In theory only the Imām, enthroned to exercise God's Sovereignty on Earth, has the power to invoke the jihād and call believers to fulfill the duty. Unless the Imām delegates his power to a subordinate, nobody has the right to exercise it without prior authorization from him. Were the jihād to be proclaimed by the governor of a province without authorization of the Imām, it would be a "secular war" and not a valid or just war. If a dissident leader, whether belonging to an orthodox or to a heterodox group, claimed the right to declare a jihād, his action would be considered disobedience to the Imām and a rebellion against the legitimate authority (Q. XLIX, 9).[16] Neither the leader nor the persons who take part in such a jihād would be rewarded with Paradise, which is granted only to those who participate in a jihād declared by the Imām.

After the downfall of the 'Abbāsid caliphate and the rise of independent rulers (provincial amīrs, sultans and others), the Imām ceased to exercise the legitimate authority even though a descendant from the 'Abbāsid dynasty continued to claim that authority from

15. Cf. Fuad Köprülü, *Les Origines de l'Empire Ottoman* (Paris, 1935), chap. 3.
16. See Shaybānī's *Siyar,* trans. Khadduri, *op. cit.*, pp. 230–31.

exile in Cairo after he had left Baghdad. In the altered circumstances, independent rulers were often compelled to wage secular wars that were not validated as just wars by the proper authority, but the scholars were divided on the matter.

In Persia, where the Shī'ī creed prevailed from the opening of the tenth/sixteenth century, the powers of the Imām during his absence (ghayba) were divided between the Shah and the Mujtahids (scholars)—the latter exercised the spiritual power of the Imām and the former his civil power. Since the jihād is a war that must be proclaimed by the joint civil and spiritual powers in order to be just, its proclamation by the Shah must be confirmed by the mujtahids if it were to be valid and just. Were the Shah to declare war without the validation of the mujtahids, it would be a secular war and therefore not a jihād or just war. In the event that the mujtahids were to assume civil powers and exercise both civil and spiritual powers on behalf of the Imām during the ghayba, they would be the agent of the Imām, as the present regime in Iran established by the Revolution of 1979 under the leadership of Āyat-Allāh Khumaynī demonstrated. Khumaynī may claim to speak on behalf of the Imām (until his return to re-establish peace and justice), but Khumaynī cannot act alone as the Imām.

In the dispersed authority of the caliphate throughout the rest of Islamic lands following the fall of Baghdad, secular rulers began to exercise civil authority and enforce the Law in consultation with the ulamā' (scholars). Even before the fall of Baghdad, the provincial governors had already been exercising internal control over their provinces as *de facto* rulers, but after the downfall of the 'Abbāsid dynasty some became fully independent heads of state, although in theory their authority remained subordinate to the Caliph. In the latter part of the nineteenth century, the Ottoman Sultan was proclaimed Caliph in accordance with the Constitution of 1876 which empowered him to proclaim the jihād, although this prerogative was not always exercised without challenge. In 1914, when World War I broke out, the Sultan-Caliph proclaimed the jihād against Great Britain and France, but Ḥusayn B. 'Alī, the Sharīf of Makka and a great grandson of the Prophet, proclaimed a counter-jihād in 1916 and sided with Britain against Germany, the ally of the Caliph. The believers were thus divided on the question as to which of the two proclamations of the jihād was valid.

The rationale for waging war, on the grounds of justice, without reference to the jihād, may be traced back to the time of the philosopher al-Fārābī.[17] He was perhaps the first Muslim scholar to divide wars into just and unjust on the grounds of whether they were to serve the personal desire or interest of the Ruler or to promote the general good of the people. According to Fārābī, just wars are as follows:

1. wars in the defense of the city against foreign attacks
2. wars to assert valid claims against a foreign people who failed to honor the city's rights
3. wars against foreign people who refused to accept a public order considered by the city to be the best and most suitable for them
4. wars against a foreign people whose place (satus) in the world is considered by the city to be that of servitude (slavery) as the best and most suitable for them.

The unjust wars, considered to serve the personal desire and glory of the Ruler, are as follows:

1. wars motivated by the Ruler's personal advantage such as lust for power, honor or glory
2. wars of conquest waged by the Ruler for the subordination of peoples other than the people of the city over which he presides
3. wars of retribution, the object of which can be achieved by means other than force
4. wars leading to the killing of innocent men for no reason other than the Ruler's propensity or pleasure for killing.[18]

Fārābī, making a distinction between the Virtuous City and other cities on the basis of the concept of the general good, held that only the Ruler of the Virtuous City is competent to proclaim a just war; all other rulers, motivated by lust and other mundane propensities, are incompetent to wage just wars. Presenting the philosophic notion of the *bellum justum,* Fārābī maintained that only the Imām has the legitimate authority to proclaim a just war. All other wars, presumably waged by chiefs without legitimate authority, must be considered unjust.

Writers who came after al-Fārābī, expressing their disapproval of warfare in Islamic lands, held that all wars, in forms other than the jihād, were abnormal and therefore unjust. Ṭurṭūshī described them

17. See chap. 4, section on Rational Justice as an Ideal Justice.

18. Fārābī, *Fuṣūl al-Madanī,* ed. D. M. Dunlop (Cambridge, 1961), pp. 146–47 (Arabic texts), 56–57 (trans.).

as social anomalies;[19] and al-Ḥasan B. 'Abd-Allāh, who wrote a work on statecraft two centuries later (708/1322), called them social diseases.[20] Both counselled rulers to cope with them by adequate military preparation. It was, however, Ibn Khaldūn, considering warfare from a different social perspective, who warned that wars were not casual social calamities; they have been recurring ever since man made his appearance on Earth. Man, he said, is by nature warlike. The question of making a distinction between just and unjust wars is therefore irrelevant. This naturalistic view of war was consistent with his general theory of society. However, he made concessions to Law by considering the jihād a just war, although he admitted that most rulers who went to war were not motivated by the duty of jihād but by lust for power and personal ambition.[21] Thus wars in Islamic lands were no longer weighed on the classical scale of the jihād. Like other aspects of social justice, the new scale of just war had to await reconsideration when conditions began to change in the modern age.[22]

19. Ṭurṭūshī, *Sirāj al-Mulūk* (Cairo, 1319/1901), pp. 150–53.

20. Ḥasan B. 'Abd-Allāh, *Athār al-Uwal fī Tartīb al-Duwal* (Cairo, 1295/1878), pp. 167–68.

21. See chap. 8, pp. 186–87; and Ibn Khaldūn's *al-Muqaddima,* II, 65–79.

22. See chap. 9.

8

Social Justice

Among some of man's [evil] qualities are injustice and aggression against one another. He who casts his eye upon his neighbor's property will lay his hand upon it to take it, unless he is held back by a deterrent, just as the poet [al-Mutanabbī] said: "Injustice is a human trait; if you find a good [just] man, there must be a reason why he is not unjust."

—Ibn Khaldūn

Social justice is justice in accordance with the operative norms and values, apart from the norms and values embodied in the Law, which the public is prepared to accept by habit, inertia, or other reasons. In contrast with the idealist concepts of justice—Divine, natural or rational—social justice (often used to include distributive justice) is essentially positive in character; it is the product of custom and human experience rather than the dictates of Reason.[1] Aristotle, who coined the term "distributive justice," used it not in the social but in the numerical and quantitative sense. The broader qualitative sense, which modern writers seem to imply by it, will be used later in this study.[2]

Today, some Muslim writers who have accepted the modern sense of the term sought to Islamize it and rationalize its adoption by an attempt to trace its origin either to a textual source or to an opinion of a classical jurist. But earlier scholars who dealt with social justice tended to stress positive elements—custom, practice, or other—with-

1. Just as the common law is the product of human experience (as Justice Holmes aptly said of the common law: "The life of the law has not been logic; it has been experience"), and often described by jurists as positive law, so social justice is positive justice, in distinction from natural justice, defined either as the commands of God or the dictates of Reason.

2. See chap. 9; for Aristotle's definition, see *Nichomachean Ethics*, 1131^a6–27.

out necessarily dwelling on the distributive or the collectivist aspects, as society had not yet been exposed to such radical and conflicting foreign ideas and ideals with which Muslims today are grappling.[3]

Social Justice and the Islamic Social Order

To Muslim theologians and philosophers, it will be recalled, justice was an abstract and an idealist concept, expressed in terms of excellence and perfection. They made no serious attempt to view justice as a positive concept and analyze it in terms of existing social conditions. It is true that they referred occasionally to skeptics and atheists (zindīqs) who seem to have questioned the validity of values derived from Revelation and asserted a naturalistic standard for human affairs, but no significant statement of their position has yet come to light save occasional vague references in the works of their opponents who were more interested in the refutation of the atheistic doctrines than in a complete statement of atheistic views. Skeptic writers seem to have discussed, among other things, the notion of justice and other values, but their writings failed to reach us. We have seen how the early Mu'tazila, though by no means skeptic in outlook, were denounced on the grounds that they used Reason as a method which appeared to Orthodox theologians as a threat to Revelation. In consequence, their writings were censored and destroyed, except for summaries of their views in the works of their critics. The fate of skeptics, who dared to challenge the authority of Revelation, could be no better than that of the Mu'tazila, who after all had accepted the validity of the Revelation.[4]

The impact of the Rationalists, not to speak of the Naturalists, however, was far-reaching; for, although most of their works may have been destroyed, their method continued to influence many writers who began to have a more critical attitude toward certain doctrines which had been taken for granted by earlier theologians. Some of the Mu'tazila, apart from those who sought a compromise between Reason and Revelation, questioned the dependence on Reason as an

3. For changes in the Islamic conception of justice under the impact of foreign ideologies, see chap. 9.

4. For the account of skeptic and atheist thinkers in Islam, see 'Abd al-Raḥmān Badawī, *Ta'rīkh al-Ilḥād fī al-Islām* [History of Atheism in Islam] (Cairo, 1947). For the meaning of Mulḥids and Zindīqs, see al-Muṭarrazī, *al-Mughrib*, I, 235.

ultimate method under the impact of classical naturalism. For instance, Abū 'Uthmān al-Jāḥiz, who accepted the Mu'tazilite doctrine of voluntarism (ikhtiyār), tried to demonstrate the absurdity of dependence on Reason as the sole method to the truth.[5] It is possible that he tried to demonstrate the need for other methods, and he himself seems to have been influenced by Aristotle's naturalism in some of his writings.[6] Ghazzālī, as noted earlier, also saw the limitations of Reason, but took refuge in the use of logic and mysticism; he was far from leaning toward the historical and inductive methods. It was al-Mas'ūdī (d. 345/956) who attempted to write history as a record of issues relevant to circumstances and conditions of the time rather than as the unfolding of God's will and predetermined events. He was perhaps the earliest scholar to deal with movements and events from a different angle and laid the grounds for the historical and inductive methods of inquiry.[7] Ibn Khaldūn, a historian and a social theorist, used the inductive method with greater depth, not only in the writing of his universal history but also in the formulation of social and political theories.

Historians were not alone in pursuing the inductive method; other social thinkers, finding Revelation inadequate, applied it with varying degree to their respective fields of inquiry. Abū Bakr al-Ṭurṭūshī (d. 520/1127), Najm al-Dīn al-Ṭawfī (d. 716/1316), and Ibn Taymīya (d. 728/1325), while remaining faithful to Revelation, employed a form of inductive method which reached its full development in the writings of Ibn Khaldūn (d. 806/1408). Ṭurṭūshī never really questioned the traditional method, but he provided us with an elaborate description of the structure of Islamic polity as he saw it, on which writers after him, especially Ibn Khaldūn, have drawn in the formulation of their social theories.[8] He considered justice as the very foundation of polity, the "foundation of foundations," in his words, and the high-

5. See Shafīq Jabrī, *al-Jāḥiz: Mu'allim al-'Aql wa al-Adab* [al-Jāḥiz: Teacher of Reason and Literature] (Cairo, n.d.).

6. In his work, *Kitāb al-Ḥayawān* [Book on Animals], al-Jāḥiz often quotes Aristotle's works as his authorities. See Ṭāha al-Ḥājirī, "Takhrīj Nuṣūṣ Aristuṭālīya," *Majallat Kulliyat al-Ādāb* (1953–54), pp. 3–23, 69–90.

7. See al-Kutubī, *Fawāt al-Wafayāt*, ed. M. 'Abd al-Ḥamīd (Cairo, 1951), II, 94–95; and Tarīf Khalidi, *Islamic Historiography: The Histories of Mas'ūdī* (Albany, N.Y., 1975), chap. 2.

8. Ṭurṭūshī wrote several works on Law and Society, perhaps the most important of which is *Kitāb Sirāj al-Mulūk* [Treatise on Light for Kings] (Cairo, 1319/1902).

est virtue with which the Ruler must be clothed.[9] He dealt with justice on two levels—he called one Prophetic, in accordance with Religion and Law, and the other political, derived from custom and the rules laid down by kings, which may be called positive justice. The latter may not be always just, especially if it runs contrary to Religion and Law, but even if it were not as just as the Prophetic justice, he contended that it would be better than the injustice (jawr) of Muslim Rulers who act contrary to the Law.[10] He noted, however, that the injustice of Muslim Rulers was not necessarily the product of caprice and evil, but often the failure of counsellors to warn rulers of the evil consequences of their unjust rule. But the public, he added, should be made aware of its responsibilities for the Ruler's unjust acts, as he (Ṭurṭūshī) had often heard many people say that the Prophet said: "Your Ruler's [acts] are [the reflection of] your acts, and as you are, so your Rulers would be."[11] After a search in the textual sources, Ṭurṭūshī found that the meaning of this saying is implied in the Revelation, in which God said: "So We make the evildoers friends of each other for what they have earned" (Q. VI, 129). From this Revelation as well as from his experiences, Ṭurṭūshī became convinced that unless Prophetic justice is supported by a feeling of public responsibility, to urge rulers to put justice into practice, injustice rather than justice is likely to prevail.[12] In other words, Ṭurṭūshī suggested the possible existence in society of a new form of justice which might, in combination with Prophetic justice, create a social form of justice which is positive in nature; but he did not explore the sources of such a new form of justice, nor did he indicate how the public could put forth a claim that would obligate Rulers to put it into practice. This line of reasoning had to await changes of conditions when thinkers became aware of the need for further inquiry into the nature of social justice.

Social Justice and the Concepts of Political Law and Public Interest

It was in the field of Law that an investigation of the social aspect of justice was attempted. Ibn Taymīya, by developing the concept of the

9. *Ibid.*, p. 45.
10. *Ibid.*, p. 47.
11. This saying is a Tradition attributed by many writers to the Prophet (see Ṭurṭūshī, *Sirāj*, p. 100), but it is not reported in the early compilations of Traditions.
12. Ṭurṭūshī, *op. cit.*, pp. 100–101.

"Siyāsa Shar'īya" (political law) as a supplement to the Sharī'a (Revealed Law), and Najm al-Dīn al-Ṭawfī, who proposed "maṣlaḥa" (public interest) as a source of Law, made it possible for other thinkers like Ibn Khaldūn to investigate the broader sources of positive justice and formulate a new theory of social justice. The contributions of Najm al-Dīn al-Ṭawfī and Ibn Taymīya were perhaps indispensable, for without them, the method which Ibn Khaldūn pursued in his inquiry into the structure of society might not have reached a relatively high level of positivism.

Ṭawfī and Ibn Taymīya were contemporary jurists—Ṭawfī was probably born in 657/1259 and Ibn Taymīya in 661/1263—but since the latter dealt with a broader concept of positive justice, his scope and method will be considered first.

From early life, Ibn Taymīya's upbringing and scholarly interest were closely connected with the events and circumstances which occasioned the shifting fortunes of Islām during the seventh/thirteenth and eighth/fourteenth centuries, when its authorities were threatened by the Crusade's expeditions from Western Christendom, and by the Mongol invasions from Central Asia.[13] Needless to say, these conditions had a profound impact on the development of his views on Law and Religion, the product not only of the traditional method of textual interpretation but also of his grappling with the practical questions of the day. By a combination of the deductive and the inductive methods, Ibn Taymīya was able to develop the concept of "political law" (siyāsa shar'īya), embodying a notion of justice drawn from textual (Qur'ān and Traditions) and social (secular) sources. This was a

13. Ibn Taymīya was born at Ḥarrān (in eastern Turkey today) in 661/1263 and fled with his family to Damascus before the approaching waves of Mongol invasions into Islamic lands when he was only seven years old. He received his education in Damascus, where his father became a teacher, and took an active part in the defense of the city as well as in subsequent attacks which brought him into prominence with the rulers of Syria and Egypt, who often sought his counsel as a popular religious leader on many questions of the day relating to Religion and Law. But his contacts with the high authorities aroused the suspicion and jealousies of other religious leaders, especially in Egypt, who objected to his method of interpretation of the textual sources and to his innovative religious and legal views. He was called three times to answer questions of legal doctrines, and preferred to remain in prison than to change his mind on questions upon which he had developed his own opinion. He died in prison in 728/1328. For his life see Ibn Khallikān, *Wafayāt al-A'yān,* IV, 20–22; al-Kutubī, *Fawāt al-Wafayāt,* I, 62–82; M. Abū Zahra, *Ibn Taymīya* (Cairo, 1952); and H. Laoust, "Ibn Taymiya," *Encyclopaedia of Islam,* new ed., III, 950–55.

departure from the classical doctrines of law and justice. How did Ibn Taymīya arrive at his concepts of law and justice?

Like al-Ghazzālī, Ibn Taymīya made a distinction between the validity of universals (kulliyāt) derived from Revelation, and of universals for which there is no Revelational evidence. The former, dealing with religious and legal matters, must be accepted without question; but the latter, the product of Reason and precedent, belongs to an entirely different category, and therefore can be the subject of discussion among scholars. The surest way to establish the validity of universals concerning which there is no Revelational evidence is by particulars (juz'iyāt) applicable to specific situations. In other words, Ibn Taymīya proposed that while some particulars derived from Revelational evidence can establish the validity of universals, the validity of universals that cannot be established by Revelational evidence must rest on particulars in accordance with the prevailing practice and custom. It is hardly necessary to say that this is the method of "induction" defined by Aristotle, whose system of logic had a profound influence on Muslim thinkers, as "a progression from singulars to universals."[14]

In his work on political law, Ibn Taymīya tried to maintain a balance between the idealism of deduction and the realism of induction—a realism based on positive sources of law, such as precedent and custom, provided they were in conformity with the purposes (maqāṣid) of Sharī'a. In almost all of his writings, he sought to serve the general interest (maṣlaḥa) of believers which he, in agreement with earlier jurists, held as the ultimate end of the Law. This end can be achieved through the Siyāsa Shar'īya.[15] The unity of Religion and Law (State), which exists in principle, must be carried out in practice. Without the effective power (shawka) of the State, he held, Religion and Law would be in danger. Conversely, without the constraints of the Law, the State (presided over by despotic Rulers) degenerates into an unjust and tyrannical organization. Only in the pursuit of justice

14. Aristotle, *Topics,* 1.12. 105^{a}13–14.

15. See Ibn Taymīya, *Kitāb al-Siyāsa al-Shar'īya fī Iṣlāḥ al-Rā'ī wa al-Ra'īya* [Book of Juridical Policy for the Improvement of the Ruler and Ruled], ed. Nashshār and 'Atīya (Cairo, 1951); French trans. H. Laoust (Cairo, 1939), and English trans. Farrūkh (Beirut, 1966). For the meaning and development of the term "siyasa Shar'īya" by followers of Ibn Taymīya, see 'Abd al-Wahhāb Khallāf, *al-Siyāsa al-Shar'īya* (Cairo, 1350/1930); and 'Abd al-Raḥmān Tāj, *al-Siyāsa al-Shar'īya wa al-Fiqh al-Islāmī* [Juridical Policy and Islamic Jurisprudence] (Cairo, 13721/1953).

can the State be expected to fulfill the ends for which it was established. The justice that Ibn Taymīya strove to achieve was obviously a new concept enshrined in the Siyāsa Shar'īya, which might be called social justice, as its aims were to serve the public interest. Since the power of Islam was in a state of decadence, social justice was the means by virtue of which that power (shawka) might have been rehabilitated. More specifically, Ibn Taymīya held that social justice would bridge the gulf between the Ruler and the Ruled (al-Rā'ī wa al-Ra'īya) and ultimately improve social conditions and enhance the power of Islam.

As a step to improve the existing standard of justice, Ibn Taymīya sought to reform the family law because the family is central in the community. For instance, he insisted that the husband cannot legally divorce his wife by three pronouncements combined in one declaration of repudiation. Nor can the wife be legally divorced were the husband to pronounce it in a conditional declaration (e.g., in an oath) or in a state of drunkenness, contrary to the prevailing opinion of Ḥanbalī jurists (the school of law to which he belonged), who considered such a divorce to be binding. Ibn Taymīya held that the jihād (*bellum justum*), in order to be just must be a defensive war. Such a view was contrary to the prevailing doctrine advocated by Shāfi'ī, that the jihād was a permanent war against the unbelievers (kuffār) regardless whether it was defensive or offensive.[16] As to the prisoners of war released by the Mongols following the negotiations in 699/1298, he held that the Christian prisoners should be included as a matter of justice, since they had been taken prisoners with Muslims and therefore should have been equally dealt with as citizens of the State regardless of differences in religion.[17]

In court hearings, Ibn Taymīya insisted that procedural justice must be strictly observed if rulers were to fulfill the ends of the Law. Once called to Court to answer a question of dogma, he refused to appear before the Ḥanafī judge Jalāl al-Dīn al-Rāzī (d. 745/1344) on the grounds that *(a)* the judge was one of the parties involved in the dispute, and *(b)* the Court, established to deal with legal disputes, lacked jurisdiction over matters of dogma.[18] He also defended the right of a Christian accused of having insulted the Prophet in 693/

16. See chap 7.

17. See Abū Zahra, *op. cit.*, pp. 38–39.

18. See Ibn Taymīya, *Miḥnat Shaykh al-Islām Ibn Taymīya*, ed. M. H. Fiqqī (Cairo, 1372/1935), pp. 9–33; Abū Zahra, *op. cit.*, pp. 56 and 58.

1293, on the grounds that there was insufficient evidence as a matter of procedure, although he upheld the rule that whoever insults the Prophet is liable for punishment.[19] He was, however, in favor of the punishment of believers and unbelievers, whenever they were engaged in activities against the State.[20]

Like Ibn Taymīya, Najm al-Dīn al-Ṭawfī lived in an age in which Islam was in a state of decadence and the believers suffered oppression under despotic rulers. He sought to improve conditions by an emphasis on the use of public interest (maṣlaḥa) as a basis for legal decisions on the grounds that it is the ultimate end of Law. He came into conflict with his peers who were opposed to the use of public interest as a guiding principle for the interpretation of textual sources.[21]

However, public interest (maṣlaḥa) as a source for legal decisions was no innovation in Ṭawfī's time; it had already been used, as noted earlier, by al-Ghazzālī and others. Indeed, it is said that Mālik (d. 179/795), founder of a school of law, was the first to use it, and the Ḥanafī jurists recognized it as guiding principle through analogical reasoning. Ṭawfī supported Ghazzālī's use of public interest (maṣlaḥa) as a basis for legal decisions irrespective of other sources of Law, provided it was applied to cases of vital interests (ḍarūrāt). But he sought to universalize the principle to be applicable to all cases of public interest and went so far as to say that even if the principle of public interest were to contradict a textual source, it should override that source on the grounds that the Law (Sharī'a) was laid down to protect public interest as the ultimate purpose of the Divine Legislator.[22]

19. He wrote, on this occasion, his first great work, *Kitāb al-Ṣārim al-Maslūl 'ala Shātim al-Rasūl* (Hyderabad, 1322/1905). See Laoust, *op. cit.*, p. 951.

20. In the war between Islam and the Crusades, Ibn Taymīya denounced Christians and Shi'ites who aided the Crusaders against Muslims (see Abū Zahra, *op. cit.*, pp. 129–37).

21. Najm al-Dīn al-Ṭawfī was born at a small town near Baghdad circa 657/1259. Although he belonged to the Ḥanbalī school of law, stressing Traditions and opposed to analogical reasoning (qiyās) as a source of law, he insisted on the use of personal reasoning (ijtihād) which prompted opponents in Cairo to accuse him of having been a Shī'ite, since the Shī'ites held that the door of ijtihād was still open and he was born in a region where Shī'ism prevailed. From Baghdad, he visited Damascus, where he met Ibn Taymīya and other scholars, and finally settled in Egypt where he died in 716/1316. For his life, see Muṣṭafa Zayd, *al-Maṣlaḥa fī al-Tashrī' al-Islāmī wa Najm al-Dīn al-Ṭawfī* [Public Interest in Islamic Legislation and Najm al-Dīn al-Ṭawfī] (Cairo, 1954), pp. 67–88.

22. For the text of Ṭawfī's treatise on maṣlaḥa, see Muṣṭafa Zayd, *op. cit.* (Appendix).

Ṭawfī's argument in favor of the use of public interest as an overriding principle is based partly on a Tradition from the Prophet which states: "la ḍarar wa la ḍirār" (no injury shall be imposed nor shall it be inflicted as a penalty for another injury), and partly on precedent and custom which determine in practice what particular public interest should be protected. Like Ibn Taymīya, Ṭawfī pursued an inductive method to define and determine public interest and sought by this method to improve social conditions. Needless to say, such a concept of social justice is positive in character, intended to promote general welfare and reduce social vices (mafsada).[23] Although the principle of public interest found no great support in Ṭawfī's age—indeed, Ṭawfī was ahead of his time—it was ably defended by the Mālikī jurist Abū Isḥāq al-Shāṭibī (d. 790/1388) and recognized, in the broader social sense, by Ibn Khaldūn. In the modern age, under the impact of Western legal thought, the principle of public interest (maṣlaḥa) has become the basis for the nationalization of private property in some Islamic lands. It has also been invoked to justify the adoption of collectivist principles as a means to achieve distributive justice.[24]

Ibn Khaldūn's Concept of Social Justice

Ibn Khaldūn's notion of justice may seem to have been derived from his study of and personal experiences with the operating forces of society irrespective of the Islamic traditions. But the opinions of scholars vary today on the questions of whether his inquiry into society derived from a purely secular or religious perspective. Some, who have been impressed by his inductive method in which he used secular concepts such as the "'aṣabīya" (a form of social solidarity based on kin affiliation), considered him a secular thinker; others reaffirmed the view that he grew up in a tradition of Islamic law and philosophy and formulated theories of society essentially within the context of the Islamic tradition.[25] It is possible to substantiate both points of view, if

23. Zayd, *op. cit.*, pp. 117 and 127.

24. For the origin and development of the concept of Maṣlaḥa (public interest) in Islamic law, see my article "Maṣlaḥa," *Encyclopaedia of Islam*, new ed.

25. The first to call attention to Ibn Khaldūn's secular outlook was De Slane, who provided a scholarly edition of the Muqaddima (Prolegomena) and translated it into French. Others, including Bouthoul, Ṭāha Ḥusayn and 'Ayyād, have supported this

one were merely to look into statements that may support one or the other viewpoint, as the later editions of the *Prolegomena* (Muqaddima) contain a number of statements on various branches of Islamic learning that have been added to it after he settled in Egypt.[26] It is not always easy to know the extent of Ibn Khaldūn's fidelity to traditions; for this reason the *Prolegomena* should be read as a whole for an understanding of his social concepts. Moreover, in his *Autobiography* (al-Ta'rīf), Ibn Khaldūn provides us with illuminating aspects of his life and thought which might be helpful if read side by side with the *Prolegomena.*[27] Since in this study we are primarily concerned with Ibn Khaldūn's concept of justice, an answer on whether his concept of justice is essentially secular or religious can be given perhaps only from this particular perspective.

Ibn Khaldūn's upbringing and early life in Tunis, where he was born and received his early education, were in accordance with the Islamic tradition. He studied religion and jurisprudence before he was introduced, under the influence of one of his learned teachers, to theology and philosophy, about which he wrote summaries of the works he read on these subjects.[28] Very soon, however, he entered into public service which carried him from one court to another, serving in various capacities under the Rulers of North-West Africa and Spain. But his aspiration to combine scholarship with service in high offices, stemming from family tradition as well as from his own interest in learning, though partially achieved, proved rather disappointing to him as he had to serve under regimes which proved unstable and with Rulers and Courtiers who proved fickle and unreliable. Despite offers

---

point of view (see bibliography). The view that Ibn Khaldūn grew up in the Islamic tradition and that his social theories form a sicence of culture ('umrān) within the framework of that tradition is explicit in M. Mahdi, *Ibn Khaldūn's Philosophy of History* (Chicago, 2nd ed., 1964). More recent studies on his socio-political ideas reaffirm the secular outlook. See 'Alī al-Wardī, *Manṭiq Ibn Khaldūn* (Cairo, 1962); M. Rabi, *The Political Theory of Ibn Khaldūn* (Leiden, 1967); and Fuad Boali and Ali Wardi, *Ibn Khaldūn and Islamic Thought-Style* (Boston, 1981).

26. See Sāṭi' al-Ḥūṣrī, *Dirāsāt fī Muqaddimat Ibn Khaldūn* (Cairo, 2nd. ed., 1953), pp. 117–35.

27. The autobiography, forming an appendix to Ibn Khaldūn's universal history, has been edited and published in a separate volume. See Ibn Khaldūn, *al-Ta'rīf bi-Ibn Khaldūn wa Riḥlatuh Gharban wa Sharqan*, ed. M. al-Ṭanjī (Cairo, 1951). Hereafter, it will be referred to as the *Autobiography.*

28. See Ibn Khaldūn, *Lubab al-Muḥassal fī Uṣūl al-Dīn*, ed. L. Rubio (Tutwan, 1952); and *Shafā' al-Sā'il Li-Tahdhīb al-Masā'il*, ed. M. al-Ṭanjī (Istanbul, 1958).

to continue in high offices, he decided to withdraw from public service in his early forties and devote himself completely to scholarship.[29]

In his retreat at the citadel of Abū Salāma,[30] where he passed four years in contemplation and study (776/1374–780/1378), he was able to isolate himself from the outside world and devote his time and efforts to the writing of his major work on history. His intent at first was to write a history of Islam in North Africa. He began to ponder on the material which Muslim historians had compiled and found it unsatisfactory to explain the rapid rise and fall of the regimes under which he served. Although he did not state the purpose for the writing of his history, hints in his *Autobiography* about disappointment with public service indicate that he perhaps wanted to understand the underlying forces which caused the shift in his fortunes. Were they the result of personal failure or the product of causes beyond human control? This and other questions must have crossed his mind and prompted his efforts to understand in depth the nature of the social processes and the underlying forces that produced them. In his attempt to find the causes of his failure in public life, he was ultimately addressing himself to a question of justice. If he were responsible for the events that led to his withdrawal from public life, his failure must have been a form of retributive justice; but if his failure

29. Since the life and thought of Ibn Khaldūn may be found in several published studies including his *Autobiography*, only a few landmarks and events might be useful to note in this study. He was born to a well-known family in Tunis on Ramaḍān 1, 732/May 27, 1332. After study and a short service under the regime of his birthplace, he went to Fās (Fez) in 754/1354 where he became involved in political rivalry (including imprisonment). He left for Granada (Andalusia) in 763/1362, where he served some three years as a counsellor and a diplomat. In 765/1365 he was called by the Sultan of Bijāya to serve as Ḥājib (Court Chamberlain), combining political and academic positions for hardly a year. After his patron's demise, he left for Biskara in 767/1366 where he passed the next six years in political rivalry and intrigue among competing factions. Unable to achieve his ambition, he decided to withdraw from politics and seek peace and learning at the citadel of Abū Salāma in 776/1375. After four years of contemplation and writing—he wrote the first draft of the Prolegomena (*al-Muqaddima*) and the history of North-West Africa—he returned to consult works in the libraries of Tunis for the completion of his History. Unable to extract himself from political intrigues, he decided to proceed to Egypt where he sought peace of mind and learning in 794/1382. He served as a teacher and judge for almost a quarter of a century—including an interlude of a political venture in Damascus to meet Tamerlane in 802/1400—and began to revise and enlarge his work on the History. It was in Egypt that he realized the need for justice as a means to overcome decadence and improve society. He died in 806/1408.

30. Its location today is in the province of Uran (Oran) in Algeria.

were the product of forces and conditions over which he had no control, his withdrawal from public life would then be right and just.

How did Ibn Khaldūn respond to this challenge?

His answer to this question in the *Prolegomena* is not the same as in the *Autobiography*. In the *Prolegomena*, justice is discussed as a social concept in the context of a theory of society whose processes were determined by social forces beyond the control of man. In other words, the concept of justice may be regarded as an apologia for his inability to control the social forces and repair the injustices resulting from them. Ibn Khaldūn must have derived inner satisfaction from his decision to withdraw from public life and a relief from the responsibility for the prevailing injustices. After he settled in Egypt, however, he looked at the matter from a different perspective. In the latter part of his life, he seems to have realized, as Ibn Taymīya did before him, the significance of Law in repairing social conditions and restraining decadence and degeneration through his participation in the administration of justice. Justice appeared to him as a more important social concept than before, and he was determined to play the role of a reformer and achieve justice rather than to merely submit to the verdict of theories about society. In both capacities he showed an interest in justice—in the first, he was a social theorist, and in the second, he was a social reformer. But his perception of justice was necessarily different from each of the two. As a theorist, it was not unnatural that he should take a detached attitude and his theory of society was deterministic. As a judge who must administer justice with impartiality, he took the role of a participant in the social process which he tried to influence in accordance with the scale of justice he held in his hand. In that capacity he could no longer submit to a deterministic view of the social process. What prompted Ibn Khaldūn to change his attitude toward society and what is the significance of his views? Before an answer can be given, perhaps a brief summary of his theory of society and its relevance to justice might be in order.

In the *Prolegomena*, Ibn Khaldūn's main concern is an analysis of the Great Society[31]—its structure, the social forces (dynamics) operat-

31. In the *Prolegomena*, Ibn Khaldūn uses the term "dawla" (state) in a general and a particular sense. The first (dawla 'āmma) is equivalent to the Great Society and the other is defined in the narrow sense of a dynasty or regime (polity). The Great Society is ecumenical in character and equivalent to Islamdom, the counterpart of Christendom in Medieval Europe. The term Islamdom was first used in the *Muslim World* (its editor was then Edwin Calverly) and in my *War and Peace in the Law of Islam* (Baltimore, 1955).

ing from within, and the resulting social processes affecting the life and destiny of man. In structure, the basic unit is the state (in the narrow sense), as Ibn Khaldūn used it specifically to denote polity or political regime. The Great Society (Islamdom) consists of a variety of states, some at the height of power, others in decadence, and still others in the making. The state as a unit, like the individual, has a limited life-span (the life-span of each is three generations, or roughly one hundred and twenty years); but Islam as the Great Society continued to exist since the rise of Islam. Changes in society, including the rise and fall of states, are caused by major social forces working within each unit. These forces are the 'aṣabīya and religion. The first (a form of social solidarity) may be found in nomadic societies and tends to stir the strongest passion for warfare and destruction, leading to constant conflicts among them. Religion, on the other hand, is a spiritual feeling of brotherhood which is likely to mature in sedentary or urban communities, and is therefore a more benign force than the 'aṣabīya. But when religion was combined with 'aṣabīya in the nomadic society, as in the case of the adoption of Islam by the Arabian tribes, it created unity of purpose and led to the establishment of Islamdom.

Religion and 'aṣabīya, however, do not always operate in unison. In Islamdom, says Ibn Khaldūn, the unity between religion and 'aṣabīya lasted only three decades after the rise of Islam. The Caliphate, embodying justice and other Islamic ideals, turned into a temporal (secular) rule under the Umayyads, who stressed a dynastic form of government. From that time the unity between religion and 'aṣabīya began to fall apart and the nomadic tribes fell back on 'aṣabīya to sustain their existence. Islam as a religion, however, continued to exist as a social force. The Rulers tried to enforce the Law, but its ideals were abandoned—superseded by the social habits and self-interest of the men in authority. As a result, the 'aṣabīya remained as the single most potent force which prompted the nomadic tribes to resume their periodic assault on urban communities and the cycle of rise and fall of states was again in full swing.[32] Needless to say, the scale of justice was no longer dependent on Law and Religion, but on other values. It was determined by the operating public order in each state. According to

32. Ibn Khaldūn has provided a summary of his theory of the cyclical rise and fall of states and the role of 'aṣabīya in his *Autobiography* (see pp. 314–45), but a full account of it is in the *Prolegomena* (see I, chap. 2; trans. I, 249ff.).

Ibn Khaldūn, three types of states might be distinguished on the basis of their scales of justice.

First, the category of states whose public order is essentially derived from Revelational sources; its scale of justice is enshrined in Religion and Law.

Second, the category of states whose public order is dependent on laws laid down by man; its scale of justice consists of values which are essentially secular in nature, based either on rational or customary norms. Since these values are not derived from Law and Religion, the scale of justice is necessarily imperfect as only God and the Prophet provide the perfect and ideal standard of justice. This kind of justice is therefore largely dependent on the Ruler. In theory, the Ruler claims to promote the welfare of his people, and they in turn are expected to be loyal to him. This scale, the central theme in all mirrors of princes, is derived from Persian traditions, and Ibn Khaldūn considered it a model of a just scale, because the Persians deemed it necessary that their Rulers should possess qualities which insure justice. The scale of justice under such a public order is essentially rational, but it is far from being perfect, as the law is secular and can by no means be restrictive of the authority of a Ruler who has the monopoly of power.

Third, the category of states whose public order consists of a mixture of secular and religious laws. This kind of an order prevailed in Islamdom after its transformation from a caliphal to a kingly form of government. In principle, Rulers were bound by Law and Religion, but in practice they pursued their own self-interest, determined by social habits, requirements of state security, and the ambition of courtiers. It follows that this kind of justice is neither ideal nor purely rational, but a form of social or positive justice, consisting of the norms and practices that had prevailed in Islamic society.[33]

After he settled in Egypt in 784/1382, Ibn Khaldūn began to examine justice from an entirely different perspective. In particular, his notion of justice and other values were considered in the light of his new experiences as a teacher and a judge in Cairo. Before he settled in Egypt, he was so preoccupied in the struggle for power that he scarcely had the time to attend to the administration of justice, but this did not mean that he was indifferent to oppression or injustice.

33. Ibn Khaldūn, *Prolegomena*, II, 1ff. (Ibn Khaldūn describes the administration of justice under such a regime); Mahdi, *op. cit.*, pp. 232–53.

Only after his retreat to the citadel of Abū Salāma and later his self-exile in Egypt did he have the time to ponder on his past, to look with a fresh eye on existing conditions in Islamdom, and to refine some of his ideas in the light of new experiences.

Upon his arrival in Cairo, he was at first favorably impressed with the capital about which he had heard such high praise before. Above all, he was overpowered by its material wealth, the grandeur of its buildings, and the growth in its population. Soon after, however, when he became more intimately acquainted with its social institutions, he began to detect the moral corruption and injustices manifested in society, with which he had similar experiences in North-West Africa. As a judge, he became aware of the abuses and irregularities in the administration of justice and set out with strictness and impartiality to enforce the Law and fight against them. His experiences as a teacher and a judge proved invaluable, for he became convinced that his task was not only to refine his social theories but to put them into practice.[34]

It was thus in Egypt that Ibn Khaldūn began to realize that justice was central in the social theory of society. From these experiences—indeed, from his earlier experiences in North-West Africa—he found that the Law had fallen into disregard. He became convinced that unless it was rehabilitated, the Great Society (Islamdom) would be completely demoralized and destroyed. As a teacher and a judge, he saw his task to be the prevention of moral decline and destruction by strict enforcement of the Law. Justice loomed large on his horizon and the role of the judge ranked even higher in the social order. He became determined in the last few years of his life to fight corruption and injustice, despite opposition from his peers who accused him of palpably lacking in his knowledge of the Law and of inconsistency in its strict enforcement without regard for the manners and customs of a country in which he was a stranger.[35]

Ibn Khaldūn's critics may have been right in pointing out that he was no great expert in the Law nor did he have the experience in judicial procedure. Indeed, he had contributed no special study on Law, not even a text-book, although he taught Mālikī jurisprudence in Egypt for years. His brief account of the subject in the *Prolego-*

34. For critique of the administration of justice in Egypt see Ibn Khaldūn's *Autobiography*, pp. 254–60.

35. Ibn Khaldūn, *Autobiography*, pp. 254–60.

mena[36] and his Inaugural Lecture on Mālik's *Muwaṭṭa'*, the leading text-book on Mālikī law,[37] are too general and reveal no great depth in the field. Before he settled in Egypt, his interest in Law and justice was not central, as he was primarily concerned with the formulation of a general theory of society. But after he became a judge in Egypt, he did indeed demonstrate an ability in the administration of justice, despite criticism by opponents who claimed that he was not fit for the office because he had no prior experience with judicial procedure.[38]

Ibn Khaldūn, essentially a social thinker, looked at the matter from a different angle. He was quite conscious of the fact that Egypt, not unlike other parts of North-West Africa with which he was quite familiar, was in a state of decadence, and he considered the office of judge an important check to deter further degeneration and decline, if the process were impossible to reverse. In his *Autobiography*, he deplores the spread of bribery, irregularities in judicial procedure and other corrupt practices which he was determined to stop.[39] He set an example of integrity and impartiality by refusing to be influenced by personal or political pressures or by bribery. His impartiality was demonstrated by treating all parties in a dispute alike, whether plaintiffs or defendents; he rejected the testimony of witnesses who proved lacking the requisite qualifications; and he applied discretionary decisions (ta'zīr) in order to check oppression and injustice. For his strictness and impartiality he had to pay the price of dismissal from office four times. For the last quarter of a century, he spent his life on the bench and in classrooms, concerned mainly with the teaching and application of the law in an effort to demonstrate that the pursuit of justice was the key to repairing social conditions. Thus his task in Egypt was not to expound a new concept of justice—he had indeed already dealt with the theoretical aspect in the *Muqaddima*—but to apply the standard of justice as it existed in his time. He proved loyal to Islamic tradition by his earnest effort to pursue procedural justice almost to perfection.

36. Ibn Khaldūn, *Prolegomena*, III, 1–25; trans. III, 3–32.

37. Ibn Khaldūn, *Autobiography*, pp. 297–311.

38. Because of his long involvement in politics, Ibn Khaldūn's appointment as a judge was questioned in some quarters, including a trenchant personal attack by Ibn 'Arafa, but in reality he proved equal to the task to which he was entrusted. See Muḥammad Abū Zahra, "Ibn Khaldūn wa al-fiqh wa al-Qaḍā'," *A'mal Mahrajān Ibn Khaldūn* [Proceedings of Ibn Khaldūn's Celebrations] (Cairo, 1962), pp. 633–34.

39. Ibn Khaldūn. *Autobiography*, pp. 257–58.

Ibn al-Azraq on Social Justice

Perhaps a discussion of social justice from the perspective of one of Ibn Khaldūn's commentators might be useful, as it might throw some light on the impact of Ibn Khaldūn's social theories on thinkers in the generation that came immediately after him. In his work on statecraft,[40] Ibn al-Azraq accepted Ibn Khaldūn's concept of social justice, though not its procedural aspect. Like Ibn Khaldūn, he grew up and received his early education in Western Islamdom, but he settled and spent the rest of his life in eastern Islamic lands after he had passed most of his life as a judge and a counselor in Spain and North Africa.[41]

Like Ibn Khaldūn, Ibn al-Azraq contended that man is by nature oppressive and unjust. He took it almost for granted that both rulers and ruled tend to pursue the path of injustice unless checked by certain restraining forces. As a judge, both by training and experience, he was interested above all in the administration of justice; he therefore addressed himself in his work on statecraft to the question of how justice can be achieved.[42]

Ibn Khaldūn, it will be recalled, pinned his hopes on the authority of the Law (Sharī'a) and on judicial procedure. Ibn al-Azraq, having spent most of his life as a judge, seems to have had second thoughts about the prospect of achieving justice through judicial procedure. We know very little about his judicial experience, except that he was highly praised by his contemporaries as a man of integrity and good reputation, but no records exist to verify how competent he could be as a judge. From his work on statecraft, however, we learn that he seems to have preferred to persuade rulers to check injustice and

40. Abū 'Abd-Allāh Ibn al-Azraq,*Badā'i' al-Sulūk fī Ṭabā'i' al-Mulk* [Marvels of State Conduct and the Nature of Authority], ed. 'Ali Sāmī al-Nashshār (Baghdad, 1977), 2 vols.

41. Ibn al-Azraq was born in Malaqa (Malaga), Spain, in 832/1427. He received his education in Law and other branches of learning in Gharnāṭa (Granada) and served as a judge at Malaqa and other towns before he became Chief Judge of Granada under the Sultan Abū al-Ḥasan. When Granada came under the threat of Christian rulers, Ibn al-Azraq went on a mission to seek in vain the support of other Muslim rulers in North Africa and Egypt. Frustrated by failure to secure support, he accepted the office of judge in Jerusalem in 896/1491. Hardly had he served a few months than he suddenly died in the same year. For his life, see al-Sakhāwī, *Al-Ḍaw al-Lāmi'*, IX, 20–21; and Nashshār's introduction to Ibn al-Azraq's *Badā'i'*, pp. 7–19.

42. Ibn al-Azraq, *Badā'i'*, I, 226–29.

promote justice through administrative processes, rather than through judicial procedure, perhaps either because he saw the futility of dependence on the courts or because he found from personal experience that rulers could by persuasion be prevailed upon to espouse the cause of justice. Ibn Khaldūn found that rulers with whom he was engaged in a struggle for power were almost always greedy and attentive only to personal interest; he therefore sought to achieve justice through judicial procedure. Ibn al-Azraq, however, viewing social justice as a concept broader than strictly procedural, believed that rulers were the most effective instrument to achieve justice because of their prestige and the power they wield over their people. In his treatise on statecraft, he maintained that it was quite possible to prevail upon rulers to espouse justice by two means: First, by demonstrating that the evil consequences of injustice would undermine the regime and lead eventually to its destruction; second, by making clear the advantages to be obtained from a policy based on justice which would enhance the prestige of rulers and consolidate their regimes. Because justice is prescribed by Religion and Law, Ibn al-Azraq held that rulers might be prevailed upon to pursue justice by inspiring them with the highest religious values and by the reward of Paradise.[43]

Both Ibn Khaldūn and Ibn al-Azraq were not aware that justice has more manifold aspect than procedural. But both lived in an age when the Islamic community was in decadence; Ibn Khaldūn analyzed this decline and indicated its causes and processes. Their dependence on the administrative and the judicial procedures is an admission of failure to improve the social order; they were therefore satisfied with the strict enforcement of the Law as a means of restraining the process of degeneration. Unlike Ibn Taymīya, who advocated improvement of the social order by the political law (siyāsa shar'īya), Ibn Khaldūn and Ibn al-Azraq were satisfied if the Law as they knew it were to be faithfully observed. This was not the view of a social reformer, and their endeavors (especially those of Ibn Khaldūn) were confined to analysis and explanation, rather than repair, of the social process. The positive view of social justice had to await the rise of a new generation of thinkers when conditions began to change the Islamic order in the modern age.

43. *Ibid.*, pp. 224–26, 229–36.

9

Changes in the Concept of Justice under Modern Conditions

The Earth shall be the inheritance of My [God] righteous [just] servants.

—Q. XXI, 105

One day in the pursuit of justice is worth more than sixty years in prayer.

—The Prophet Muḥammad

Before we discuss the changes in the Islamic conception of justice in the modern age, perhaps a summary of the Islamic theory of justice and its various underlying principles and sources might be illuminating at this stage. We have seen how manifold were the aspects of justice advanced by the various schools of thought and how diverse were the viewpoints of the men of learning in each school. Yet despite all the diversities and differences of opinion among schools and scholars, all agreed that in its ideal form Islamic justice was an expression of the *jus divinum.* Its sources and general assumptions may be summed up as follows:

First, originating from so high a Divine source, justice became known only through the evidence made available to man. According to some, such evidence could be found only in the Revelation; others insisted that Reason was necessary for understanding it. Both methods were finally recognized, but Revelation was and continued to be regarded as providing the overriding evidence.

Second, justice, identified with Divine qualities, was not a simple concept for the scholars to define in human terms. Some considered it the embodiment of the highest human virtues, but others, viewing it as direct emanation from God, equated it with Perfection. They all agreed that, whether by Divine or human standards, it was an ideal notion which man sought to realize in meaningful human virtues.

Third, the subjects of Divine Justice were those who believed in the One and Just God; all others—indeed, the rest of mankind—were the object of that Justice. Like God's Law, Divine Justice is not only perfect, it is eternal, irrespective of time and place, and designed for universal application to all men. Even if men who did not believe in the One God were to seek refuge in it, they would not be denied access to it.

Fourth, the standard of justice, whether determined by Reason or Revelation, indicated for men the paths of right and wrong, so that all, each according to his light, would pursue the right and reject the wrong in order to achieve the good in this world and salvation in the next—in a word, to achieve happiness in both.

Scholars, however, had disagreed on how Divine Justice would be realized on Earth, not to speak of the hereafter. The differences between one school and another—indeed, often between one scholar and another in each school—proved exceedingly difficult to reconcile, and the great debate that ensued shifted from a discussion of one aspect of justice to another, revealing the concerns and aspirations of each generation about the meaning and purpose of justice and how these would be realized in relevance to existing conditions.

Apart from differences arising necessarily from changing circumstances, one of the continuing causes of disagreement among scholars was methodological: failure to relate the theory of justice to practice. By its very nature, Divine Justice is an abstract concept, and the great majority of men who sought to define it considered the matter from the perspective of the destiny of man without regard to reality; those who defined it in terms of reality dealt with it on two levels—Divine and human—but were not able to relate the one to the other.[1] Only in the modern age, under the impact of Western secular thought, did Muslims begin to focus the debate on the nature of justice from a

1. The notable example of scholars who dealt with justice on two levels were the philosophers and writers on ethical justice. In dealing with human or Rational justice, however, they set one ideal standard without regard to reality (see chaps. 4 and 5), and the writers who dealt with social justice and paid attention to reality failed to formulate a synthesis combining elements of both the ideal and real (see chap. 8).

different perspective and apply a pragmatic method relevant to modern conditions.

The debate on justice first began concerning its political aspect. In a political community, committed to the doctrine that the locus of sovereignty is in Heaven and its exercise was delegated to the Prophet, it was taken for granted that political justice was an expression of God's Will as interpreted and put into practice by the Prophet. God, on His throne in Heaven, was the ultimate Ruler, and the Prophet—His mouthpiece—was the proximate Ruler. But after the Prophet's death, when no clear guidance was provided for "succession" (the Imamate), the legitimacy of succession became the centerpiece of the debate on political justice. For if the Prophet's successor proved to be lacking in legitimacy, his decisions would not be the expression of God's Sovereign Will, but the dictates of his own will; therefore, his acts would be impious (fisq) and unjust. The debate on political justice thus turned to the question of legitimacy, which divided the political community first into political factions (parties); later, when each party sought justification of its position on religious grounds, those factions gradually developed into credal communities. So the debate on justice was bound to turn from a political to religious and theological aspects—first as a by-product of the discourse on political questions (legitimacy) and then on essentially theological doctrines (God's Will and Justice) and their relevance to the destiny of man.

The debate on theological justice, however, was not confined to theologians, as it touched on the broader questions of scope and method and how Divine Justice would be defined in human terms. Philosophers and other thinkers were drawn into the debate, and the theological discourse not unnaturally touched on philosophical, ethical, and other aspects. As a result, another dimension was introduced into the debate, and the philosophers and other thinkers began to discuss justice as an expression of Reason and of man's responsibility for his acts. So the debate branched out into almost all aspects of human relationships for which justice might provide a standard of action.

When the debate on justice began, the discourse which occurred among rival political leaders (political justice) and jurist-theologians (theological justice) rested almost exclusively on Revelation, embodied in the two authoritative sources—the Qur'ān and Traditions. Reason as evidence was first introduced into the debate by the early Qadarites, but it was more systematically used in theological discussion by the Mu'tazila. It was initially rejected by almost all of the theologians (though not by the jurists) and only tacitly accepted by Ash'arī and his followers as subordinate to Revelation.

Where the Mu'tazila failed, the philosophers (al-falāsifa) succeeded in another attempt at establishing Reason as a method in its own right, because they made a concession to Revelation: the truth arrived at by Reason was the same as that embodied in the Revelation. However, the philosophers made it clear that they dealt with justice on two levels—Divine and human: one from God, and the other the product of Reason. Of the major philosophers, only Ibn Rushd, differing from the prevailing view, maintained that Rational Justice was not the same as Divine Justice, even though the truth was ultimately the same. In taking this position, he tried to assert a naturalistic view of human justice which would distinguish it from Divine Justice.

Attempts to introduce a third dimension into the great debate on justice were made by a few thinkers who sought to stress its secular elements. But such attempts met strong opposition, notwithstanding that the scholars who proposed the secular dimension tried to justify it on Revelational grounds. Of those who stressed this approach, only Ibn Khaldūn proposed a secular (social) concept of justice in no uncertain terms, and he made it clear that, on the operational level, the standard of justice was the product of social habits, customs, and local traditions which were not always consistent with Revelation and Reason. But Ibn Khaldūn's analysis of society had little or no impact on contemporary thinkers, and when he himself became involved in the administration of justice (after settling in Egypt), he found that it was impossible to apply a secular standard which was inconsistent with the prevailing spirit of the age. The significance of his concept of social justice became more meaningful to thinkers in the modern age when the Islamic society, under the impact of Western secular thought, became aware of the need for a new dimension.

The Scale of Divine Justice Reconsidered

Muslim thinkers began to reexamine the classical conception of justice when they became aware that its relevance to reality was significantly outdistanced by the material advantages which man derived from the standards of justice in Western society. But before a Western secular standard of justice could be tolerated, the Islamic society had to overcome long-standing inhibitions against secularism which Western Christian society itself had experienced in its struggle to achieve a secular standard. Bearing in mind that Islam is some six centuries younger than Christianity, adjustment to secularism is bound to take time, even though the possibility of adjustment is not unprecedented in Islam's own struggle to come to terms with life.

Foreign elements of justice were assimilated into the Islamic body politic in the past, provided they were introduced through recognized channels (consensus, analogy, and others). But in the modern age, the confrontation between Islam and Western society, leading to a loss in power and a threat to its sovereignty, generated continuous tensions and violent changes. The threats grew even more alarming when Western pressures continued, in one form or another, long after the domination of European Powers had begun to recede. For this reason, Muslim scholars were divided on the question of adoption of Western measures of justice into two schools: One, which may be called the Revivalist (often popularly called Fundamentalist) school, consisting of scholars who rejected foreign standards as inconsistent with Islamic standards on the grounds of secularism. Second, the Modernist school, consisting of scholars who received their education in the West or in institutions modelled after Western patterns, advocated the adoption of secular standards under the influence of Western ideals without regard to their relevance to Islamic traditions. Some of the Muslim scholars were not opposed to certain foreign elements of justice which did not contradict Islamic principles, but the wholesale adoption of foreign concepts under the impact of modern ideological winds—nationalism, socialism, and others—was entirely unacceptable to most scholars. The great debate on justice was turned again to the question of whether the adoption of foreign (secular) elements was at all consistent with Islamic traditions, just as the advocates of Rational Justice in the past were opposed by most theologians on the grounds that their dependence on Reason compromised Revelation.

Neither school of thought could provide a new standard to the satisfaction of a society in need of rehabilitation. Yet a nexus between Islamic and Western standards which combines possibilities of continuity and change was necessary if the conscience of the community were to be set at rest. Such a constructive approach was offered by

Jamāl al-Dīn al-Afghānī (1839–97) and his principal disciple, Muḥammad 'Abduh (1849–1905), who sought to bring about cooperation between the two rival schools and offer a compromise combining Islamic and Western standards of justice.[2]

After a journey to several Islamic lands—Iran, Afghanistan, India, Egypt, and Turkey—Afghānī was struck by the glaring despotism of Muslim rulers and the widespread injustices inflicted by both rulers and courtiers on their subjects. The rulers, in their turn, had either directly or indirectly fallen under the domination of European Powers which forced them to grant concessions to foreigners at the expense of public interest, which aggravated the injustices to their people. The limitations imposed on the authority of Muslim rulers by foreign Powers did not only tarnish the dignity of rulers in the eyes of their subjects, but also impaired the legitimacy of their authority, presumably derived ultimately from God's Sovereign Will. Before a new standard of justice combining Islamic and foreign (secular) elements relevant to modern conditions could be accepted by the believers, Afghānī held that Muslim rulers should put an end to foreign domination and reestablish the legitimacy of their authorities. But how could such an objective be achieved?

Muslim rulers, according to Afghānī, could achieve this objective first by reform within the regime presided over by each ruler and secondly by cooperation among the rulers in their stand against foreign domination. To achieve the first step, Afghānī proposed that rulers should grant their subjects the right of participation in the exercise of authority by calling on elected assemblies to discuss public affairs in accordance with the principle of consultation (shūra) which stipulates that public affairs are open for discussion between rulers and subjects (Q. XXVII, 32; XLII, 36). In his call for elected assemblies, Afghānī sought to combine Islamic and Western principles of political justice which would command the respect of the various shades of opinion. Such a measure of reform could provide not only legitimacy for rulers but also support in their stand against foreign pressures. To achieve the second step, Afghānī proposed cooperation among Muslim rulers through their participation in a Pan-Islamic movement which had already been in progress and to which an impe-

2. The ideas and roles of Afghānī and 'Abduh as social reformers are dealt with in another work, to which the reader may be referred, entitled *Political Trends in the Arab World* (Baltimore, 1970 and 1972), chap. 4.

tus had been given by Afghānī's own call to Muslims to support it. Were all Muslim rulers, supported by their peoples, to stand against foreign domination, no foreign Power could possibly interfere in Muslim domestic affairs or find an opening to extend its influence into Islamic lands.[3]

Afghānī's proposals may seem essentially negative in nature, confined to the termination of foreign control and the reestablishment of legitimacy. True, he spent the whole of his life in the pursuit of these objectives by peaceful as well as revolutionary methods, and he died without achieving them. But he never gave up his hope that Islam, with its impressive spiritual potential and the inherent power of its peoples, would eventually be liberated from its fetters. In his spare moments, Afghānī did give some thought to what the ideal standard of justice should be for Muslims once foreign domination had come to an end. Indeed, he conceived of a standard not only for Muslims but for mankind as a whole, derived from Islamic traditions and experience as well as from the experiences of other nations. In his treatise on the refutation of the materialists,[4] he maintained that only in societies that possess higher religions capable of providing a set of spiritual and social checks on rulers which would restrain them from oppression and injustice could man lead a happy life.

But what do those restraining factors teach us, one may ask? Religion, said Afghānī, teaches three fundamental principles: First, that man is the most honorable creature who rules over the Earth; second, each man maintains that his own is the most honorable people in the world and that other peoples' beliefs are wrong; three, that every man is urged to achieve his perfection on Earth in preparation for the eternal and happy life in the hereafter. In the preparation for his perfection, man is warned against the acceptance of beliefs based on evil and wickedness, leading to oppression and injustice; he is also

3. Afghānī's call for Pan-Islamism has often been associated with the ideal of Islamic unity under the rule of one Caliph (Imām) which some leaders had advocated; in reality, however, Afghānī did not call for the unity of Islamic lands under one supreme ruler, but called for concerted action by Muslim leaders for the liberation of Muslim lands from foreign domination without necessarily entering into unity. See Jamāl al-Dīn al-Afghānī, *al-Waḥda al-Islāmīya wa al-Waḥda wa al-Siyāda* [Islamic Unity and Unity and Sovereignty], ed. 'Izzat al-'Attār (Cairo, 1938).

4. Jamāl al-Dīn al-Afghānī, *al-Radd 'Ala al-Dahriyīn* [Refutation of the Materialists], originally written in Persian and rendered into Arabic by Muḥammad 'Abduh (Cairo, 1344/1925). French trans. by A. M. Goichon, *Refutation des Materialistes* (Paris, 1942).

urged to adopt virtues which inspire love for the truth, righteousness, and justice. Those virtues, according to Afghānī, are the following:

First, the virtue of shame (al-ḥayā') which restrains man from committing certain acts for which he would be blamed and might affect adversely his good reputation. Afghānī considered this virtue much more important than laws in the maintenance of peace and order; for, if the veil of shame were lost, perhaps no penalty save capital punishment could prevent man from committing shameful acts.

Closely connected with shame is the virtue of pride and lofty-mindedness (al-ibā'). It has the same effect as shame in avoiding indecency and evil.

Second, the virtue of trust (al-amāna) which provides the very basis for honest dealing between man and man; it is indeed the invisible thread that unites the social fabric of society. Without trust it would be impossible for men to work together and carry on business to the satisfaction of all.

Third, the virtue of telling the truth. Truth is the key to an understanding of social relationship and for men's dealing with one another. For in the absence of truth, leading to confusion and distrust, lying would prevail, and the consequential destruction of the foundation of the social order would be inevitable.

The three virtues—shame, trust, and the truth—are the pillars on which the standard of order and justice is founded. In his emphasis on virtues as the human qualities necessary for the achievement of justice, Afghānī was speaking with the voice of classical Muslim scholars. But as a modern scholar who sought to identify Muslim with Western standards, he stated in no uncertain terms that these virtues were not only essential for the maintenance of order and justice in Islamic society, but for the maintenance of order and justice throughout the world. Were those virtues to vanish, he said, society would be exposed to the danger of foreign domination and oppression, as Islamic lands had experienced at the hands of European Powers.[5]

Muhammed 'Abduh, Afghānī's principal disciple, shared his master's views on justice and other matters and he supported him in his endeavors to achieve these goals. After failure of the 'Urābī revolt (1882), in which he had participated, 'Abduh saw the futility of Afghānī's methods, and after his return to Egypt from exile (1888),

5. *Ibid.*, pp. 36–46. See also Afghānī's *Khāṭirāt* [Memoirs], ed. Muḥammad al-Makhzūmī (Beirut, 1931), pp. 250–55; 316–26; 340–45; 445–49.

his ideas began to take shape independently of his master's influence. Although he continued to take an interest in justice and other measures of reform, he looked at them from a different point of view. Like Ibn Khaldūn, he devoted the rest of his life after he returned to Egypt to speculate not on the theory but on the application of justice—procedural justice in particular—whether in the position of judge (Qāḍī) or Grand Muftī. In the discharge of his task he realized the importance of the judicial system and he was determined to achieve justice through its processes. But he also realized the need for the reform of the judicial system, in the efficiency of which the West excelled, to meet the demands of changing conditions. Since it has become fashionable, almost irresistible, throughout the world to adopt Western skills, Muslims could no longer afford to ignore them. Some judges and scholars still held, in the tradition of the Revelationists, that Western innovations were incompatible with Islamic concepts, but 'Abduh argued that Western judicial processes were not inherently incompatible with Islamic procedural justice. Both in his capacity as judge and later as Muftī, 'Abduh set the example of how justice should be administered and how the Law was to be interpreted. True, some of his legal opinions, such as the Transvaal fatwa, declaring it lawful for Muslims to eat the flesh of animals slaughtered by Christians and Jews, and the fatwa permitting Muslims to deposit money in Postal Savings Banks which yield interest, were attacked by scholars who adhered to the literal interpretation of the Law in the tradition of the Revelationist scholars of old.[6] But 'Abduh paid no attention to criticism and insisted that the Law should be interpreted by Reason. In the case of conflict between the literal meaning of the Law and Reason, 'Abduh argued, the latter should be given priority, as Rationalist scholars had indeed advocated in the past.

By this method, 'Abduh provided a common ground for modern Rationalist and Revelationist scholars and saw no inherent incompatibility between the two schools of thought. He succeeded in his call for the reform of the judicial system and in the interpretation of the Law in accordance with Reason.

After his death, 'Abduh's arguments in favor of Western standards were taken up by Modernists who advocated the wholesale adoption

6. See M. Rashīd Riḍa, *Ta'rīkh al-Ustādh al-Imām Muḥammad 'Abduh* (Cairo, 1947), II, 113–18; III, 84; Muḥammad 'Umāra, *al-'Amal al-Kāmila li al-Imām Muḥammad 'Abduh* (Beirut, 1972), II, 78–95.

of Western concepts of justice, but some objected to this method concerning which they had certain mental reservations. Since 'Abduh did not work out a coherent theory of Law and justice, his disciples were divided into two schools: the Modernist, which may be called the modern Rationalist, advocated the adoption of Western standards; and the Revivalist (in the tradition of classical Revelationist), which took a more conservative attitude toward reform. The first school, while remaining loyal to 'Abduh's moral values, stressed his Rationalism and advocated the adoption of secular standards of justice. The other school, claiming to conform more closely to 'Abduh's method, took a more conservative, almost apologetic attitude in order to defend Islamic standards in the face of the influx of secular standards. This attitude, especially as espoused by 'Abduh's principal disciple Muḥammad Rashīd Rida (d. 1935), stamped the Revivalist school with traditional Revelationism, and the school lost direct touch with the new generation. Failure to agree on a common standard led to conflicts between the two schools which affected adversely the process of reform on all levels.

Political Justice Reconsidered

Like the scholars in the early Islamic period, the Modernists who tried to draw on Western standards began to adopt measures touching on the very foundation of Islamic society—the standard of political justice. New codes of law, judicial procedures, and constitutional instruments were adopted gradually from the early years of the nineteenth century, which eventually led to the transformation of the state from an Islamic (universal) state into a modern (national) state. These measures were objected to by scholars who insisted on Revelational standards, but the cooperation between Modernists and Revivalists under the influence of Jamāl al-Dīn al-Afghānī and his disciples, which culminated in the promulgation of the Ottoman constitution of 1876, proved to be a short-lived arrangement. From this turning point to the present, no common ground for constructive cooperation among Modernists and Revivalists has yet emerged. For this reason, the Turkish reformers following World War I took the drastic step of replacing almost completely Islamic standards with Western standards. The leading Muslim state (Turkey), the product of a revolutionary movement which was in progress during the latter part of the Ottoman period, disestablished the Islamic state and Islamic law (except the portions dealing with strictly religious and ritualistic practices), and eventually replaced them by Western concepts of law and authority. By taking this drastic step, the Islamic standards of political and legal justice were declared null and void. The other aspects of Islamic justice—theological, ethical, philosophical and others—though remaining outside the pale of the state (by the very act of separation between state and church), necessarily became of academic interest, and were considered irrelevant to a nation which had already adopted nationalism and secularism as its basic principles. Strictly speaking, Turkey no longer remained a Muslim state in accordance with the Islamic standard of justice, although an important portion of its people remained loyal to Islam and has in recent years reasserted some aspects of Islamic justice.

Turkey's unilateral disestablishment of the standard of political justice was rejected in principle by other Islamic lands, but most of them accepted, in varying degree, some Western concepts—parliamentary democracy, civil codes, and judicial procedures. This resulted in the establishment of two levels of political justice without any serious effort to harmonize them. The office of the Imamate remained in existence in theory, but no agreement was reached to enthrone an Imām. In some countries, his powers were exercised by local rulers in accordance with Islamic law, but in others, where parliamentary systems were established, the rulers were made responsible to the people, contrary to the Islamic standard of justice, and all other matters relating to religion and Islamic law were entrusted to religious authorities.

In the Afghānī-'Abduh Rational line of thought, only one jurist made an effort to resolve the problem of two levels of political justice created by the abolition of the Caliphate in Turkey—'Alī 'Abd al-Rāziq of Egypt. Egypt, whose constitutional structure was for long developing under the impact of European standards, had just been separated from Turkey during World War I, and its adoption of a constitution (1925) drawn on advanced European models aroused criticism in circles which still clung to Revelational standards. Rāziq may not have been the only man who felt the need for resolving the conflict between two standards, but he was the one with the great courage to publish a book in which he worked out an Islamic rationale for the abolition of the Caliphate and the secularization of the standard of political justice. Rāziq (1888–1966), combining a solid background in Islamic and Western thought and belonging to an influential family which took an active part in Egyptian politics, was in an eminent position to take the bold step in presenting an answer to the unresolved issue.[7]

Rāziq's rationale is based on two premises: first, the Caliphate, as the instrument for the exercise of Divine authority, is not inherent in Islam as a system of religion and therefore not necessary; and second, the separation between state and religion and consequently the standard of political justice would not depend on Revelation. In support of the first premise, Rāziq argued that the Revelation is silent on the matter; vague references to the subject give no ground for Caliphal authority. Nor does consensus or any other authoritative source provide guidance for its need as a form of government as defined by Muslim scholars.

From this premise Rāziq turned to the other—the separation of religion from state. This separation necessarily led to the separation of political and legal standards of justice closely connected with acts of state, from theological and moral standards connected with religious principles and values. The Prophet, said Rāziq, exercised political power necessitated by the special circumstances of his time; but his action should not be taken to imply that it was part of his religious mission. His mission was completed with his death. After him the political community was bound to establish some form of government, because it could not revert to the former state. Entrusting authority to Abū Bakr set a precedent for the Caliphate, but his office was political and not religious in nature. It was in succeeding generations that a religious significance was attached to this office—a significance which the Caliphs found in their interest to encourage. From this Rāziq concluded that the Caliphate had outlived its usefulness and might be allowed to vanish as political conditions have radically changed. Concerning the separation of political and legal justice from theological and moral justice, Rāziq held that all civil matters did not call for the association of religious with civil authorities. The Prophet never insisted that he was the best informed on civil matters. Only the principles regulating the spiritual life of believers are valid for all time

7. For a brief account of his life and thought, see my *Political Trends*, pp. 213–18.

and unchangeable; all other matters should be regarded as secular and regulated in accordance with standards of justice subject to change in accordance with the needs and aspirations of society.[8] Rāziq's rationale for possible changes in Islamic standards provided validity for the newly established national regimes in Egypt and other Arab countries. Yet both the Egyptian authority and the advocates of Revelational standards rejected it on the grounds of secularism; only Rashīd Riḍa, who claimed to have pursued 'Abduh's liberal reform method, offered a formula which would link parliamentary democracy with the Caliphate, provided the Muslim scholars were represented in the elected assemblies. Thus the Caliph, head of state, would hold the ultimate authority, and parliament, exercising legislative power, would enact all laws, provided they were in conformity with the Sharī'a. Riḍa, however, did not deal with the problem of the relationship between the Caliph and other Muslim states that came into existence after World War I.[9] 'Abd al-Razzāq al-Sanhūrī (d. 1968), a Modernist, offered the formula designed to entrust the Caliph with the titular office of the head of a confederation of independent Muslim states—a confederation which he called the Muslim League of Nations—to which is entrusted the ultimate religious authority while the secular power would be dispersed and distributed among the heads of the various Muslim states.[10] Neither formula was acceptable to Modernists and Revivalists nor provided adequate satisfaction to the needs of society: the Western standard proved unsuitable without adaptation to local values and traditions, and the Islamic standard was inadequate for a society that had been undergoing significant changes under the impact of Western material and technological innovations. As a result, conflicts and tensions and the double loyalty to two standards aggravated the conscience crisis in society. Only after half a century of almost continuous internal conflicts and tensions did the Muslim authorities, under popular pressure, begin to adapt and har-

8. For text of Rāziq's work, see 'Alī 'Abd al-Rāziq, *al-Islām wa Uṣūl al-Ḥukm* [Islam and the Sources of Authority] (Cairo, 1925); French trans., "L'Islam et les bases du pouvoir," by L. Bercher, in *Revue des ètudes Islamiques*, VII (1933), 353–91; VIII (1934), 163–222.

9. Rashīd Riḍa, *al-Khilāfa aw al-Imāma al-'Uzma* [The Caliphate or the High Imamate] (Cairo, 1341/1922); French trans., *Le Califat dans là doctrine de Rașid Rida*, by H. Laoust (Beirut, 1938).

10. A. Sanhoury, *Le Califa: Son évolution vers une Société des Nations Orientales* (Paris, 1926).

monize Western and Islamic standards. No theory of political justice has yet emerged, however, and the sovereignty of God, dispersed into more than two dozen independent political entities, is gradually being transformed into sovereign national republics, and the standard of political justice in each has been remodelled somewhat differently from the other, notwithstanding that the constituent elements in each are a combination of Islamic and foreign concepts.

A standard of political justice acceptable to the public is obviously needed. Some of its components, closely related to the social and legal standards of justice, are today the subject of animated debate in various Islamic countries, but no clear pattern has yet emerged. Ethical justice, though closely related to theological and philosophical justice, is indirectly dealt with in the debate on legal and social justice, but it has not yet been fully scrutinized by Modernists. Scholars who have taken an interest in religion (theology) and philosophy have yet to explore the aspects of justice relating to their fields.[11] The two major aspects of justice with which Muslim scholars—Revivalists and Modernists—are deeply preoccupied today are the social (distributive) and the legal aspects of justice. The latter will be dealt with first as an example of the debate among scholars on legal justice.

The Debate on Legal Justice

Three codes of legal justice are chosen to illustrate the methods pursued to provide standards designed to meet society's needs—the civil code, the code of personal status, and the penal code. Since these codes have aroused intense controversy between Modernists and Revivalists, it might be illuminating to discuss the basic principles and issues involved in the preparation of each one. Let us discuss first the steps taken in the enactment of the Islamic civil code.

The jurists who prepared a modern Islamic civil code have on the whole pursued an empirical method, proceeding from one step to another in a practical manner to bring the classical standard to terms

11. A modernist attempt at formulating proposals for a new religious (essentially theological-moral) standard was made by Muḥammad Iqbāl in the early twentieth century. While Iqbāl's writings attracted the attention of a few Western scholars, it had virtually no important impact on Islamic countries outside the Indian sub-continent. See Muhammad Iqbal, *The Reconstruction of Religious Thought in Islam* (Oxford, 2nd ed., 1934).

with life. In the preparation of such a code, the first step which they undertook was to codify those relevant parts of Islamic law which related to obligation and contract, thus forming a modern Islamic civil code (although by no means embodying all aspects of a civil code), which came to be known under the name *al-Majalla,* issued in 1869.[12] Derived in the main from one school of law (the Ḥanafī school, although recourse had also been made to other schools), the code was a significant landmark in the evolution of a modern standard of legal justice. However, the *Majalla* (although the Western influence is shown only in the form in which it was drafted) established a precedent for the possibility of change in Islamic standards. The next step was to deal with the substance of justice.

From this point of view, Islamic lands may be divided into three categories. First are those countries that followed Islamic law without significant changes in their standards of justice: northern and central Arabia (now called Sa'udi Arabia) conformed primarily to the Ḥanbalī school of law; southern Arabia, consisting of the Yaman (which officially followed the Zaydī law), 'Adan (Aden) and the southern coast, conformed to the Shāfi'ī school; and south-east Arabia followed partly the 'Ibāḍī school of law (the official school in 'Uman) and partly the Shāfi'ī school. Second are those countries that followed Islamic law with some modifications as codified by the Ottoman authorities. After the breakup of the Ottoman Empire, most of the successor states—'Iraq, Syria, Palestine, Transjordan (now Jordan), and Libya—continued to follow the *Majalla.* Third, those countries that adopted the French Civil Code as a model—Egypt, Lebanon, Tunisia, Algeria, and Morocco—remained loyal to Islamic law only with regard to matters of personal status. Similarly, Muslims in southern Asia (Pakistan, Bangladesh and others) developed codes of law which were essentially Islamic in substance but which had been modified by local traditions after these countries passed under foreign control.[13]

12. The full name of the code is *Majallat al-Aḥkām al-'Adlīya* [Digest of the Principles of Justice]. For the origins and nature of the code, see S. S. Onar, "The Majalla," in Khadduri and Liebesny, eds., *Law in the Middle East* (Washington, D.C., 1955), I, chap. 12.

13. The classic case is the development of Islamic law in the Indian sub-continent into a system of law that came to be known under the hybrid Anglo-Muḥammadan law to meet the needs of Muslims in that region. See H. J. Liebesny, *The Law of the Near and the Middle East* (Albany, N. Y., 1975), pp. 118–25.

This situation remained essentially unchanged until World War II, when the countries that had been under foreign control gradually achieved independence. Their experiences with the administration of justice demonstrated that neither a purely Western nor an exclusively Islamic standard proved satisfactory without some modification. A conflict between two schools of thought ensued: the Modernists, advocating a complete change, denounced the strict conformity to the Islamic standard as incompatible with modern conditions; and the Revivalists demanded full restoration of Islamic standards. To the Revivalists the issue was of greater significance; Western codes adopted in Islamic lands under foreign control were never really recognized as part of the Islamic legal system (indeed, there were two parallel legal systems in existence), but upon achieving independence, when the Western codes were to be integrated into the existing legal systems, these codes were bound to be modified. Egypt and 'Iraq, representing two entirely different sets of civil codes—the latter was Islamic and the former French—showed readiness to adopt new civil codes, as both had come to the conclusion that neither one was adequate to the need of each.

'Iraq took the first step when 'Abd al-Razzāq al-Sanhūrī, the Egyptian jurist, was invited to head a committee to draft a new civil code. The work of the committee, despite interruptions, was completed and enacted into law in 1951. Before the law came into force in 'Iraq, it was adopted, not without modification, by Syria in June 1949. Meanwhile, a new civil code for Egypt was prepared by Sanhūrī and came into force in October 1949. The code was derived primarily from the French Civil Code and from Egypt's own experiences with the administration of justice when the national courts assumed full jurisdiction after the abolition of the Mixed Courts.

In the preparation of the draft civil codes for 'Iraq, Syria, and Egypt, Sanhūrī pursued a practical approach by adopting a standard of justice consisting essentially of Western elements—French, Swiss, German, and others—which he considered compatible with Islamic principles. The blend of Western and Islamic principles became the basis of a new standard of legal justice for these countries as well as for others which were to adopt it. Sanhūrī retained a few concepts from the Islamic standard which had no equal in Western standards, such as the Shuf'a sale, and he modified others that were not quite compatible with the Islamic standard, such as the sale of property not available for immediate delivery.[14] But he found it exceedingly difficult to justify the use of "interest" (fā'ida), a Western concept, for which there is no equivalent in Islamic standards. On the contrary, the Islamic concept of usury (riba), which the Revelation and Traditions repudiate, was considered by most Muslim scholars to include "interest."

Drafting the 'Iraqī Civil Code, Sanhūrī consciously avoided grappling with the problem of interest, partly because it was not dealt with in the *Majalla,* the code that had been in force in 'Iraq, and partly because it would arouse the opposition of scholars who considered it contrary to Islamic standards. In practice, however, interest had already become part of the economic system, notwithstanding that its use in business transactions had yet to be justified. In Egypt, the situation was somewhat different from 'Iraq as its former civil code, a replica of the French Civil Code, took interest for granted, and the question of its justification in accordance with Islamic standards had not yet arisen. This situation, however, completely changed when Egypt decided to bring its new civil code into harmony with Islamic standards. Since interest had become part of the economic system and was recognized under the former civil code, Sanhūrī was bound to justify it on Islamic grounds.

It is true that Muslim scholars in Egypt—indeed, in all other Islamic lands—equated interest with usury and most of them insisted that it should be prohibited. However, some were prepared to agree with Modernists that a distinction between usury as a transaction between money-lenders (murābin: usurers) and interest as a transaction between economic institutions (banks and others) and investors must be made. But such a subtle distinction between interest and usury was rejected by the Revivalists on the grounds that it was not

14. The drafting committee adopted the Western concept of sale partly on the basis of the practice prevailing in 'Iraq and partly on the strength of the opinion of a classical jurist, Ibn al-Qayyim al-Jawzīya, whom we met before (see chap. 6, section on Equity and Judicial Procedure) and who proposed that if the reason for prohibiting sale with deferred delivery did not arise, the sale would be valid. See Munīr al-Qāḍī, "Bay' al-Ma'dūm" [Sale of Property Not in Evidence], *Majallat al-Qadā',* II (1936), 19–29). For Sanhūrī's draft code concerning sale, see *ibid.,* pp. 223–394 (including a memorandum on the method pursued). For text of the enacted 'Irāqī Civil Code, see Kāmil al-Samarrā'ī, ed., *al-Qānūn al-Madanī al-'Irāqī* [The 'Irāqī Civil Code] (Baghdad, 1951).

very significant and should be discounted.[15] Sanhūrī, accepting without hesitation the distinction between interest and usury, recognized interest but he failed to provide a rationale for it.[16]

For a long time, the concept of usury, as defined in the Revelation, has been the subject of debate among scholars to determine whether its meaning (which literally is "increase") would be binding in all kinds of transactions. In the Revelation, the texts read as follows:

> God has permitted sale and forbidden usury. (Q. II, 276)
>
> O believers, devour not usury, doubled and redoubled, and fear your God . . . (Q. III, 125)
>
> And for their [Jews] taking usury, that they were prohibited, and consuming wealth of the people in vanity . . . (Q. IV, 159)
>
> And what you give in usury, that it may increase upon the people's wealth, increase not with God . . . (Q. XXX, 38)

Since there is the possibility of profit in all business transactions, which is obviously a kind of increase from sale as well as from other transactions, the meaning of usury as a kind of "increase" in the Revelation must be taken as a special kind and must be distinguished from other kinds. According to the leading jurists—Mālik, Shāfi'ī and Ibn Ḥanbal (three of the four founders of the recognized Sunnī schools of law)—the concept of usury was construed to mean increase only in lending transactions, but not necessarily in other kinds. Their position was based on Traditions from the Prophet which run as follows:

> Let no one exchange gold for gold save in equal quantities, or increase one quantity against the other. Let no one exchange silver for silver save in equal quantities, or increase one quantity against another. Let no one exchange anything at hand for another not in evidence.[17]

15. See Shaykh 'Abd al-'Azīz Ibn Rashīd, *Mā Huwa al-Riba al-Muḥarram* [What Is the Prohibited Usury?] (Alexandria, n.d.); 'Alā' al-Dīn Kharūfa, *al-Riba wa al-Fā'ida* [Usury and Interest] (Baghdad, 1381/1962).

16. Having known Sanhūrī from his works as well as a friend over the years, I have the greatest respect for and sympathy with his contribution to legal secularism (see my *Political Trends in the Arab World*, pp. 239–44); but my own studies in Islamic law have shown that he has not really been able to resolve the theoretical question of the harmony between Western and Islamic legal standards.

17. Mālik, *al-Muwaṭṭa'*, II, 632–33; Bukhārī, *Ṣaḥīḥ*, II, 31; Muslim, *Ṣaḥīḥ*, XI, 8–12. For a different wording, see Abū Dāwūd, *Sunan*, III, 249 (trans. Khadduri, *Islamic Jurisprudence*, p. 210).

Al-riba (usury) is to be found in al-nasī'a (deferred payment).[18]

Other jurists, however, have taken the position that increase as a principle should be applicable to all kinds of transactions and not specifically to lending transactions which had been prevailing in pre-Islamic society. Abū Ḥanīfa, founder of a leading school of law, while he accepted usury in principle, he limited its applications to highly usurious cases. In practice, however, the opinion of other jurists, confirmed by consensus (ijmā'), that any kind of increase was equated with usury prevailed and became binding on succeeding generations. As a result, people in need of credit were often compelled to resort to casuistic methods (al-ḥiyal al-Shar'īya) in order to justify the practice of usury, and the standard of legal justice thus tended to be divorced from reality. Despite the protest of Ḥanbalī scholars, the Ḥanafī jurists continued to assist money lenders by casuistic methods on the grounds that the principle of prohibition was applicable only to highly usurious cases. The widespread practice of usury, in a society morally opposed to it in principle, created a resentment which has been aggravated in the modern age by high interest rates following the introduction of Western business methods into Islamic lands.

Not only did Islam experience a conscience crisis; Western Christendom had passed through similar experiences. In Europe the Jews felt free to lend money to gentiles; but Christians were not allowed to practice usury according to the canon law. They debated the question for a long time before it was finally resolved in the sixteenth century.[19] To resolve the problem of usury in Islam, it may not necessarily take as long as it did in Europe, but Muslims have yet to grapple with it. Most scholars are not unaware that the classical concept of usury is no longer compatible with reality, but they have not yet been able to work out a formula acceptable to the public. The principal points which are still being debated may be summed up as follows:

1. Should interest, though it may have a certain common element with usury, be equated with usury?

2. Should the concept of interest be defined strictly in the sense of an increase in business transactions, regardless of whether it is used for productive or consumptive purposes?

18. Mālik, *op. cit.*, II, 633; Muslim, *op. cit.*, XI, 11; Abū Dāwūd, *op. cit.*, III, 248 (trans. Khadduri, *op. cit.*, p. 211).

19. For the controversy about usury in Western Christendom, see B. N. Nelson, *The Idea of Usury* (Princeton, 1949), and a bibliography on the subject, pp. 167–220.

3. Should the interest rate determined by an agreement between money lenders be equated with that determined by the authorities?

Revivalists, though admitting the validity of such subtle distinctions, have not yet been reconciled to accept a secular concept of interest. At bottom, the problem is not substantive but methodological. Like their classical predecessors, the Revivalists are bound to recognize eventually new concepts to meet the need for new conditions. Ibn Taymīya, it will be recalled, had already set a precedent in developing the concept of political laws (siyāsa Sharʿīya) as a concession to social reality. Whether in the form of political laws or new legislation by representative assemblies, the demand for accommodation can be justified on the grounds of necessity. Indeed, necessity has already been accepted as a principle in Islamic jurisprudence and the *Majalla* conceded that it can supersede certain specific rules.[20] Thus a prohibited act may, in accordance with this principle, become permissible if compelling circumstances require the relaxation or the suspension of the act. Since interest has become an integral part of the economic system, usury should be considered obsolete and no longer binding according to the principle of necessity.

Second, the enactment of codes of personal status:

The Modernists who prepared civil codes to meet immediate needs failed to provide a fully convincing rationale to resolve the conscience crisis. In the preparation of the code of personal status, however, the Revivalists made it crystal clear that they would not depart from the principles of the Islamic standard. In substance, the code which they laid down may not have been up to expectation; in method, however, it was the product of a more careful scrutiny of the Law and provided the necessary nexus between old and new standards which set the public conscience at rest.

Unlike the *Majalla,* enacted in 1877, the Law of Family Rights (dealing with all matters of personal status) was not possible to enact until 1917 when the Ottoman Empire was on the verge of collapse. Except in form, this code conformed in substance to the classical standard and remained in force (not without changes to meet local differences) in the successor states until it was replaced by modern

20. The *Majalla* (Art. 21) states that "necessities may supersede certain prohibited acts" (al-ḍarūrāt tubīḥ al-maḥḍūrāt).

codes.[21] The classical standard, however, remained essentially the same without significant changes in substance. Polygamy was reasserted in principle, although the Egyptian and Syrian codes provided procedural restrictions, and divorce remained the privilege of the husband. Very soon changes in the scale of family relationships were bound to take place owing to improvement in social conditions and the spread of education in urban society.

In the postwar years, several Muslim countries, in response to popular demands, began to introduce significant changes in the status of women, but only two countries—Tunisia in 1956 and 'Iraq in 1959—abolished polygamy and put women on a status of equality with men. Despite opposition, the Tunisian code is still in force, but the 'Iraqī code, under pressure of Revivalists arguing that the Revelation cannot be repealed in principle, was modified in 1963. The modified code recognized polygamy but qualified it with certain restriction (provided permission was granted by the judge on the basis of specific reasons given to justify the taking of a second wife), which virtually rendered polygamy a dead letter in practice. The 'Iraqī code, however, retained the Shī'ī provisions concerning inheritance, which were considered more liberal. While the Tunisian code may be taken to represent the viewpoint of Modernists, the 'Iraqī code, which granted women virtually equal privileges but fell short of granting equality of status, struck a compromise between the viewpoints of Revivalists and Modernists.[22]

The Tunisian code contains three basic principles which made a radical change in the classical standard of justice in favor of women. First, the abolition of polygamy (Article 18) was justified on the grounds that it is impossible for a husband to be just in his relationships with more than one wife in accordance with the Revelation (Q. IV, 129). Second, women were granted the right to divorce just as men could under the classical law, provided that the divorce in either case was obtained through a court hearing in which the reason for the divorce was given (Articles 30–31). Third, women were granted equal

21. In Turkey an entirely new code of personal status was adopted when the Sharī'a as a whole was abolished, but in all the successor states it was observed, and it is still in force for Muslims in Lebanon and Israel.

22. For texts of the Tunisian and 'Irāqī codes, see N. T. Sanūsī, ed., *Majallat al-Aḥwāl al-Shakhṣīya* [Tunisian Code of Personal Status] (Tunis, 1956); and Kāmil al-Sāmarrā'ī, ed., *al-Aḥwāl al-Shakhṣīya* [The 'Irāqī Code of Personal Status] (Baghdad, 1973).

rights in all of their relationships with men, including inheritance. These provisions were justified on the strength of the principle of equality, although Revivalists are not sure that the provisions are all in conformity with Islamic standards.[23]

Like 'Iraq, the other Islamic countries recognized plural marriage in principle but laid down restrictions ranging from those granting in practice full status to women, to others that stipulated relatively less severe restrictions. Moreover, the restrictions were to be either self-imposed, as in the case of Morocco, or subject to court hearings, as in the case of several other countries including Egypt and Syria.[24] Apart from the Tunisian code, the codes of other Muslim countries seem to be consistent with Islamic standards and provide a link between Islamic and modern standards.

Modernists maintain that the abolition of polygamy in Tunisia is justified on the grounds of the Revelation which warns husbands: "But if you fear you will not be just, then only one [wife];" and "You will not be able to be just between your wives, even though you be eager to do so" (Q. IV, 129). Long before the Tunisian Code was enacted, Muḥammad 'Abduh had often argued on the strength of the Revelation that no man could possibly be just to more than one wife under modern conditions of life.[25] Revivalists, however, contend that the Revelations referred to in the Tunisian Code are only qualifying clauses to other Revelations (Q. IV, 4, 128–30) and therefore cannot possibly supersede or repeal the overriding Revelation which states: "If you fear that you cannot act with justice towards the orphans, marry such women as seem good to you, two or three or four . . . " (Q. IV, 4). No Modernist, to the best of my knowledge, has ever tried to justify the limitation of plural marriage on the grounds of justice, not in reference to a specific qualifying clause, but as the ultimate purpose of the Revelations as a whole. Nevertheless, it seems relevant to ask whether the Quranic legislation was meant to confirm the licentious pre-Islamic practice of polygamy or to reform it by imposing quantitative and qualitative restrictions on its practice.

23. For the argument in favor of equality between men and women, see 'Allāl al-Fāsī, *Maqāṣid al-Sharī'a al-Islāmīya* [Purposes of Islamic Law] (al-Dār al-Bayḍā' [Casablanca], 1963), pp. 241–44; cf. Abū Zahra "Family Law," in Khadduri and Liebesny, eds., *Law in the Middle East*, I, 132–78.

24. For texts of the various codes of personal status, see Ṣalāḥ al-Dīn al-Nāhī, ed., *Family Laws* (Baghdad, 1956).

25. See Rashīd Riḍa, *op. cit.*, II, 113–18; Muḥammad 'Umāra, *op. cit.*, II, 78–95.

The Prophet, as a social reformer, did not attempt to bring about complete change; rather he sought to effect gradual change in marital relationships, although the ultimate purpose seems clear in retrospect. Viewed from this perspective, it would seem that the Revelation concerning marriage sought to reform the practice of polygamy to the extent possible at the time, rather than to ratify it. By restricting the practice, the Revelation's logical end was to transform marriage from a polygamous to a monogamous relationship. The Revelation thus was not intended to endorse polygamy but to legitimize monogamy. In taking this broader view, the Tunisian code has not strayed far from the purpose of the Revelation, which is to achieve justice, and may well be considered to have set a precedent for other countries if the time should ever come for their codes of personal status to be revised.

In comparing the endeavors of scholars who prepared the codes of personal status with those who laid down the civil codes, it seems obvious that Modernists, although they set an example by providing a synthesis between Western and Islamic standards, were not very original, as the bulk of the subject matter of the civil codes was borrowed from European codes. The Revivalists who laid down the codes of personal status began to look at the question from the opposite direction—to re-examine the concepts of justice that were no longer adequate for Islamic society and to revise them in the light of the experiences of both Islamic and other societies. In attempting to reform Islamic standards from within, in contrast with Modernists who depended heavily on Western law, they proved more constructive by providing codes that seem to meet immediate necessities and to command public respect.[26]

Third, the Islamic Penal Code:

The Revivalists, however, have shown perhaps less flexible position in the preparation of a draft code of penal justice than in the codes of personal status. Apart from the countries that still conform to classical standards, Egypt is the first country that has shown readiness to modify its Western penal code, which has long been in force, and to bring it into harmony with Islamic standards. When the Azhar University, the leading Islamic institution of learning, was invited to participate

26. The writer has drawn freely from his articles, "Marriage in Islamic Law: The Modernist Viewpoints," *American Journal of Comparative Law*, XXVI (1978), 213–18; "Some Contemporary Concepts of Islamic Law," *World Congress on Philosophy of Law and Social Philosophy* (Wiesbaden, 1982), pp. 81–85.

in the preparation of a draft penal code by the People's Assembly, its scholars submitted a set of proposals with no significant change from the standard of classical penal justice.[27] In brief, the Revelation provides that offenses are forbidden acts for which punishments are determined by either a legal penalty (ḥadd) or discretionary act (ta'zīr). The offenses are as follows: theft (al-sariqa), brigandage (al-ḥirāba), fornication and adultery (al-zina), drinking of wine (al-shirb), false accusation of indecency (al-qadhf), and apostasy (al-ridda). The punishment for theft is amputation of the right hand; for brigandage it is death, if the objective were a threat on life, and amputation, if the offense were confined to property. The punishment for fornication is one hundred lashes, and for adultery it is stoning to death for both the man and the woman; for drinking (including involvement with any kind of intoxicating beverage) it is eighty lashes; and for apostasy, the punishment is death, unless the apostate is prepared to repent.[28] These penalties were precisely defined in an explanatory memorandum, and the circumstances as well as the manner in which they should be applied were carefully described.[29] In principle, the draft code did not depart from the classical standard, but showed greater flexibility in procedure which rendered some penalties, such as apostasy, to be a dead letter since the moment the apostate changed his mind or denied that he had apostatized, he would not be liable for punishment.[30] This penalty, however, is contrary to the principle of religious freedom which Egypt has accepted under the Universal Declaration of Human Rights. It is also contrary to the spirit of the Revelation which states that "there is no compulsion in religion" (Q. II, 257), although this text is construed by most commentators to mean freedom in the choice of Islam, but not in turning one's back to it.[31]

Revivalists are not all in agreement that the classical standard of penal justice should be embodied in the new penal law, including some who were on the Azhar faculty such as Shaykh Maḥmūd Shaltūt,

27. For text of the proposals, see The High Committee (of al-Azhar) for the Review of Legislation in Conformity with the Sharī'a, *Mashrū' Qānūn al-Ḥudūd al-Shar'īya* [Proposals for the Islamic Penal Code], ed. 'Abd al-'Azīz Hindī (Cairo, 1978).

28. See *ibid.*, pp. 14–22.

29. For the explanatory memorandum, see *ibid.*, p. 24ff.

30. See *ibid.*, p. 22.

31. The explanatory memorandum states that the acceptance of communism, which repudiates belief in God, amounts to the repudiation of Islam. *Ibid.*, p. 46.

a former Rector, and others.[32] Although the Revelation is clear about some penalties, such as homicide, it is not as clear about other penalties, such as drinking. The Revelation only warns men against the harmfulness of drinking and does not necessarily call for punishment. Above all, the ultimate purpose of the Revelational penalties is not to undermine, but to promote peace and order, and to urge men to avoid committing indecent and offensive acts; indeed, the Revelation does not prescribe retributive justice for all wrongs, as some belong to God who will punish wrongdoers on the Day of Judgement. Moreover, Modernists are not all prepared to accept a standard of penal justice drawn only on Islamic standards. For a modern standard of penal justice to be meaningful, it must be drawn on both Islamic and Western standards, modified in accordance with society's needs. Were Egypt to enact a penal code combining the best elements from Islamic and Western standards, its code would likely be a model for other Islamic lands.

The Debate on Social Justice

The form of social justice which Modernists and Revivalists began to debate in the modern age is known to Western thinkers as distributive justice. This term, coined by Aristotle, was not unknown to Muslim scholars, but it was used in the quantitative and not in the modern social sense. Revivalists who agreed with Modernists on the need for the adoption of one form or another of distributive justice have disagreed on the evidence for its justification as well as on the method of adoption. The Modernists, considering its adoption as an expression of the general will, were influenced in the main by Western ideals and they maintained that distributive justice was in the public interest and therefore, they argued, there was no need for justification on Islamic grounds. The wholesale adoption of foreign concepts by Modernists, paying little or not attention to Islamic standards, was entirely unacceptable to Revivalists, not to speak of conservative scholars. Indeed, some of the Revivalists who did not object to certain foreign measures were opposed to the method of accepting them without a nexus which

32. Maḥmūd Shaltūt, *Fiqh al-Qur'ān wa al-Sunna: al-Qiṣāṣ* [The Jurisprudence of the Qur'ān and Tradition Concerning Penalties] (Cairo, 1946).

would provide a rationale for harmonizing foreign and Islamic standards. Such a nexus was indeed necessary, as it would keep the conscience of the community at rest.

At first the debate began on private ownership and the relationship between property and the individual. Before Islamic society was exposed to foreign economic doctrines—often summed up under the categories of collectivism and free enterprise—Islam had in the past maintained a standard consisting of both categories, perhaps with an emphasis on libertarian principles as the trends in its development down the centuries seem to indicate. When Muslims began to adopt European concepts (coinciding with the domination of some Islamic lands by European powers), Islam's economic system became increasingly linked with the European system, and its standard of justice was necessarily influenced by European standards. Disparity between landlords and the merchant community (often referred to as "capitalist") on the one hand and peasants and workers on the other, gradually began to widen, which adversely affected the religious and ethical standards of justice and contributed to social and political unrest. As a result, European collectivist doctrines found an opening into Islamic society, and their advocates—first the intellectuals, and later the working classes—began to argue that Islamic concepts of social justice were opposed to vested interest and the rich who accepted a Western capitalist scale of justice.

The advocates of both collectivism and free-enterprise sought to justify their doctrines on Islamic grounds, as there is ample evidence in the textual sources in favor of both. The controversy centered on whether the Islamic standard was in conformity with social (distributive) justice or opposed to it. This question may perhaps be answered, or at least clarified, by a discussion on whether the relationship between property and the individual is essentially based on egalitarian or libertarian principles.

In theory, all property belongs to God on the grounds that He has created everything in Heaven and Earth. The Revelation, often reminding men that God is the ultimate Sovereign on Earth, states:

> Is not indeed what is in Heaven and what is in the Earth belongs to God? (Q. X, 56)
>
> Is not, verily, whoever is in the Heavens and whoever in the Earth belongs to God? (Q. X, 66)

Implied in these texts is the principle that ownership of property belongs *ab initio* to God. God has granted men only the right to enjoy property; for, as the Revelation states, men were admonished:

> Have you not seen, God has subjected to you whatever is in the Heaven and Earth? (Q. XXXI, 19; Q. ILV, 12)
>
> It is He who created for you all that is in the Earth. (Q. II, 29)

The other basic principle, which qualifies the first, is that God, though ultimately the owner of property, has granted men the right of "possession." It is not clear from the Revelation, however, whether God has granted the right of possession to men collectively without the intention of distribution among individuals or whether He left to men the mode or modes of distribution. Opinions on the subject varied, as texts from the authoritative sources were cited in support of either point of view. From the early Islamic period when opposing views on the subject were proposed, one school maintained that the purpose of the Revelation was to keep property in the possession of men collectively, even though some might make exclusive use of it. Others argued in favor of distribution and the inherent right of the individual to acquire and transfer property from hand to hand.

The first school of thought (that God has left the possession of property to men collectively) may be found in early legislation, especially in the decrees concerning the acquisition of lands by conquest from neighboring countries. The jurists held that since all lands belong to God, the enemy territory that passed under Islamic control should remain in possession of the state on behalf of the believers collectively rather than to be divided among them individually.[33] But lands previously owned by individual Muslims remained in their exclusive control. Thus, the two principles of collective and individual ownership were indeed recognized, although the principle of collective ownership was not applied to movable property. Nevertheless, the other school of thought, which argued in favor of private ownership, continued to influence the development of the Law and to affirm the principle of private ownership. In time it was taken for granted that private ownership had become the established principle, qualified by an increasing number of restricting acts reflecting the pressure of groups which still argued that the principle of collective ownership

33. See Abū Yūsuf, *Kitāb al-Kharāj* [Book of Taxation] (Cairo, 1352/1934), pp. 23–27.

was valid. In other words, individual ownership (freedom) may be said to have become the overriding principle, qualified by collectivist restrictions (equality).

Two sets of restrictions may be noted: (1) restrictions provided by the Revelation, and (2) restrictions established by precedents and given expression in legal digests. Although the two textual sources—Revelations and Traditions—seem to recognize the overriding principle of individual ownership, there are texts which qualify individual freedom in favor of collectivism. These restrictions, as we have already had occasion to discuss, may be summed up as follows: the legal alms (zakāt), the usury (riba), the pious foundation (waqf), the preemption (shuf'a), restriction on inheritance right by wills, and confiscation of private ownership by the state. The acceptance of these principles obviously reflected concessions of free enterprise to distributive justice.[34]

In the modern age, when Modernists, under the influence of European ideologies, began to advocate social justice, Revivalists at first reacted negatively, partly because these ideas originated in non-Islamic societies, but primarily because they were based on a materialist philosophy, devoid of moral and spiritual values. Later, beginning in the post-war years, when the younger generation became disenchanted with the slow progress achieved under an oligarchic older generation, they began to attack them on the grounds that they were oppressive and unjust. Although the young generation was divided into two groups—one group which called for distributive justice in accordance with Western standards, and another which advocated a form of social justice in accordance with Islamic (collectivist) standards—the uneasy alliance between these two groups was negative in character because of the inherent conflict between two opposing philosophies; therefore, it was not expected to endure too long. By invoking Islamic principles in favor of distributive justice, the radicals (often called Islamic Communists or Islamic Marxists) sought to attract confirmed believers to their ranks; but the moderates, who were not unaware of the inherent incompatibility between the two systems, preferred to develop their own Islamic standard of social justice.[35]

34. See chap. 6, section on Substantive Justice.

35. For a discussion of the background and conflicting principles of these groups, see my *Political Trends in the Arab World* (Baltimore, 1970), chaps. 4–5.

Several Muslim groups began to make their appearance in response to public concern about the falling away from Islamic standards. Two representative groups may be chosen as examples of those who directly addressed themselves to social justice: the Muslim Brotherhood (al-Ikhwān al-Muslimūn) of Egypt, and the Islamic group (al-Jamā'ā al-Islāmīya) of Pakistan. Their appeal (especially that of the Brotherhood) was not confined to one particular country but to all other Islamic lands. The Muslim Brotherhood, under the leadership of Ḥasan al-Bannā (d. 1951), was organized in the mid-twenties, but it became more articulate and vocal in its call for new economic doctrines after World War II. The Islamic group, under the leadership of Abū al-A'la al-Mawdūdī (d. 1979), was organized after the establishment of Pakistan and sought to assert Revelational standards against collectivist doctrines, although its emphasis was in the main on credal and devotional matters.

The Brotherhood of Egypt dealt in particular with the political and economic reorganization of society. It reproached young men who turned their eyes to foreign economic systems when Islam, it asserted, possessed the ideal standard. The combined merits of all Western doctrines could, the Brotherhood claimed, be found in Islamic standards. The basic principle of social justice, according to the Brotherhood, was to be found in the Revelation which states: "But do not give the fools property that God assigned to you" (Q. IV, 4); and in a Tradition in which the Prophet said: "Lawful wealth belongs to him who is good." As stated earlier, Islam recognizes the principle of private ownership and the right of disposition and the transfer of property from hand to hand, provided that public interest and the promotion of the community's welfare are protected. It also urges believers to exploit natural resources for the good of the community as prescribed in the Revelation.[36] From these and other Islamic teachings,the Brotherhood concluded that the economic life of the community should be based on just standards. In order to achieve this goal, the Brotherhood called for industrialization, nationalization of public utilities, and acquisition of all foreign firms and capital by the state. The Brotherhood, though asserting free enterprise in principle, urged the state to play a greater role in the organization of economic life.

36. Ḥasan al-Bannā, *Mushkilātuna* (Cairo, n.d.).

But in general, it aimed at keeping a balance between freedom and equality.[37]

The Islamic group, while in agreement with the Brotherhood in its opposition to collectivist standards, stressed individual ownership more strictly and rejected state ownership of land, although state ownership of land had its precedents in early Islamic practice. Like the Brotherhood, it was prepared to come to terms with life and accept modification of Islamic standards, yet it stressed more strictly traditional values. Unlike the Brotherhood, however, the deep concern of the Islamic group was not for social justice in the narrow distributive sense, but in the broad sense that Islam, as a way of life, provided an equitable standard, and the group hoped that all Muslims in the Indian sub-continent would accept its ideas.[38] After the establishment of Pakistan, the Islamic group demanded that the new state should be a republic based on Islamic standards. The constitutions of Pakistan (1950, 1962), recognizing Western standards of justice, stressed free enterprise and paid only lip service to Islamic (Revelationist) standards of social justice—a point often reiterated in official pronouncements. Describing Pakistan as an Islamic republic, the Islamic group sought to reassert Islamic standards in all walks of life, but the Modernists were nevertheless able to transform the Islamic community into a modern national state.[39]

Some Muslim countries which were prepared to accept moderate collectivist (distributive) standards of justice, at first saw no reason to justify them on Islamic grounds. Turkey was perhaps the first Muslim country that adopted collectivist standards, but they were neither called socialist nor were they justified on Islamic grounds. Turkey had

37. For a discussion of the Brotherhood's economic ideas as a whole, see Sayyid Quṭb, *al-'Adāla al-Ijtimā'īya fī al-Islām* [Social Justice in Islam], trans. J. B. Hardie (Washington, D.C., 1953); *Ma'rakat al-Islām wa al-Ra'smālīya* [Struggle between Islam and Capitalism] (Cairo, 2nd ed., 1952). For a brief summary, see Khadduri, *Political Trends,* pp. 81–84; Richard Mitchell, *The Society of the Muslim Brothers* (London, 1969).

38. For Mawdūdī's political and economic ideas, see Abū al-A'la al-Mawdūdī, *Mas'alat Malakīyat al-Ard fī al-Islām* [Question of Land Ownership in Islam], trans. Ḥaddād (from Urdu) (Damascus, 1956); and "Economic and Political Teachings of the Qur'ān," in Sharif, ed., *History of Muslim Philosophy* (Wiesbaden, 1963), pp. 78–98.

39. For the controversy of the various Muslim groups over the constitutional structure of the newly created state of Pakistan, see E.I.J. Rosenthal, *Islam in the Modern National State* (Cambridge, 1964), chap. 8.

already disestablished Islam as a political and legal system (though not Islam as a religion) by revolutionary actions, and sought to justify the adoption of collectivist doctrines, called "etatism," on secular grounds (nationalism, *raison d'état*, and others), and not on Islamic grounds.[40] It was relatively easy for Turkey to renounce Islam as a system, because the Turks claimed that Islam had not been part of their national heritage. Other Islamic lands—the Arab countries in particular—refused to follow the example of Turkey. And yet all Muslim countries have adopted some collectivist measures in varying degree without the intention of renouncing or compromising Islamic standards.

Some of the Arab countries which claim Islamic standards to be part of their national heritage have made greater strides by adopting socialist (distributive) standards without recourse to Islam. True, some Modernists have argued that these standards should be justified on purely secular grounds (nationalism and other principles), but others preferred to pay lip service to Islam as justification for their adoption. The slogan of Islamic socialism, used by some in favor of distributive justice, is neither profound nor indeed original, as it combines Islamic and European concepts which are inherently incompatible. Some scholars, such as Khālid Muḥammad Khālid (Egypt) and Musṭafa al-Sibā'ī (Syria), deemed it necessary to stress Islamic principles as a link with the Islamic heritage; but Modernists (e.g. the Ba'th Party and other nationalist groups), under the spell of collectivist doctrines, sought justification on national (secular) grounds and paid lip service to Islam only as part of the Arab national heritage, although some, considering nationalism as an overriding principle, stressed a purely secular standard. Those conservative nationalists who held leftist views clung to the Revelational standard which considered the egalitarian principles (such as the zakat and other measures) as the very basis of Islamic socialism.[41]

40. In the post-war years, when the Turks turned to free enterprise standards, they were justified on the grounds of democratic rather than on Islamic standards, although Islamic religious and moral standards have been reasserted on various occasions in recent years.

41. For the first groups, see Khālid Muḥammad Khālid, *Min Huna Nabd'* [From Here We Start] (Cairo, 1950), trans. Fārūqī (Washington, D.C., 1953); Musṭafa al-Sibā'ī, *Ishtirākīyat al-Islām* [Islam's Socialism] (Damascus, 2nd ed., 1960); for modernists, see the works of Michel 'Aflaq and Munīf al-Razzāz; e.g., 'Aflaq, *Fī Sabīl al-Ba'th* (Damascus and Beirut, 1959 and 1962), and Razzāz, *Ma'ālim al-Ḥayāt al-'Arabiya al-Ḥurra* (Cairo and Beirut, 1953, 4th ed., 1960).

No complete synthesis of Islamic and collectivist standards of justice has yet emerged. Attempts at making such a synthesis may well be imminent in such proposed plans as the "Islamic equilibrium" (al-takāful al-ijtimā'ī) in which a balanced system combining egalitarian and free enterprise principles may be achieved. The term "takāful" (equilibrium), agreeable to Modernists and some Revivalists, combines measures of the two systems, but a synthesis of the two has yet to be achieved.[42]

It is perhaps unlikely that a synthesis which is acceptable to all shades of opinion is expected to emerge soon, since each group is still insisting on one standard or the other. It is possible, however, that a consensus might emerge in favor of a standard evolving out of several proposed plans, provided they were thrown open to public debate and tested by experience. This seems to be a healthy approach to accepting a standard of justice which consists of elements derived from Islamic and other modern standards. Although many a Modernist may prefer a standard based essentially on freedom, the majority seems to be in favor of egalitarian principles, even if they were to lead to restrictions on private ownership. To Revivalists, such a standard might be justified on the grounds of equality and brotherhood which are the foundations of the Islamic political community.

Does this mean that the modicum of libertarian principles which is wanting in the standards of some Islamic lands will remain indefinitely subordinated to egalitarian principles? Once a large measure of distributive justice is achieved, we are inclined to believe, it is likely that individual freedom would be in greater demand, and some form of a balance between egalitarian and libertarian principles might be achieved to the satisfaction of Modernists and Revivalists. The validity of this viewpoint seems borne out in the constant demand for greater freedom voiced by intellectuals, not to speak of other groups who have already accepted certain measures of distributive justice, not only for their own middle or upper-middle class, but for the nation at large. Such a demand for freedom, inherent in all societies, is a reminder to mankind that, if social justice is to endure, it must

42. For a discussion of the concept of equilibrium in the contexts of modernism and Islam, see Ismā'īl Mazhar, *al-Takāful al-Ishtirākī* [The Socialist Equilibrium] (Cairo, 1960); 'Abd-Allāh 'Alwān, *Al-Takāful al-Ijtimā'ī fī al-Islām* [The Social Equilibrium in Islam] (Aleppo, 1963).

depend ultimately on libertarian and not only on egalitarian principles.

The Reassertion of Revelational Justice

In more recent years, an extreme Islamic resurgence, rejecting all possible compromises in Islamic standards, has swept several Islamic lands. But this reassertion of Revelational standards, reminiscent of Ḥanbalism and Ash'arism in one form or another, is not new in Islamic lands. In the modern age, there have always been extremist members in almost all Revivalist groups, who rejected compromises and insisted on strict application of Revelational standards. Perhaps the most vocal and articulate of such extremists is Āyat-Allāh Rūḥ-Allāh Khumaynī, whose teachings were given expression in the Islamic Revolution of Iran in 1979. It is not our purpose to discuss the principles and goals of the Iranian Revolution, which has yet to be studied and analyzed by scholars, but to sum up the ideas and ideals of a leading Muslim thinker about justice which might throw light on the stream of thought of other co-religionists who are struggling to set the Revelational standards aright. Khumaynī has written several works dealing with a variety of subjects long before the Revolution, in Iran and in exile, especially in Najaf, where he lectured and issued many messages to his followers. But his ideas about justice are set forth in particular in a book on Islamic government.[43]

"Islam," said Khumaynī, "is committed to truth and justice." Although these concepts are not defined in Khumaynī's writings, their meaning becomes fairly clear from his discussion of the broad purposes and structure of the proposed Islamic government. By truth he meant the truth of the Revelation, and by justice he meant Divine Justice. Both are embodied in the Revelation as the ultimate source of authority—the authority proceeding from God, delegated to be exercised by the Prophet on behalf of God, and after him to the Imām. As

43. Āyat-Allāh Rūḥ-Allāh Khumaynī, *Ḥukūmat-i Islāmī* [Islamic Government], trans. Hamid Algar (with other statements and speeches of Khumaynī), under the title *Islam and Revolution* (Berkeley, 1981), pp. 27–149. For an analysis of the broader ideas and ideals of Khumaynī, see "Iran: Khumaynī's concept of the 'Guardianship of the Jurisconsult,'" in *Islam in the Political Process*, ed. J. P. Piscatori (Cambridge, 1983); pp. 160–80; and R. K. Ramazani, "Khumayni's Islam in Iran's Foreign Policy," in *Islam in Foreign Policy*, ed. A. Dawisha (Cambridge, 1983), pp. 9–32.

a Shī'ī scholar, Khumaynī accepted the legitimacy of the Imām in accordance with the principle of designation—the designation of 'Alī, the first Imām, by the Prophet, and then to 'Alī's descendants in direct line. The Imām, according to the Shī'ī doctrine, understood the full meaning of the truth and was instructed to rule with justice. But the last of the Imāms, who disappeared but will return in the capacity of al-Mahdī (messiah), left the community of believers like a flock without a shepherd, at the mercy of unjust rulers.[44] During the absence of the Imām it was taken for granted that the mujtahids (scholars) would provide guidance for shī'ī believers. In Iran, the Shah began to exercise civil authority from the sixteenth century, presumably on behalf of the Imām, leaving matters of Religion and Law to the mujtahids. Not all the mujtahids, however, stood together against the Shah when corruption and injustice prevailed, since they held that their task was to render advice but not to engage in political activities. Khumaynī maintained that the duty of the mujtahids was not merely to render advice; for if their advice were disregarded, they were duty-bound to take over authority and put an end to corruption and injustice. He appealed to the mujtahids to establish a regime presided over by the faqīhs (jurists), called the wilāyat-ī faqīh (governance of the jurists), and assume all powers in accordance with the Sharī'a. In other words, the Sharī'a, replacing all civil legislation, is the only Law on the strength of which all decisions—political, social, and others—would be taken.

There seems to be nothing very original in Khumaynī's system of government as stated in his writings, since it is essentially the same set of principles embodied in the Shī'ī standard of justice in accordance with the Twelvers' or the Ja'farī's sub-division which prevails in Iran. The significance of Khumaynī's proposals, however, is not that they were new in substance, but that they were laid down in a well-formulated program of action to meet immediate demands. Khumaynī, an activist leader, called on all scholars to reassert their religious duty by exercising an authority that has already passed under the control of secular, tyrannical, and unjust rulers. It is the duty of the scholars, he said, to cooperate and stand against the tyrant (al-taghūt)—the ruler who has been misguided by evil propensities—so that the rule of Law and Justice would be restored. Not only did the tyrant become unjust

44. See chap. 2.

and oppressive, he added, but he had also fallen under foreign pressures and adopted material and corrupt practices which ran contrary to Islamic standards. Khumaynī's call to stand in opposition to injustice was not only directed to scholars in Iran but to scholars all over Islamic lands where corruption and materialism have prevailed. Indeed, when Khumaynī began to preach his ideas, he was then in Najaf ('Iraq) where he spent over a decade in exile, and his book on Islamic government was given as lectures to young men studying Islamic law and theology before it was published in both Arabic and Persian languages.[45]

Khumaynī's immediate concern was, of course, with conditions in Iran, but his call for the "truth and justice" was a message to scholars all over Islamic lands to unite against rulers who failed to resist foreign pressures and allowed materialism to prevail. After his return, Khumaynī made no secret of his intention to stir the Islamic Revolution not only in Iran, but also in neighboring countries. Indeed, extreme elements which reasserted Revelational standards in Egypt and Saudi Arabia, to mention but two examples, responded by political agitation and uprisings against the authorities, and the Shī'a in 'Iraq and the surrounding Gulf area made no secret of their readiness to support Khumaynī's revolutionary call. Had he offered himself as leader of an Islamic Revolution, irrespective of denominational differences, as he seemed to have implied in his initial call, his impact on the resurgence of Islam might have been deeper and more widely spread; but his involvement in the immediate needs and expectations of Iran necessarily limited the area of his influence and reduced the validity of his call to a Shī'ī standard of justice. The deeper involvement of Khumaynī with the affairs of Iran and with the activities of its Supreme Council, over which he presided, the more his movement is reduced to and identified with Iranian Shī'ism which is often associated with

45. In 1964 Khumaynī was sent into exile because of his open criticism of the Shah's policies. He went to Turkey before settling in Najaf, where he continued to incite the public against the Shah both with his writings and contacts with dissidents. While Khumaynī was in exile, his elder son was assassinated in Najaf, presumably by Iranian instigators. Because of his political activities against the Shah, Khumaynī was served notice to leave 'Irāq. He went to Paris in September 1978, where he was more actively in contact with Iranian revolutionary activities. He returned to Iran in January 1979, after the Shah's departure, and participated actively in the construction of the Islamic Republic of Iran. For a brief summary of his life, see Hamid Algar, *op. cit.*, pp. 13–21.

Persian nationalism. But Khumaynī's ideas and ideals rose above national denominations, since he spoke with the voice of an Imām preceding the era of nationalism and his call was addressed not only to the Shī'a but to all who believed in his universal message of "truth and justice" all over the world.

Conclusion

In the course of our study, we have often alluded, directly or indirectly, to some of the lessons which might be drawn from Islam's experiences with justice, whether on the national or the international plane. It might not be out of order to sum up some of the broader aspects of those experiences in a few final words which would bring our study to a close.

Not unlike other nations which possessed well organized religious systems, Islam has demonstrated again the truth that, despite diversity of standards, the believers maintain that a "higher" standard of justice must be found, consisting of a higher order of norms and virtues which mankind aspires to realize on Earth. It was this conviction which lured Muslim scholars to enter into a great debate on justice in an effort to discover the elements that constitute the *jus divinum* and to find ways and means which could make it more meaningful in their life on Earth. Failure to achieve such a goal seems never to have deterred or discouraged them from holding the enduring assumption that man possesses an inherent sense of justice which urges him to be just. Man, to believers, is by nature just. Whether guided by Revelation or Reason, or even by social habits, he constantly endeavors to pursue the path of justice as a duty for the good of the community. If a higher scale of justice were ultimately realized, it would be potentially applicable to both the national and the international planes.

No less significant is Islam's experience with the method of accommodation to changing conditions which enabled its standard of justice to endure up to the modern age. For centuries, the debate on justice—indeed, the debate on several other Islamic standards—took the form of an alternation between forward and backward steps—the introduction of change followed by a violent reaction against it—rather than a steady and peaceful process of adaptation of an old standard to a new one. Despite the recurrence of many forms of reaction, the process of accommodation and the assimilation of foreign elements continued, and the debate on justice never really completely stopped. Such a process of alternation between forward and backward steps (without necessarily implying that it is inherently cyclical in nature) seems to have characterized the debate on justice from a relatively early period, when the debate on legitimacy (political justice) ensued between Qadarites and Jabarites. It continued to alternate in the debate on other aspects of justice between Mu'tazilites and Ash'arites which, broadly speaking, came later to be virtually a contest between Rationalism and Revelationism. Not infrequently, the debate culminated in violence, but the process of change paid no attention to abstract doctrines, and adaptation and assimilation triumphed at the end.

In the modern age, following a long period of stagnation and decadence, the scholars have resumed the debate on justice with renewed vigor in order to meet the new challenges of life created by pressures from within and from without Islamic society. We have seen how differently the scholars responded to pressures—some sought to resume the debate with caution and to absorb the foreign elements that imposed themselves upon society, without significantly changing its standards; but others, considering the changes inadequate by drawing only on textual sources, were impatient with the slow process of change and advocated the adoption of European and Western measures without paying attention to their adverse impact on Islamic standards. As a result, the process of change did not always take the form of adaptation and assimilation, but appeared as the wholesale adoption of foreign notions, carried out by the state without regard to their relevance to Islamic standards. Muslim scholars, deeply concerned about the outcome of such changes, frequently appealed to the public to rise up against the men in authority who failed to heed their warnings. The so-called Islamic upsurges thus were not unlike the reassertion of the Revelational standards of old, rallying not necessarily against change *per se,* but against the method adopted by Modernists in carrying out changes.

Following two world wars, Islam has experienced several violent repercussions resulting from quick changes carried out under enormous pressures to catch up with Western advances without regard to Islamic standards. But these repercussions were obviously not a new phenomenon and have recurred more conspicuously in countries which have undergone more thorough changes than others—the Muslim Brotherhood in Egypt, the Islamic group in Pakistan, and more recently the Islamic Revolution, led by Khumaynī, in Iran—to produce violent reactions. These reactions were not confined to lands stricken with violence, but extended to countries where the believers were conscientiously stirred in response to calls to rally with others affected by foreign pressures. The Islamic world, said one keen observer, is like a "sounding box"; each violent upheaval in one country thus caused resounding repercussions in others in an attempt to ensure that Islamic standards were not undermined as a whole. Their ultimate aim was, of course, not merely to defend Islam against occasional incursions, but to protect the integrity of Islamic standards.

Since the Islamic society has inadvertently chosen the alternating "forward" and "backward" steps as a method to achieve social change, the two alternating steps may be regarded as complementary and not in opposition. Whenever the forward step advances rapidly, the reaction of the other is to bring about a pause, not necessarily to undo or negate the impact of the forward step but to allow a breathing space for society to assimilate it before taking another stride. It is indeed not an unhealthy sign that society pauses to take stock of the enormous changes which have taken place and to gather momentum before taking further strides. The recurrence of revivalism thus is not without value. The process of absorption without assimilation creates tensions which call for a pause without which order, not to speak of justice, might be exceedingly difficult to re-establish.

On the international plane, Islam's conception of justice has undergone significant changes, partly owing to the integration of Islamic countries within the community of nations but mainly because of the transformation of Islamdom into a set of sovereign states. In the course of these changes, Islamic as well as other states have accepted the principle that religious doctrines should be separated from the standard of justice in international relations.

Perhaps an even more significant change was the adoption by Islam of the principle of peace, replacing the classical principle of the permanent state of war between Islam and other communities. All Muslim states today have accepted peace as normal condition among nations ever since the Ottoman Empire entered at the height of its power into a peace treaty first with France (1535) and later with other non-Muslim states.[46] The concept of the jihād as just war, becoming inadequate as a basis of Islam's relations with other nations, has been gradually changing into secular war to be invoked by the head of state whenever he felt it was necessary, without the need of a sanction by religious authorities. War, in the form described by Ibn Khaldūn long before Islam joined the modern community of nations, has become a state instrument (a secular war) in almost all Islamic lands and superseded the jihād as a religio-juridical concept.

The participation of Muslim states in the maintenance of peace and security and other corollary principles considered necessary for cooperation among nations gradually became acceptable to Islam—the principle of equality, reciprocity, and territorial sovereignty (the byproduct of the break-up of the Islamic universal state) and others. These principles, the essential attributes of the modern state system, became binding not only on Muslim states but also on others and are considered the very foundation of the modern community of nations. No less significant is the impact of the secular character of Western law on the development of the Islamic legal system as a whole, which led to the adoption of secular rules and practices by many a Muslim country and their eventual integration into the Islamic administration of justice. This gave rise to a set of complex problems proceeding from the Western concept of territorial sovereignty and national identity, such as the movement of nationals, conflict of laws, boundary and river questions, and others. In the absence of guidance from the classical doctrines, Muslim states felt compelled to draw on the experiences of Western nations for the improvement of their system of the administration of justice.[47]

46. For a brief account of this treaty and its significance in the relationship between Islam and other countries, see my *Islamic Law of Nations*, pp. 63–65.

47. A case in point which provides an excellent example of the consequences of the change of the division of the world from the two divisions—dār al-Islām and dār al-Ḥarb—to a modern state system in which Muslim states have become equal members is in the application of the law of inheritance. In the past, the division of the world into two realms had the effect of debarring a Muslim from the right of inheritance whenever he left the dār al-Islām to become a resident in a non-Muslim country, but the incorporation of the dār al-Islām into the modern community of nations allowed the individual to retain his right of inheritance even if he became a citizen of that country. The main reason for the change of ruling is not only because the state of war between Islam and non-Muslim countries is no longer in existence (superseded by peace), but also because Muslim countries have accepted a secular standard of justice governing the relations among members of the modern community of nations. For a discussion of how this change in the application of the law of inheritance began, see 'Azīz Khankī, *Ikhtilāf al-Dārayn* (Cairo, 1934).

In reviewing Islam's experience in its competition and rivalry with Western Christian countries, what conclusions are likely to be drawn from such experiences, one may ask? Four possible lessons might be found here.

First, the Islamic-Christian conflict and competition, which endured over a long period, demonstrated that no nation could claim the monopoly of one standard of justice, whether Divine or otherwise, and that diverse national standards could co-exist and might eventually be reconciled to form a common standard for the community of nations. In view of the acculturation between Islam and other nations, diversity of values might enrich the human heritage as a whole, if each nation were to co-exist with other nations and take a tolerant attitude toward the other's scale of values.

Second, the confrontation between Islam and Western Christendom demonstrated that religious doctrine as a basis for the relationship among states tended to create divergent standards of justice which rendered the task of reconciliation between them exceedingly difficult; only when religious doctrine was relegated to the domestic level did Islam, and later other nations, agree on a common standard of justice devoid of religious dogma. The historical experiences of Islam and Christendom demonstrated that the fusion of religion or any other form of ideology with the foreign conduct of the state tended to complicate and hamper the possibilities of reconciliation and agreement on a common standard of justice derived from their historical experiences and common interests. It is unfortunate that when Islam and Christendom, following a long period of rivalry and conflicts, finally learned to divorce ideology from the principles and practices governing their relationship, both have found themselves today confronted by nations advocating new standards of justice, derived either from religious or other ideological doctrines, which their followers appear to insist on re-introducing into the relationship among nations.

Third, today both Muslim and Christian (Western) nations—indeed, all other members of the community of nations—have tacitly agreed that the standard of justice governing the relationship among nations should ultimately be determined by a confluence of the national interests of all nations, although each nation does not necessarily have to disavow its own values. Western nations claim to weigh their national interests on the scale of rational and objective standards, whereas Muslim leaders still assert certain values and subjective criteria. Indeed, neither Western nor Muslim leaders are prepared to compromise their national interest, but Western leaders attempt to pursue their national interest by dexterous and flexible means which Muslim leaders often consider inconsistent with their values and moral ends. Among nations, it may be asked, what the relationship between means and ends ought to be? Perhaps, we may argue, neither one should be completely divorced from the other, as the subordination of one to the other raises a moral question.

But should morality, like religion, be divorced from the standard of justice among nations? We have just noted that both Islam and Western nations have been compelled to relegate religious doctrine to the domestic level. But the divorce of religious doctrine from the foreign conduct of states does not necessarily mean that the standard of justice among nations should be devoid of moral principles. Indeed, the historical experiences in the relationship between Islam and Christendom demonstrated a paradox: that religious doctrine as a basis for the conduct of state promoted conflict and continuous hostilities, but religion as a source of moral values prompted Muslims and Christians to respect certain concepts of justice still considered important in the relationship among nations (see Appendix). The historical experiences of Islam—indeed the historical experiences of all mankind—demonstrate that any system of law and justice on the national as well as well as the international plane would lose its meaning were it divorced completely from moral principles.

Appendix: Human Rights in Islam

No subject is more closely connected with the concept of justice than "human rights," since justice would be meaningless if the fundamental rights of man were to be unrecognized or ignored by society. In the Revelation, it will be recalled, the two concepts of justice and rights were implied in the abstract term of "al-ḥaqq," which is one of the ultimate goals of the Law. The jurist-theologians, in their discourses on justice, often said that, whereas the object of the Law is justice, its subject matter is the rights and duties of man.

Islam did not deal with "human rights" merely as individual rights, but as rights of the community of believers as a whole (Q. III, 106). In the pre-Islamic society of Arabia, the individual counted for little by himself. Islam, like other higher religious systems, sought to reform the social order and liberate the individual from lingering traditions that had subjected him to the group. Above all, Islam sought to accord the individual a higher level of esteem and self-respect, recognizing no distinction among believers—such as race, class, or color—save their membership in the Islamic brotherhood (Q. XLIX, 10).

However, though Islam sought to liberate man from servitude and

Toward the closing days of the United Nations Conference at San Francisco (1945), the editors of the *Annals of the American Academy of Social and Political Science* solicited papers for a special issue on human rights from a number of scholars (some were members of the American as well as foreign delegations) intended to stimulate public interest in human rights to which several references were made in the U.N. Charter. As a member of the delegation of 'Iraq, I was asked to contribute a paper on "Human Rights in Islam," which appeared in the special issue of the *Annals* (February 1946), 243, 77–81. Since I have given some further thought to the subject, the present paper is more than a mere reproduction of the original, published over thirty years ago.

grant him equality of status, slavery as a system was not abolished by the Law, and women were not completely emancipated. It may seem strange indeed that women and slaves should suffer a degraded position and that the public order did not grant them equality of status. Slavery as a system and the inequality of women, however, have not been laid down by the Divine Legislator, as the Qur'ān provided no rules which pertained to slavery. It would indeed be inconceivable to ascribe the institution of slavery to God, were the Qur'ān to recognize it in principle. And yet Islamic law provided detailed rules governing the relationships between masters and slaves and men and women. Why did Islamic law provide rules for a system which seemed so inconsistent with the principles of equality and brotherhood that the Revelation laid down, it may be asked.

In most ancient societies, slavery and the inequality of women had long been rooted in their public orders and the Prophet, a social reformer who preferred gradual over revolutionary methods, deemed it necessary to urge believers to emancipate slaves, and he provided liberal rules for improvement of the status of women rather than to abolish slavery or put women on equal footing with men at once. But his ultimate purpose was clear; he intended to eliminate slavery and put women on equal footing with men. For this reason, the Qur'ān did not deal with slavery. It did, however, provide legislation granting women certain rights which they had not possessed before.[1] The Traditions, however, though recognizing slavery, called on men to emancipate slaves almost as a religious duty. Just as the *jus naturale* recognized no slavery, so the Revelation, the embodiment of the *jus divinum,* did not recognize it, although both the Roman *jus civile* and Islamic law dealt with it in accordance with the traditions and conditions of both Roman and Muslim societies.

Non-Muslim subjects in Islamic lands were not accorded equal rights with Muslims, although they were considered subjects of the state and granted the right to practice their religion and observe their canon laws with relative freedom. They formed separate communities by themselves. In accordance with charters issued by the Prophet and the early Caliphs, they were allowed to live in peace and security and conduct their everyday business without restrictions as long as they

1. There is an implied reference to female slaves in the Revelation (Q. IV, 3–4), but this did not necessarily mean recognition of the principle of slavery.

respected the laws of the land. Nor were they denied justice, if they sought resource to Muslim courts. The status of a "Dhimmī" (protected person) would be changed to full status the moment he had made the declaration to join the community of believers by reciting the formula of the profession of faith.[2] In the modern age, legal disabilities have been gradually removed, beginning with the Tanzimāt (reform) decrees issued under the Ottoman Empire in 1839 and after. Under the new constitutional laws of the modern national state, Muslims and non-Muslims enjoy equal rights, but a few lingering inhibitions may still exist in varying degree from one country to another. The new principle of national identity, replacing religious identity, is intended to ultimately supersede the lingering inhibitions, although it has introduced a new rule which denied privileges to Muslims, the subjects of one national state, in the event they entered another Muslim (national) state. The principle of national identity, based partly on territorial sovereignty but mainly on ethno-cultural differences, caused certain difficulties to non-Muslims in their relationship with European Powers who claimed the right of protection over religious minorities. In reality they sought to protect them not necessarily in the name of humanity, but to assert foreign capitulatory rights in the Ottoman Empire, the leading Muslim state since the fourteenth century. Under the regimes of Arab states, while the status of Christians was improved mainly because they accepted the national identity accorded to them, the position of the Jews has deteriorated considerably as a consequence of the establishment of Israel, not as a national home for the Jewish people, but as a sovereign state and against Arab consent. Needless to say, the Arab-Israeli conflict today is not a conflict between Islam and Judaism, in accordance with the standard of the *jus divinum,* but an Arab-Israeli conflict in accordance with the doctrine of nationalism which originated in European society and under whose impact both Jews and Arabs have put forth conflicting national claims. The problem of national minorities thus arose just as the problem of religious minorities was on its way to being resolved.

Apart from the broad principles of human rights, Islam accorded the individual a set of specific rules governing human relationships

2. See chap. 7. For the legal status of non-Muslims in Islamic lands, see my *War and Peace in the Law of Islam,* chap. 17.

which might well be reviewed within the context of the comprehensive Universal Declaration of Human Rights, adopted by the United Nations in 1948. Based on several references to human rights in the UN Charter (Articles 1, 55, 56, 68 and 76), this Declaration has been accepted by the Muslim states which participated in the preparation of the Charter at San Francisco in 1945. In the commission of eight, which was established to prepare the draft Declaration, Lebanon (a country of mixed population of Muslims and Christians) was elected a member, presumably to represent the Islamic bloc, and its delegate was appointed as the rapporteur of the Commission.[3] All Muslim member-states, except Saudi Arabia (which abstained), voted in favor of acceptance of the Declaration by the General Assembly of the United Nations (December 10, 1948).[4] The Universal Declaration of Human Rights, though obviously not a legally-binding instrument, is perhaps the most important standard of human rights accepted by an international organization, comprising the norms and values of civilized nations that might be regarded as morally binding, not only on the members of the United Nations but on the community of nations as a whole.

It is perhaps scarcely necessary to discuss the broad outline of the hopes of mankind for what the right of the individual ought to be, concerning which Muslim states are in agreement, since there are several studies dealing with this subject. It is proposed to discuss only the most important human rights that Islam had recognized in the past and those which Muslim states have accepted after the United Nations Declaration of Human Rights was issued.

1. The principles of dignity and brotherhood, originally the preserve of believers, are now acknowledged by Muslim states as the rights of all men in accordance with the Universal Declaration of Human Rights (Article 1). Religion as the symbol of identity in the Muslim brotherhood is now being superseded by national identity on the national plane and by the spirit of cooperation among nations on the international plane (Articles 6 and 15). Apart from Turkey, no Muslim state has officially taken the step to separate religion from state, but in practice there is a growing tendency, especially in north-

3. The chairman of the Commission, Mrs. Roosevelt (U.S.A.) and its rapporteur, Charles Malik (Lebanon), were assisted by a number of experts who were acquainted with Islamic teachings.

4. See note 6.

ern Arab countries, to regard religion as a personal matter in varying degree.

2. Equality among members of the community is perhaps the principle most emphatically stressed, not only in the narrow legal but in the wider social sense, as Islam recognizes no distinction on the basis of race color, or class. Moreover, Islam has shown tolerance towards other religious groups within its territory in the past and has therefore been quite prepared to accept the principles of equality and tolerance on the international plane (Articles 2, 3, 6 and 7).

3. Respect for the honor, reputation, and family of each individual are rights recognized in the law of Islam; they are also rooted in the traditions of many communities that had become part of the larger Islamic community. Needless to say that the extension of these rights to the international plane (Article 12) was most welcome by Muslim states.

4. The right of each individual "to be presumed innocent until proved guilty according to law" (Article 11) is implied in the principle of "presumed innocence" (al-aṣl barā'at al-dhimma), set forth in the *Majalla* (Article 8) and in modern legislation. However, the guarantees necessary for defense in procedural justice have not, as noted before, been fully provided. In the modern age, a number of Muslim states have adopted several measures to provide such guarantees, though these vary considerably from one country to another.

5. Individual freedom in Islam is perhaps the most difficult to relate to the modern concept of freedom referred to in the Declaration (Articles 18–20), as freedom in the strict legal sense was used essentially as the opposite to slavery, although freedom as a political and philosophical concept was not unknown to Muslim scholars. As a philosophical concept, it was used to denote man's capacity to create his acts, including the exercise of free choice (ikhtiyār) in human affairs. But this concept came into conflict with the doctrine that all human acts are the creation of God. This doctrine, which stressed the utter dependence of man on God's Will, left little or no room for the freedom of the individual in human affairs and allowed rulers to exercise authoritarianism under the guise that their acts were the expression of Divine Will. In the modern age, there has been an increasing tendency to limit authoritarianism under the impact of the Western concept of individual freedom which allows man to exercise a free will in human affairs.

However, freedom to change one's own religion, which touches on man's relationship with God, falls into another category. It is true that conversion into Islam must be achieved by persuasion and not by violence, according to the Revelation (Q. II, 257); but once the individual has adopted Islam, he should not "turn his back to it," according to the Tradition, as the change of religion is considered apostasy punishable by death unless the individual repents.[5] Yet, in matters which pertain to human conscience, it is inconceivable that God would prescribe death, and the Revelation has indeed clearly stated that there should be no compulsion in religion (Q. II, 257). Like other higher religions, the Islamic Revelation has left matters of belief (imān) to the individual, as only God will ultimately decide such matters on the Day of Judgement (Q. II, 214; XVI, 108). Nor was it the practice of the Prophet to punish man for the change of his religion by death, for in his treaty with the people of Makka (signed in 8/630), he left all matters of faith to human conscience and allowed those who adopted Islam to renounce it, if they so wished, without molestation.[6] After the Prophet's death (10/632), however, when some of the tribes renounced Islam, the authorities in Madīna resorted to violence to bring them under control; but this was a political act for which a religious sanction was invoked and it should not be considered applicable to individual cases. The Tradition that "he who changes his religion should be killed," originating during the wars of apostasy after the Prophet's death, was endorsed by state acts and was subsequently accepted as part of the Law. In the latter days of the Ottoman Empire, however, a decree was issued to suspend the death sentence for apostasy. Today most Muslim states have accepted the UN Declaration which calls for freedom of conscience and religion, including freedom to change one's own religion or belief (Article 18).[7]

Article 20 (3), which states that "the will of the people shall be the basis of the authority of government," provides another principle

5. See Bukhārī, *Ṣaḥīḥ* (Leiden, 1864), II, 251; Mālik, *al-Muwaṭṭa'* (Cairo, 1951), II, 736; Abū Dāwūd, *Sunan* (Cairo, 1935), IV, 126.

6. See Ibn Hishām, *Kitāb al-Sīra,* ed. Wüstenfeld (Göttingen, 1860), II, p. 747; Wāqidī, *Kitāb al-Maghāzī,* ed. Jones (Oxford, 1966), II, 611–12.

7. Saudi Arabia, which abstained from voting on the Declaration, seems to have been prompted to do so in order to avoid the consequential acceptance of an obligation which would be in conflict with Islamic law. See Ganji, *International Protection of Human Rights* (Geneva and Paris, 1962), p. 45, n. 12.

which may come into conflict with the Islamic principle of political justice. The source of all authority, according to the Revelation, is God, as noted before; only its exercise was delegated to men. In the modern age, however, most Muslim states have accepted the principle that authority resides with the people, though its incidence may be construed to mean that it did not necessarily originate from the people but that, having been delegated by God to the people, it now resides (or, in the words of the U.N. Declaration, its basis rests) with the people. Article 20 (3), so interpreted, can therefore be considered consistent with the Islamic principle of political justice.

Finally, with regard to other principles stressed in the Declaration, such as the principle of private property, the right to work, the right to education, and others, most Muslim countries seem to be prepared to grant such rights to the individual, especially the oil-producing countries which have provided free educational facilities to all citizens on all levels. They have also provided opportunities for workers and peasants to work and to form cooperative societies to improve public welfare and raise the standard of living. The right to form trade unions, however, has not yet been acknowledged, as unions are still considered to be a form of political parties that exists only in a limited number of Muslim countries. Since such a right has been recommended under the Declaration as a form of "the right to freedom of opinion and expression" (Article 19), workers are justified to press their claim to it in a society that asserts egalitarian principles.

Glossary

'adl: justice
'ādil: just man
amān: safe-conduct; pledge of security
'aql: reason

bāṭil: void
bid'a: innovation

caliph: head of state. *See* Imām

ḍarar: harm; injury
ḍarūra: necessity
dawla: state; dynasty
dīn: religion

fā'ida: profit; interest
faqīh (pl. fuqahā'): jurist; scholar of the Sharī'a
farḍ (pl. farā'iḍ): duty
fāsid: invalid
fāsiq: impious
fatwa (pl. fatāwa): legal opinion
fiqh: jurisprudence; law
firqa (pl. firaq): sect
fisq: impiety
furū': rules

ghayba: occultation, absence of the Imām in his corporeal existence but not in spirit (Shī'ī doctrine)

ḥadd (pl. ḥudūd): penalties (prescribed in the Qur'ān)
ḥadīth: Tradition (from the Prophet)
ḥalāl: lawful, permitted act
ḥaqq (pl. ḥuqūq): right; truth
ḥarb: war (secular). *See* jihād
ḥikma: wisdom; divine wisdom
ḥukm: judgement; ruling
ḥusn: beautiful; good
ḥuzn: sorrow

'ibāda (pl. 'ibādāt): worship; devotional duty
ibāḥa: permission
i'jāz: miracle of the Qur'ān
ijmā': consensus; agreement
ijtihād: individual reasoning on matters of law or the creed
ikhtiyār: free-will; voluntarism
ikrāh: compulsion; coercion
Imām: head of state; leader in prayer; head of a school of law or a creed
imān: inward belief
irjā': suspension (of judgement)
'iṣma: sinlessness; infallibility
ishtirākīya: socialism

jabr: compulsion; doctrine of involuntarism

jā'iz: permitted
jawr: injustice
jihād: just war

kāfir: unbeliever (in the message of the Prophet)
kalām: theology (originally was used in the sense of speculative theology and applied to the Mu'tazilites, but later applied to all theologians)
khayr: public good
kufr: unbelief; heresy

luṭf: Divine grace

majalla: digest of law
maṣlaḥa: interest; public good (public interest)
milk: private ownership
muftī: jurisconsult (jurist who gives a legal opinion). *See* fatwa
mujtahid: scholar who exercises ijtihād. *See* ijtihād
mulk: authority; sovereignty
murtadd: apostate

nīya: intent

qadar: power (Divine); doctrine of voluntarism
qāḍī: judge
qānūn: law (secular)
qiyās: analogy
qubḥ: evil

ra'y: opinion
riba: usury

shafā'a: intercession
shahāda: testimony
Sharī'a: Islamic law
shāhid: witness
shahīd: martyr
shūra: consultation (on public affairs)
siyar: conduct of state (in international affairs)
sūfī: mystic
sunna: custom; rule based on the Prophet's precedent

tafsīr: commentary (on the Qur'ān)
taklīf: obligation of observing the Law (sharī'a)
taqīya: dissimulation (Shī'ī doctrine)
ta'wīl: allegorical interpretation (Sunnī doctrine); esoteric knowledge of the Imām (Shī'ī doctrine)
tashrī': legislation
tawḥīd: Oneness (doctrine that God is One)
ta'zīr: discretionary power of the judge

'ulamā (sing. ālim): scholar
'uqūba (pl. 'uqūbāt): penalty

vizīr (wazīr): minister (head of the administrative system, responsible directly to the Caliph)

walāya: pledge of loyalty to the Imām
wasaṭ: middle; the golden mean

Select Bibliography

A bibliography consisting of a complete list of the works that have bearing on the Islamic conception of justice is perhaps unnecessary, as the compilation of such a list will probably have to include almost all of the books relating to Islamic thought. It is, therefore, the purpose of this bibliography neither to be exhaustive nor to reproduce all the works cited in the footnotes, but rather to provide the fundamental primary and modern works that have more direct bearing on the substance of the subject. Fairly exhaustive bibliographies of classical works can be found in Ibn al-Nadīm's *Kitāb al-Fihrist,* edited by G. L. Flügel (Leipzig, 1871), translated by Bayard Dodge, *The Fihrist of al-Nadīm* (New York, 1970); Ḥajjī Khalīfa's *Kashf al-Zunūn,* edited by G. L. Flügel (Leipzig and London, 1835–38); and C. Brockelmann's *Geschichte der Arabischen Litteratur,* 2nd ed. (Leiden, 1943–49), with three supplementary volumes (1937–42). The reader may also refer to the relevant articles in the *Encyclopaedia of Islam* (old and new editions) which provide guidance for classical and modern works.

Primary Sources

'Abd al-Jabbār, Qāḍī Abū al-Ḥasan. *Al-Mughnī.* Edited by Khawlī, Ahwānī, Madkūr, and others. 14 vols., some lost. Cairo, 1958–65.

———. *Sharḥ al-Uṣūl al-Khamsa.* Edited by 'Abd al-Karīm 'Uthmān. Cairo, 1384/1965.

———. *Kitāb al-Majmū' fī al-Muḥīt bi al-Taklīf.* Edited by J. J. Houben. Beirut, 1962.

Abū Dāwūd, Sulaymān B. al-Ash'ath al-Sijistānī. *Sunan.* 4 vols. Cairo, 1354/1935.

Abū Yūsuf, Ya'qūb. *Kitāb al-Kharāj.* Cairo, 1352/1934.

Āmidī, Abū al-Ḥasan 'Alī. *Kitāb al-Iḥkām fī Uṣūl al-Aḥkām.* 3 vols. Cairo, 1347/1928.

Ash'arī, Abū al-Ḥasan 'Alī. *Maqālāt al-Islāmiyyīn.* Edited by Ritter. Istanbul, 1929. New edition by M. 'Abd al-Ḥamīd. 2 vols. Cairo, 1369/1950–1373/1954.

———. *al-Ibāna 'an Uṣūl al-Diyānah.* Translated by Walter C. Klein. New Haven, 1940.

Badawī, 'Abd al-Raḥmān, ed. *Al-Uṣūl al-Yunānīya bi al-Nazarīyāt al-Siyāsīya fī al-Islām*. Cairo, 1954.

Baghdādī, Abū Manṣūr 'Abd al-Qāhir B. Ṭāhir. *Kitāb Uṣūl al-Dīn*. 2 vols. Istanbul, 1346/1928.

———. *Kitāb al-Farq Bayn al-Firaq*. Edited by M. Zāhid al-Kawtharī. Cairo, 1948. English translation, pt. I, by Kate C. Seelye; pt. II, by A. S. Halkin. Tel Aviv, 1935.

Bāqillānī, Qāḍī Abū Bakr. *Kitāb al-Tamhīd*. Edited by R. J. McCarthy. Beirut, 1957.

———. *Kitāb al-Inṣāf*. Edited by Zāhid al-Kawtharī. Cairo, 1382/1963.

Bazdawī, Abū al-Yusr Muḥammad B. 'Abd al-Karīm, *Kitāb Uṣūl al-Dīn*. Edited by H. P. Linss. Cairo, 1383/1963.

Bukhārī, Abū 'Ahd-Allāh Muḥammad B. Ismā'īl. *Kitāb al-Jāmi' al-Ṣaḥīḥ*. Edited by M. Ludolf Krehl. 4 vols. Leiden, 1862/1908.

Fārābī, Abū Naṣr. *Al-Fuṣūl al-Madanī*. Edited and translated by D. M. Dunlop. Cambridge, 1961.

———. *Kitāb Arā' Ahl al-Madīna al-Fāḍila*. Edited by A. N. Nādir. Beirut, 1959.

———. *Kitāb al-Siyāsa al-Madanīya*. Edited by F. M. Najjār. Beirut, 1964.

———. *Kitāb Taḥṣīl al-Sa'āda*. Hyderabad, 1346/1926.

———. *Kitāb al-Tanbīh 'ala Sabīl al-Sa'āda*. Hyderabad, 1346/1927.

Ghazzālī, Abū Ḥāmid. *Kitāb Iḥyā' 'Ulūm al-Dīn*. 4 vols. Cairo, n.d.

———. *Kitāb al-Iqtiṣād fī al-I'tiqād*. Edited by 'Ādil al-'Awwa. Beirut, 1969.

———. *al-Munqidh Min al-Ḍalāl*. Edited by Farīd Jabr. Beirut, 1959.

———. *Mishkāt al-Anwār*. Edited by A. 'Affīfī. Cairo, 1383/1964.

———. *Ma'ārij al-Qudus fī Madārij Ma'rifat al-Nafs*. Cairo, 1963.

———. *Mizān al-'Amāl*. Edited by Sulaymān Dunya. Cairo, 1964.

———. *al-Qisṭaṣ al-Mustaqīm*. Edited by Victor Shalhat. Beirut, 1959.

Ḥillī, Ḥasan B. Yūsuf. *al-Babu 'l-Ḥādī 'Ashar*. Edited by Miller. London, 1928.

Ḥujwīrī, 'Alī B. 'Uthmān. *The Kashf al-Maḥjūb*. Translated by R. A. Nicholson. Leiden and London, 1911.

Ibn 'Arabī, Muḥyī al-Dīn. *Kitāb Naqsh al-Fuṣūs*. Hyderabad, 1367/1948.

———. *Fuṣūs al-Ḥikam*. Edited by Abū al-'Alā 'Affīfī. Cairo, 1365/1946.

———. *Kitāb Iṣṭilāḥ al-Ṣufīya*. Hyderabad, 1367/1948.

———. *Rasā' il Ibn al-'Arabī*. 2 vols. Hyderabad, 1367/1948.

Ibn al-Azraq, Abū 'Abd-Allāh. *Badā' i' al-Sulūk fī Tabā' i' al-Mulk*. Edited by A. S. al-Nashshār. 2 vols. Baghdad, 1977.

Ibn Anas, Mālik. *Al-Muwaṭṭa'*. Edited by 'Abd al-Bāqī. 2 vols. Cairo, 1370/1951.

Ibn Bābawayh, Muḥammād B. 'Alī (Shaykh Ṣadūq). *A Shī'ite Creed*. Translated by Fyzee. London, 1942.

Ibn Ḥanbal, Aḥmad B. Muḥammad. *Al-Musnad*. Edited by Aḥmad Shākir. 15 vols. Cairo, 1368/1949–1375/1956.

Ibn Ḥazm, Abū 'Alī. *Kitāb al-Akhlāq wa al-Siyar*. Edited and translated into French by Nada Tomiche. Beirut, 1961.

———. *Al-Iḥkām fī Uṣūl al-Aḥkām.* 4 vols. Cairo, 1345/1926.
———. *Kitāb al-Faṣl fī al-Milal wa al-Ahwā' wa al-Niḥal.* Edited by 'Abd al Raḥmān Khalīfa. 5 vols. Cairo, 1321/1903.
Ibn al-Jawzī, 'Abd al-Raḥmān. *al-Ḥasan al-Baṣrī.* Edited by H. Sandūbī. Cairo, 1350/1931.
Ibn Khaldūn, 'Abd al-Raḥmān. *al-Muqaddima.* Edited by Quatremère. 3 vols. Paris, 1858. English translation by Rosenthal, Franz. *The Muqaddimah: An Introduction to History.* 3 vols. London, 1958.
———. *Kitāb al Ta'rīf bi-Ibn Khaldūn wa Riḥlatuh Gharban wa Sharqan.* Edited by M. al-Ṭanjī. Cairo, 1951.
Ibn Khalil al-Tarābulusī, 'Alā' al-Dīn Abū al-Ḥasan 'Alī. *Kitāb Mu'īn al-Ḥukkām.* Cairo, 1300/1882.
Ibn al-Murtaḍa, Aḥmad Ibn Yaḥya. *Kitāb al-Munya wa al-Amal.* Edited by Thomas Arnold. Hyderabad, 1316/1899.
———. *Kitāb Ṭabaqāt al-Mu'tazila.* Edited by S. Diwald-Wilzer. Beirut and Wiesbaden, 1961.
Ibn Qayyim al-Jawzīya, Shams al-Dīn Abū 'Abd-Allāh Muḥammad. *I'lām al-Mu'waqqi'īn.* 4 vols. Cairo, n.d.
Ibn Rushd, Abū al-Walīd. *Kitāb Faṣl al-Maqāl.* Edited by A. Nādir. Beirut, 1961. Translated by Hourani, George F. *Averroes on the Harmony of Religion and Philosophy.* London, 1961.
———. *Kitāb al-Kashf 'an Manāhij al-Adilla fī 'Aqā' id al-Milla.* Edited by M. J. Müller. Munich, 1859. New edition by M. Qāsim. Cairo, 1955.
———. *Averroes' Commentary on Plato's Republic.* Edited by E.I.J. Rosenthal. Cambridge, 1956. New translation by Lerner, Ralph. *Averroes on Plato's Republic.* Ithaca, N.Y., 1974.
———. *Bidāyat al-Mujtahid.* 2 vols. Istānbūl, 1333/1914.
Ibn Sinā, Abū 'Alī al-Ḥusayn. *Kitāb al-Shifā': al-Ilāhīyāt,* vol. II. Edited by M. Yūsuf Mūsa, Sulaymān Dunya, and Sa'īd Zāyid. Cairo, 1960.
———. *Kitāb al-Ishārāt wa al-Tanbīhāt.* Edited by Sulaymān Dunya. 3 vols. Cairo, 1367/1947.
———. *Kitāb al-Najāt.* Cairo, 1331/1912.
———. *Tis' Rasā' il fī al-Ḥikma wa al-Ṭabī'īyāt.* Cairo, 1326/1908.
———. *The Life of Ibn Sīna.* Translated by W. E. Gohlman. Albany, N.Y., 1974.
Ibn Taymīya, Taqī al-Dīn. *al-Siyāsa al-Shar'īya fī Iṣlāḥ al-Rā 'ī wa al Ra'īya.* Edited by Samī al-Nashshār and Zakī 'Atīya. Cairo, 1951.
Isfirāyīnī, Abū al-Muzaffar. *Kitāb al-Tabṣīr fī Usūl al-Dīn.* Edited by Zāhid al-Kawtharī. Cairo, 1374/1955.
———. *Mamjū 'at Rasā 'il.* Edited by M. H. al-Fiqqī. Cairo, 1368/1949.
Jurjānī, Sharīf 'Alī. *Kitāb al-Ta' rīfāt.* Edited by G. L. Flügel. Leipzig, 1845.
Juwaynī, Imām al-Haramayn. *Kitāb al-Irshād.* Edited by M. Y. Mūsa and 'Alī A. 'Abd al-Hamīd. Cairo, 1369/1950.
———. *al-Shāmil fī Uṣūl al-Dīn.* Edited by H. Klopfer. Cairo and Wiesbaden, 1960–61.

Kindī, Abū Yūsuf Ya'qūb B. Isḥāq. *Rasā' il al-Kindī al-Falsafīya.* Edited by M. A. Abū Rīda. 2 vols. Cairo, 1950–53.

———. *Kitāb al-Kindī ila al-Mu'taṣim bi-Allāh fī al-Falsafa al-Ūlā.* Edited by A. F. al-Ahwānī. Cairo, 1367/1948.

———. *al-Kindī's Metaphysics: A Translation of al-Kindī's Treatise "On First Philosophy."* Translated by Alfred L. Ivry. Albany, N.Y., 1974.

Malaṭī, Abū al-Ḥusayn. *Kitāb al-Tanbīh wa al-Radd.* Cairo, 1949.

Mālik B. Anas. *See* Ibn Anas.

Māturīdī, Abū Manṣūr Muḥammad. *Kitāb al-Tawḥīd.* Edited by Fath-Allāh Khulayf. Beirut, 1970.

Māwardī, Abū al-Ḥasan. *Kitāb al-Aḥkām al-Sulṭānīya.* Edited by Engeri. Bonn, 1853.

———. *Adab al-Qāḍī.* Edited by M. H. al-Sirḥān. 2 vols. Baghdad, 1391–92/1971–72.

———. *Adab al-Dunya wa al-Dīn.* Edited by M. al-Saqqa. Cairo, 1973.

Muslim, Abū al-Ḥusayn Muslim B. al-Ḥajjāj. *Ṣaḥīḥ,* with Nawawī's Commentary. 18 vols. Cairo, 1929–30.

Nasafī, Najm al-Dīn. *Creed of Islam,* with Taftazānī's Commentary. Translated by E. E. Elder. New York, 1950.

Nu'mān, Qāḍī Abū Ḥanīfa. *Da'ā'im al-Islām.* Edited by Āṣif B. 'Alī Aṣghar Fayḍī [Fyzee]. 2 vols. Cairo, 1951–60.

Qifṭī, Jamāl al-Dīn 'Alī B. Yūsuf. *Ta'rīkh al-Ḥukamā'.* Edited by Julius Lippert. Leipzig, 1903.

Qu'rān. Several renderings of the Qur'ān are available in the English language, but there is no fully adequate translation. Not infrequently a modified rendering based on one or two of the following translations has been made for the purpose of this book:

Bell, Richard, *The Qur'ān.* 2 vols. Edinburgh, 1937–39.

Arberry, A. J. *The Koran Interpreted.* 2 vols. London, 1955.

Pickthall, M. M. *The Meaning of the Glorious Koran.* London, 1953.

Dawood, N. J. *The Koran.* London, 1956.

Rāzī, Abū Bakr Muḥammad B. Zakarīya. *Rasā'il Falsafīya.* Opera Philosophica, edited by Kraus. Beirut, 1973.

Samnānī, 'Alī B. Muḥammad. *Rawḍāt al-Quḍāt wa Ṭarīq al-Najāt.* Edited by al-Nāhī. 3 vols. Baghdad, 1970–73.

Shāfi'ī, Muḥammad B. Idrīs. *Al-Risāla.* Edited by A. Shākir. Cairo, 1358/1940. Translation in Khadduri, M. *Islamic Jurisprudence.* Baltimore, 1961.

Shahrastānī, Muḥammad B. 'Abd al-Karīm. *Kitāb al-Milal wa al-Niḥal.* Edited by William Cureton. London and Leipzig, 1846, 1923.

———. *Kitāb Nihāyat al-Iqdām.* Edited by Alfred Guillaume. London, 1934.

Shāṭibī, Abū Isḥāq Ibrāhīm B. Mūsa. *al-Muwāfaqāt.* Edited by Durāz. 4 vols., Cairo, n.d.

———. *Kitāb al-I'tiṣām.* 3 vols. Cairo, 1331/1913.

Shaybānī, Muhammad B. al-Ḥasan. *Kitāb al-Makhārij fī al-Ḥiyal.* Edited by Schacht. Leipzig, 1930.

———. *Kitāb al-Siyar.* Edited and translated by Khadduri, M. *The Islamic Law of Nations.* Baltimore, 1966.

Ṭabarī, Abū Ja'far Muḥammad B. Jarīr. *Jāmi' al-Bayān 'an Ta'wīl Āyy al-Qur'ān.* Edited by Maḥmūd Shākir. 15 vols. Cairo, n.d. Often referred to as Ṭabarī's *Tafsīr.*

Ṭurṭūshī, Abū Bakr Muḥammad. *Kitāb Sirāj al-Mulūk.* Cairo, 1319/1902.

Ṭusī, Naṣīr al-Dīn. Akhlāq-i Nāṣirī. Translated by Wickens, G. M. *The Nasirean Ethics.* London, 1964.

'Umāra, Muḥammad, ed. *Rasā'il al-'Adl wa al-Tawḥīd.* 2 vols. Cairo, 1971.

Wensinck, A. J. *A Handbook of Early Muḥammadan Traditions.* Leiden, 1927.

Ziriklī, Khayr al-Dīn, ed. *Rasā' il Ikhwān al-Ṣafā'.* 4 vols. Cairo, 1347/1928.

Modern Works

Abū Zahra, Muḥammad. *Ibn Taymīya.* Cairo, 1952.

Affifi, A. E. *The Mystical Philosophy of Muhyid Din Ibnu'l Arabi.* Cambridge, 1933.

Afnan, S. M. *Avicenna: His Life and Works.* London, 1958.

Anawati, G. C. *Étude de philosophie musulmane.* Paris, 1974.

Arberry, A. J. "Rhazes on the Philosophic Life," *Asiatic Review* 45 (1949): 703–13.

Atiyeh, George N. *Al-Kindi: The Philosopher of the Arabs.* Karachi, 1966.

Berman, Lawrence V. "Excerpts from the Lost Arabic Original of Ibn Rushd's Middle Commentary on the Nichomachean Ethics," *Oriens* 20 (1967): 31–59.

Cook, Michael. *Early Muslim Dogma.* Cambridge, 1981.

Corbin, H. *Histoire de la philosophie islamique.* Paris, 1964.

Dunya, Sulaymān. *Al-Ḥaqīqa fī Nazar al-Ghazzālī.* Cairo, 1947.

Fakhry, Majid. *A History of Islamic Philosophy.* 2nd ed. New York, 1983.

———. *Dirāsāt fī al-Fikr al-'Arabī.* Beirut, 1970.

———. *Al-Fikr al-Akhlāqī al-'Arabī.* 2 vols. Beirut, 1978–79.

———. "Some Implications of the Mu'tazilite View of Free Will," *Muslim World* XLIII (1953): 95–109.

Fāris, Bishr. *Mabāḥith 'Arabīya.* Cairo, 1939.

Fāsī, 'Allāl. *Maqāṣid al-Sharī'a al-Islāmīya.* Casablanca, 1963.

Frank, Richard M. *Beings and Their Attributes.* Albany, N.Y., 1978.

Gardet, L. and Anawati, G. C. *Introduction à la théologie musulmane.* Paris, 1948.

Gibb, H.A.R. *Modern Trends in Islam.* Chicago, 1946.

Goodman, Lenn Evan. "Maimonides' Philosophy of Law," *Jewish Law Annual* I: 72–107.

Hourani, George F. *Islamic Rationalism.* Oxford, 1971.

———. "The Rationalist Ethics of 'Abd al-Jabbār." In *Islamic Philosophy and the Classical Tradition,* edited by S. M. Stern et al., pp. 105–15. Columbia, S.C., 1972.

Ḥuṣrī, Saṭī'. *Dirāsāt 'An Muqaddamat ibn Khaldūn.* Cairo, 1953.

Ibn 'Āshūr, Muḥammad al-Ṭāhir. *Maqāṣid al-Sharī'a al-Islāmīya.* Tunis, 1366/1946.

Iqbal, M. *The Reconstruction of Religious Thought in Islam.* London, 1934.

Khadduri, Majid. *War and Peace in the Law of Islam.* Baltimore, 1955.

———. "Property: Its Relation to Equality and Freedom in Accordance with Islamic Law." In *Equality and Freedom: Past, Present and Future* (edited for the International Association of the Philosophy of Law and Social Philosophy). Wiesbaden, 1978.

———. "Marriage in Islamic Law: The Modernist Viewpoints." *American Journal of Comparative Law* XXVI (1978): 213–18.

Khadduri, M., and Leibesny, H. J., eds. *Law in the Middle East.* Washington, D.C., 1955.

Kholeif, Fath-Allāh. *A Study on Fakhr al-Dīn al-Rāzī and His Controversies in Transoxiana.* Beirut, 1966.

Khumaynī, Āyat-Allāh Rūḥ-Allāh. *Ḥukūmat-ī Islāmī.* Translated by Hamid Algar, titled *Islam and Revolution.* Berkeley, 1981.

Laoust, H. *Essai sur le doctrine sociale et politique de T. D. Ahmed B. Taimiya.* Cairo, 1939.

Lerner, R., and Mahdi, M. *Medieval Political Philosophy.* Glencoe, Ill., 1963.

Liebesny, Herbert J. *Law of the Near and Middle East.* Albany, N.Y., 1975.

Madkūr, Ibrāhīm B. *Fī al-Falsafa al Islāmīya.* 2 vols. 3rd ed. Cairo, 1976.

Mahdi, Muhsin. *Ibn Khaldun's Philosophy of History.* 2nd ed. Chicago, 1964.

Massignon, Louis. *La passion d'al-Husayn ibn Mansour al-Hallaj.* 2 vols. Paris, 1922. Translated by Mason, Herbert. *The Passion of al-Hallaj.* 4 vols. Princeton, 1982.

Masud, Muhammad Khalid. *Islamic Legal Philosophy: A Study of Abū Isḥāq al-Shāṭibī.* Islamabad, 1977.

Nader, Albert N. *Le système philosophique de Mu'tazila.* Beirut, 1956.

Nasr, S. H. *Three Muslim Sages.* Cambridge, Mass., 1964.

Nicholson, R. A. *Studies in Islamic Mysticism.* Cambridge, 1921.

———. *The Mystics of Islam.* London, 1963.

Obermann, Julian. "Political Theory in Early Islam: Ḥasan al-Baṣrī." *Journal of the American Oriental Society* LV (1935): 138–62.

Peters, P. E. *Aristotle and the Arabs.* New York, 1968.

Qāsim, Maḥmūd. *Ibn Rushd.* Cairo, 1969.

Quṭb, Sayyid. *Al-'Adāla al-Ijtimā'īya fī al-Islām.* Cairo, n.d.; translated by Hardie, J. B. *Social Justice in Islam.* Washington, D.C., 1953.

Rahbar, Daud. *God of Justice.* Leiden, 1960.

Rahman, F. *Prophecy.* London, 1958.

Rosenthal, E.I.J. *Political Thought in Medieval Islam.* Cambridge, 1958.

Rosenthal, Franz. *Concept of Freedom in Islam.* Leiden, 1960.

Salem, Elie A. *Political Theory and Institutions of the Khawārij.* Baltimore, 1965.

Ṣalība, Jamīl. *Al-Dirāsāt al-Falsafīya.* Damascus, 1383/1964.

Sanhūrī, ʿAbd al-Razzāq. *Al-Wajīz*. 2 vols. Cairo, 1966.
Seale, Morris S. *Muslim Theology*. London, 1964.
Shaltūt, Maḥmūd. *Fiqh al-Qur'ān wa al-Sunna: al-Qiṣāṣ*. Cairo, 1946.
Smith, Jane I., and Haddad, Yvonne Y. *The Islamic Understanding of Death and Resurrection*. Albany, N.Y., 1981.
Ṣubḥī, Aḥmad Maḥmūd. *Al-Zaydīya*. Alexandria, 1980.
Ṭyan, Emile. *Histoire de l'organisation judiciaire en pays d'Islam*. 2 vols. Paris, 1938–43.
Van Ess, Joseph. *Anfänge Muslimischer Theologie*. Beirut, 1977.
———. "Skepticism in Islamic Religious Thought." *al-Abḥāth* XXI (1968): 1–14.
Walzer, Richard. *Greek into Arabic*. Oxford, 1963.
Wardī, ʿAlī. *Manṭiq Ibn Khaldūn*. Cairo, 1962.
Watt, W. M. *Free Will and Predestination in Early Islam*. London, 1953.
———. *Muslim Intellectual*. Edinburgh, 1963.
———. *Islamic Philosophy and Theology*. Edinburgh, 1962.
Wensinck, A. G. *Muslim Creed*. Cambridge, 1932.
Zayd, Muṣṭafa. *Al-Maṣlaḥa fī al-Tashrī' al-Islāmī*. Cairo, 1954.

Index